# celebrating sacraments

To all the people who have been sacraments in my life—
especially Susan, Katie, Pat, and Tim

Genuine recycled paper with 10 % post-consumer waste.
Printed with soy-based ink.

Nihil Obstat:   Rev. John M. Sauer, STL
                Censor Librorum
                10 November 1999

Imprimatur: †Most Rev. Bernard J. Harrington, DD
                Bishop of Winona
                10 November 1999

The nihil obstat and imprimatur are official declarations that a
book or pamphlet is free of doctrinal or moral error. No impli-
cation is contained therein that those who have granted the nihil
obstat or imprimatur agree with the contents, opinions, or
statements expressed.

The publishing team included Barbara Allaire, development
editor; Jerry Windley-Daoust and Stephan Nagel, consulting
editors; Mary Duerson, copy editor; Laurie Geisler, cover and
page designer, production editor, and typesetter; Cindi Ramm,
art director; Alan S. Hanson, pre-press specialist; Genevieve
Nagel, photo researcher; Michael O. McGrath, illustrator; and
Patricia Deminna, indexer.

The acknowledgments continue on page 316.

Printing: 9  8  7  6  5  4

Year: 2008  07  06  05  04  03

ISBN 0-88489-624-2

Saint Mary's Press
Christian Brothers Publications
Winona, Minnesota
www.smp.org

*Cover student art:* Photo of shamrocks by Kim Hall, Sacred
Heart Cathedral Preparatory School, San Francisco, California;
photo of group hiking by Clare Major, Saint Joseph's Academy,
Baton Rouge, Louisiana; photo of water droplets by Swen
Swenson-Graham, Sacred Heart Preparatory School, Menlo
Park, California; photo of shells by Lindsay Van Cleave, Notre
Dame Preparatory School, Towson, Maryland

        Library of Congress Cataloging-in-Publication Data
Stoutzenberger, Joseph.
   Celebrating sacraments : / Joseph Stoutzenberger.— 3rd ed.
     p.   cm.
Includes index.
Summary: Discusses the seven sacraments of the Catholic faith
and how God communicates through the people, places, and
experiences that shape a person's life.
   ISBN 0-88489-624-2 (pbk.)
   1. Sacraments—Catholic Church—Juvenile literature.
2. Catholic Church—Doctrines—Juvenile
literature. 3. Catholic youth—Religious life.
[1. Sacraments—Catholic Church.
2. Catholic Church—Doctrines.]
I. Title.
   BX2200.S786 2000
   234'.16'08822—dc21

     00-008018

# celebrating sacraments

**Third Edition**

**Joseph Stoutzenberger**

# table of contents

# 1

# Sacraments

## encountering the sacred

creation . . . the loving presence of God

... open to seeing God ... in our everyday life

**Gracious God,** we begin this course
seeking to know you better
and to continuously discover
your loving presence in our life.
As we talk, pray, create, and explore together,
may we experience wonder
at the marvels that surround us
and find cause to celebrate a world
alive with your goodness and glory.
**Amen.**

# listening for thunder

Mice are very busy creatures. They gather seeds and grain and collect little bits of straw or sticks for their nests. Always keeping their nose and eyes to the ground, they scurry here and there looking for whatever food and bedding they can find. Normally, this is all they do and all they ever expect to do. A story from a Native American tradition, however, tells about one mouse who was different.

**One Day,** a busy little mouse began to hear a faint thundering noise in the distance. She inquired of the other mice if they too heard it. No one else did, so she decided to forget the matter and busied herself all the more. Yet she continued to hear the thundering noise. Try as she would, she could not ignore it.

Determined to discover the source of the thunder, the mouse set out on a perilous journey across the open prairie. Along the way, she encountered predators, as well as numerous animal friends who assisted her in her quest. When she finally arrived at a river—the source of the thundering noise—a frog suggested that if the mouse wished to see the river beyond the cattail reeds, she should leap as high into the air as she could. In so doing, she not only saw the river but also caught sight of the sacred mountains—powerful and brilliant, though still far away. At the same time, she also received a nickname—Jumping Mouse—from the frog.

Jumping Mouse returned to the other mice and told them of her journey, of the thunderous river, and of the sacred mountains. Some merely ignored her, some feared her, and some laughed at her, mocking her new name. But they all preferred to remain busy about their work.

Jumping Mouse decided that she must see the mysterious mountains up close, even if it meant journeying there alone. Again she was assisted by other animals of the prairie who either admired her courage or pitied her silly curiosity. When at last she arrived at a lake near the mountains, she jumped once more into the air to get a better glimpse of them. Carried by the mountain wind, she ascended higher and higher and higher—up to the mountain peaks. In the process she was changed and received another name, the name by which she has been known ever since—**Eagle.**

# Sacramental Awareness

## Listening for Thunder, Searching for Sacred Mountains

By and large, we modern people are very busy creatures—like the mice in the opening story. Cars, ATVs, snowblowers, weed whackers, televisions, CD players, computer games, and coffee grinders provide the sound tracks to our many activities. With so much busyness and noise going on, it is no wonder that we sometimes cannot hear any thunder in our life, much less take the time to think about its source. And with our nose so often close to the ground, or our eyes mesmerized by television, we fail to catch sight of the majestic mountains on the horizon.

*Student art:* Watercolor by Virginia Foy, Cor Jesu Academy, Saint Louis, Missouri

This course on the seven sacraments of the Catholic faith suggests that the **sacred**—the holy, that which is of God—is right before our eyes. But to encounter the sacred, we must, like Jumping Mouse, be willing to open ourselves up to it and let it touch our life. In doing so we discover that the world and life itself are so much bigger and more wonderful than our own narrow view can see.

This course, therefore, asks you to take a journey deep into the world around you, to listen and look without haste and with an essential openness. This can lead to a special appreciation of the sacred in the world, to what we call **sacramental awareness.** A

## God Is Everywhere

The Catholic church's view about the presence of the sacred in the world can be summed up by paraphrasing the Baltimore Catechism (a question-and-answer book of Catholic teachings that was used in much of religious education until the 1960s):

Question: "Where is God?"

Answer: "God is everywhere."

Catholic belief is that God communicates through the people, places, actions, events, and experiences that shape a person's life. God is present in and communicates with us through all of creation. God speaks and can be seen through all things. At the same time, God is not identical with creation: God transcends creation—is beyond it as the loving source of it all. B

## Dullness to the Sacred

If God can be found in the midst of life and creation, why are we not always aware of God's presence? No one simple response will fully answer this question, but people's lack of sacramental awareness can be thought of in this way: Those who cannot perceive the sacred in their life or in the world suffer from what can be thought of as sacramental dullness.

### Why Sacramental Dullness?

Why are people dulled to the presence of the holy?

**People are too busy.** The story of Jumping Mouse suggests one possible cause of sacramental dullness. People are so preoccupied with the daily routines of living that they simply cannot see or hear the signs and signals of God's presence in their life.

**A great deal of pain and suffering exists in the world.** Another reason people might not see the sacred is that a great deal of pain and suffering exists in their own life and in the world. Many people become overwhelmed by all the problems facing themselves personally and the world as a whole—broken relationships, unsatisfying jobs, war, poverty, the destruction of the environment, and so forth. When this happens their vision of life becomes dominated by gloom and pessimism. They cannot imagine that God could be present.

**People do not know where to look or what to look for.** Perhaps another reason some people have a hard time perceiving God in their midst is that they do not really know where to look or what to look for. How often have we looked for something and not recognized it, even though it was right there in front of us? We may have been expecting whatever we were searching for to look different, or to find it in a different place. C

The world and life are so much bigger and more wonderful than our own narrow view can see.
*Student art:* Oil pastel by Caroline Read, Saint Scholastica Academy, Covington, Louisiana

take a second look

Ⓒ If, in activity B, you could not identify something in creation that conveys a sense of the holy or the sacred to you, describe in writing why you think you could not.

### Taking a Second Look: A Cure for Sacramental Dullness

The antidote to sacramental dullness may be a lot like the antidote to prejudice. Prejudice toward a person or group usually melts away once we take a closer look, once we take some time to know more about the person or group. Similarly, seeing the sacred in our life and in the world requires taking a second, even closer look to see if we might have missed something the first time around. In the process we are able to shed whatever it is that dulls us to the sacred.

A Christian perspective gives us that deeper look at reality. The Christian vision is that God created us and the entire world out of love, and that this makes all of creation sacred. If we really take on this perspective, it can open up a whole new world for us.

**sacramental awareness**

## For Review

1. What does sacramental awareness reveal about God's presence to us in creation?

2. Define sacramental dullness and list three possible causes of it.

3. Briefly describe how sacramental dullness can be cured.

# Where This Course Is Going

As you have probably noticed by now, this course does not begin by immediately going into the seven sacraments of the Catholic church. That kind of start would be like walking into the middle of a movie. You may already know quite a bit about the seven sacraments, and by this time you may have celebrated several of them. Before considering the seven sacraments themselves, however, this course will explore the rich vision that sees all of creation as sacramental, as communicating God's love to us.

So this course begins by recognizing God's presence in the world and by becoming familiar with the ways God and people communicate with each other, such as through symbols, rituals, and prayer. From there the journey moves to Jesus, the center of life for Christians, and to his continuing presence in the world through the church in history. Only after this foundation is laid does the course move on to the seven official sacraments of the Catholic church. The finale, however, is a sacrament called YOU.

Perhaps you are not Catholic, and this course will be an opportunity to learn about the sacramental vision that is part of the Catholic heritage of the school you and your parents have chosen. It is hoped that you find much of the course material relevant to your life, whether you are Catholic or not.

Blessings on your work of learning and growing.

■ *Student art:* Photo by Patrick Brinkman, North Catholic High School, Pittsburgh, Pennsylvania

creation is graced

# Grace: God's Loving Presence in the World

Christians have a special way of describing God's loving presence in the world, a way that helps God's presence to be understood in a here-and-now, personal light. This central Christian belief is called grace. **Grace** is the creative, sustaining, and transforming self-gift of God that is always being offered to us.

God loves us and cares for us unconditionally, and no matter what happens, God is with us and for us. For Christians the word *grace* expresses this reality of God's gift of Self to us. In addition, God's love and concern extend not only to people but to all of creation. So to say that all of creation is sacred means that all of creation is graced.

How does God communicate this love and concern for us? How does God make this loving presence known to us? "Because God is everywhere," as an old teaching says, "God speaks to us in many ways."

## Flesh-and-Blood Communication

To understand how God communicates with us, we need to appreciate something about how we humans communicate with one another—the fact that our body language and gestures often speak louder than our words.

### Speaking with Our Body

The notion that we communicate with our body and our gestures has long been a part of human wisdom. Researchers who study what is called body language inform us that a person reveals what is going on "inside" by the way he or she acts on the "outside." If a woman is fidgeting with her watch, for example, she might be communicating that she is anxious to make the time pass. Direct eye contact can signal self-confidence or interest in another person. A blush may indicate several feelings—embarrassment, pleasure, or even anger.

Body language is not an earthshaking concept, but it does reinforce something we already know: Consciously or unconsciously, our body communicates our feelings. We "speak" with one another through physical expressions, and our nonverbal, or body, messages often speak louder than our verbal messages.

Studies have also suggested that when a spoken (or verbal) message conflicts with a body (or nonverbal) message, people more often respond to the nonverbal message. In other words, if you told a friend, "I like your new haircut," but then started to snicker, your friend would "hear" the insincerity more clearly than the spoken compliment. Or if you said to someone, "I really want to hear more about last night," but then continually yawned during the story, that person would likely feel that you didn't really want to hear what she or he had to say.

So our smiles, tears, laughter, sighs, touches, looks, open hands of friendship, closed hands of rejection, hugs—all our expressions and gestures—communicate who and what we are to one another. Our human flesh thus expresses our human spirit. Amplifying a message by using flesh-and-blood terms is the normal human way of communicating intensely. ◻

◻ List five examples of body language and the messages they communicate.

*God speaks in many ways*

E Look through a Bible and write down five descriptions that use images of nature. Choose one of the images and briefly describe how it can speak to us about God's presence.

F First, imagine that your closest friend goes away for four years and cannot communicate with you. In writing, do the following:
• Name five ways your friend continues to be present with you.
• Name five things your friend might like you to know.
• Name five things you could do to be reminded of your friend.
Second, imagine that your closest friend is Jesus. Complete the above three exercises as they might apply to Jesus.

### God's Body Language

Because we are creatures of flesh, creatures of the earth, God chooses to speak to us using the human language of physical reality. Thus God employs a kind of body language, examples of which abound.

**Examples from the Bible.** In the Old Testament, for instance, we read that Moses recognized God in a burning bush. Samuel saw God in a dream; Elijah, in a gentle breeze; Abraham and Jacob, in passing strangers. The prophets were constantly observing the world around them and seeing God:

> I [God] will be to the people of Israel like rain in a dry land.
>
> . . . . . . . . . .
>
> Like an evergreen tree I will shelter them.
>
> (Hosea 14:5–8, GNB)

In the Gospels Jesus described God's grace using images from nature—fish, birds, trees—and happenings from people's everyday lives—a father welcoming home his wayward son, a woman rejoicing at finding her lost coin, a landowner treating his workers generously. In the Scriptures, then, God speaks through the material and social world. E

**Examples from today.** The God of the Bible continues to communicate and be revealed today. The evergreen tree that gave shelter to the Israelites is still with us. Rain still brings new life to parched lands; strangers still cross our paths and become friends. And although we may not be aware of it, we are always bumping into God in the daily business of life.

By recognizing the many hints of God's grace in our life, we experience **sacraments** in the broadest sense of the term: God's loving presence made visible and tangible in our life here and now. Sacraments are not *about* God; rather,

they are meant to provide an experience *of* God—an earthy, bodily experience that is also a spiritual experience.

Later in this course, we will look at the sacraments in the more specific sense of the seven sacraments of the Catholic church. Like sacraments in the broadest sense, these are encounters with God's loving, helping presence, but in them God's power is communicated in a heightened, special way. We will save a definition of sacraments in that sense for chapters 3 and 5.

## God Speaks Through Our Friendships

The following comment by a modern Catholic theologian reveals another clue about how God communicates love and concern to people: "Perhaps the most basic sacrament of God's saving presence to human life is the sacrament of human love and friendship" (Cooke, *Sacraments and Sacramentality,* pages 81–82). In other words, we especially experience God's love and concern in many earthy and bodily ways through our relationships with other people, particularly in our friendships.

Human friendships come and go; sometimes they are rekindled, and other times they die. Nonetheless, friendships—whether short-lived or longlasting—sustain us, nourish us, keep us human, identify us as who we are. And in the Christian vision, our personal friendships reveal God's friendship with us as well. Friends who are open, honest, and caring toward each other not only let another person into their life but also make room for God. As the First Letter of John says, "God is love, and those who abide in love abide in God, and God abides in them" (4:16). F

God's friendship as grace is revealed to us in the profound intricacy of our natural world, in the words and stories of the Scriptures, in the inspiring lives of church heroes past and present, and in the intimacy between friends. And these are just some of the ways God converses with us.

## For Review

4. What is grace?

5. What role does body language play in human communication?

6. Describe three examples of God's "body language."

7. Define sacrament in the broadest sense of the term.

# Receiving God's Offer of Friendship

As you probably know from your experience, maintaining strong, healthy friendships depends on honest communication. The same is true for establishing and maintaining a friendship with God. Real communication happens when messages are both sent and received. Read the following story to see how two young teenagers experienced true communication not only with each other but also with God.

Evening comes quickly to Camp La Crosse. Already the calm that follows sunset has fallen over the patch of woods where two boys sit by a still lake. Matt, who has been quiet for most of the week, is now talking freely. Jonathan, usually loud, boisterous, and always the joker, now speaks in softer, thoughtful tones:

"Yeah, I don't see much of my dad at all," says Jonathan.

Jonathan can't believe that he is talking like this. Secrets that he has kept inside all his life he is now sharing with a near stranger.

"I have a real nice family," says Matt. "We're actually close, but no one shows it. Everyone's just busy."

Surprising himself, Matt is discovering these truths as he says them. They come from deep inside—so deep that he had not known they exist.

The two boys sit staring at the lake. They both feel captivated—under the spell of the place, the moment, the company. At camp, Jonathan has worked hard at being "Mr. Good Times." And he has been quite successful at it. He has developed his own following, a bunch of guys ready to join him in whatever practical jokes he suggests. Matt, on the other hand, has spent his week at camp doing what comes naturally for him—lying low, keeping quiet, smiling a lot, and not causing any trouble.

Yet now these two unlikely companions find themselves together really talking to each other, involved in a conversation that neither has ever experienced before—deep talk, personal talk, talk from the heart. Their conversation is the kind of talk that friendships are made of.

Of course, thirteen-year-olds don't talk about friendships much. Both boys know, however, that they are on different terms this night. They are revealing themselves and listening to each other as neither has ever done before or even thought possible. So they know this moment is special.

Jonathan and Matt were not great conversationalists—at least not until that night. That night, Jonathan put aside his mask and revealed himself as he truly was. Matt also chanced speaking about his real feelings. That unlikely evening encounter between two seemingly different persons was special indeed. For insofar as they said yes to some honest sharing and mutual giving, they made an act of friendship with each other. And whether they realized it or not, their yes to each other was a yes to God as well. Jonathan and Matt made God's presence real to each other in their open and honest communication, in their listening and responding to each other. By acting in friendship with each other, they were also acting in friendship with God.

*Student art:* Photo by Colleen Hagan, Saint Patrick High School, Maysville, Kentucky

## in the evening calm

## Sacramental Skills

In their special moment together, Jonathan and Matt were learning for the first time two important skills necessary for real communication: listening and responding. If we are to truly communicate with God, listening and responding must be a part of our understanding of sacraments. Listening and responding are the skills necessary for sacramental awareness; they help us to fully experience the beauty, the excitement, and the deep meaning of our encounters with God. Let's take a closer look at these skills.

### Listening for God

Listening skills are important for our growth throughout life. Of course, applied to sacraments, listening is not confined to our ability to hear. The art of listening implies all kinds of receptivity—the ability to receive, to take in what has been sent our way. Insofar as it involves receptivity, listening can play a critical role in overcoming what was referred to earlier as sacramental dullness.

Listening is affirming and nonjudgmental. Listening means letting go of ourselves and opening up to the outpouring of experiences through which God constantly speaks to us. Indeed, listening can be uncomfortable and even painful. What we hear when we pause and listen may not always be pleasant. That is why it is important for us to hear again and again the story of Jesus, who addresses our pain and pleasures, sorrows and joys. ©

*listen and reflect*

© Develop your ability to listen by spending fifteen minutes alone in each of the following three situations: (1) in silence, (2) listening to music, and (3) in a park or woods. Write a half-page reflection for each experience.

The seven Catholic sacraments involve receiving—for example, receiving forgiveness, receiving healing, or receiving Jesus in Communion. By developing the skill of listening (receptivity), those who experience life sacramentally or participate in the seven sacraments are making themselves fertile ground in which grace can bear fruit.

### Responding to God

Sacramental awareness requires the skill of responding. Typically, listening occurs as part of the back-and-forth communication in a conversation. Responding to another person in conversation signals that we have been taking in what the other person has communicated to us. If true listening has occurred, genuine responses flow out of us almost naturally. Even responses as simple as a nod of the head or a smile of approval can move a conversation along to deeper levels. Responses are critical to continuing communication; they tell the other person that you heard what he or she said to you.

Similarly, sacramental experiences call for a response. Whenever we are given a gift, receive a hug, or hear our name called with genuine affection, we are drawn to respond. The sacraments are meant to be experiences of being touched profoundly by God, leading to a positive response in the way people treat God, others, and themselves. Therefore, the skill of responding involves developing ways to improve our continuing conversation with God in our life.

# God's Many Precious Gems

God places in our grasp many precious gems whose beauty we can easily overlook—unless we have the skills to see them for what they are.

A young man presented himself to the local expert on gems and said he wanted to become a gemologist. The expert brushed him off because he feared that the youth would not have the patience to learn. The young man pleaded for a chance. Finally the expert consented and told the youth, "Be here tomorrow."

The next morning the expert put a jade stone in the boy's hand and told him to hold it. The expert then went about his work, cutting, weighing, and setting gems. The boy sat quietly and waited.

The following morning the expert again placed the jade stone in the youth's hand and told him to hold it. On the third, fourth, and fifth day the expert repeated the exercise and the instructions.

On the sixth day the youth held the jade stone, but could no longer stand the silence. "Master," he asked, "when am I going to learn something?"

"You'll learn," the expert replied and went about his business.

Several more days went by and the youth's frustration mounted. One morning as the expert approached and beckoned for him to hold out his hand, he was about to blurt out that he could go on no longer. But as the master placed the stone in the youth's hand, the young man exclaimed without looking at his hand, "This is not the same jade stone!"

"You have begun to learn," said the master.
(Cavanaugh, *The Sower's Seeds,* pages 8–9)

## Sacramental Moments in Daily Life

Once we begin to learn the skills of sacramental awareness, we start to recognize many events in our daily life as experiences of God's loving presence, experiences that can be called sacramental moments. Consider the following examples:

- Juanita stays in bed as long as she can. Starting at a new school in the middle of the year just has to be the most dreadful situation she has ever faced. How is she going to make it through the day? Everyone will be staring at her all day and probably laughing at her accent.

  Expecting the worst, Juanita braces herself as she is about to enter her new classroom. But instead of being greeted with judging stares and silence, Juanita is received with a huge hand-made sign strung across the wall: WELCOME, JUANITA! All the members of the class have signed it.

- The summer is not turning out at all the way Jesse had planned. Within the first two weeks of vacation, he has to go into the hospital to have his tonsils taken out. Exactly a week after he gets home from that operation, he wakes up in the middle of the night with an awful pain in his abdomen. An hour later he is back in the hospital having his appendix removed.

  Jesse is so mad when he wakes up around noon the next day that he refuses to eat or say anything. But later that day, Jesse receives a gift that helps turn his spirits around. After baseball practice that afternoon, the whole team—all of Jesse's buddies—stops by to visit: "We sure hope you get better soon, Jesse. The team doesn't seem the same without you."

- Caitlin's mom got a new job about the same time school started. It was a big promotion, and Caitlin was really happy for her mom. Unfortunately her mom often has to work late now. So the message on the answering machine doesn't surprise Caitlin when she gets home from school: "I won't get home till about eight o'clock tonight. I've called your grandma and told her to expect you for dinner."

*Student art:* Photo by Lauren Aumiller, Notre Dame Preparatory School, Towson, Maryland

⊞ Recall a sacra-
mental moment
from your own
life—an occasion
when you felt
especially attuned
to God's presence.
Write about your
experience. Include
some details and
background.

At first Caitlin resented not being able to spend as much time with her mom. They used to have a lot of fun getting dinner together and catching up with each other. These days they did that twice a week if they were lucky. But as she is walking home from her grandma's house that evening, Caitlin realizes just how lucky she is. Not only has she been able to get to know her grandma better since she has been eating there a couple of nights a week, but the times she and her mom can be together now seem even more special.

Though none of these examples may seem profound, they are, nonetheless, examples of sacramental moments— occasions in which God has graced a person's life. ⊞

Take a second look at the examples. Notice that what has been described in them echoes some of the sacraments of the Catholic church. Can you identify which ones? In the church's sacraments, some very natural, human events—like welcoming a stranger into community, helping out a sick friend, and sharing a meal together—are raised up, intensified through ritual, and celebrated as God's body language, God's communication of love. Through the seven sacraments, Catholics believe, God pours out love on us in a special way.

Recognizing sacramental moments means that we are listening to and re-sponding to God's messages of love and concern. We are letting ourselves be moved and transformed by God's grace —as Jumping Mouse from our opening story let herself be transformed by the sacred into Eagle.

*Student art:* Photo by Clare Major, Saint Joseph's Academy, Baton Rouge, Louisiana

# transformed
## by grace

## For Review

8. How did Jonathan and Matt say yes to God's offer of friendship?

9. List two skills necessary for sacramental awareness. Briefly explain why these skills are important for celebrating sacraments.

10. What is a sacramental moment? Give an example.

# Sacraments Reveal God's Love

Christians believe that the primary message spoken by God is one of love. Consequently, the world is filled with meaning, charged with the Spirit, a revelation of God's presence as grace. In that sense we are always surrounded by sacraments.

Simply stated, the two dimensions of a sacrament are as follows: (1) God acts and is present as grace, and (2) we respond to God's presence in faith and friendship. The primary message of any sacrament, then, is the good news that God is with us and for us, lovingly active in the affairs of human life. At the same time, we respond to that good news in our relationships and celebrate it as a community using symbols and rituals—the topics of the next two chapters.

# 2 Symbols

## doorways to the sacred

...look beyond the surface

O Creator God, I look lovingly at your world,
and invite it to speak to me,
helping me to see
beyond the surface of things.
May I continue to keep an eye out
for the many ways
your love is revealed to me.
Amen.

When we become more aware of the sacred in the world around us, we can see that God is communicating with us all the time. This chapter considers how communication can happen through the use of symbols. Symbols, in turn, are key to the seven sacraments of the church.

The following incident describes a particularly "enlightening" example of how symbols can communicate meaning:

# flame of hope

## During the visit

of Pope Paul VI to the United States in 1976, thousands of people witnessed a marvelous occurrence. The pope was addressing a full house at the huge Madison Square Garden in New York City on a hot, steamy day. All of a sudden, the electricity failed, causing a blackout. The whole arena was in pitch darkness. You could not see your hand in front of your face.

After a few moments of restless re-action in the crowd, someone in one corner of the vast arena lit a match. Miraculously, it seemed, you could see throughout the whole arena, although dimly.

A murmur went up from the crowd. The symbolic impact of the moment was clear: In the darkest hour, even one small flame of hope casts a great light.

# Communicating Through Symbols

Imagine that you were in Madison Square Garden when the incident in the opening story happened. Like everyone else there, you too would probably have realized the powerful symbolism of a small light illuminating such a large, dark space and carrying the meaning of hope. Communicating through the use of symbols is a universal hu-man characteristic. It is some-thing we do all the time.

## Creating "Meaning Pictures"

Broadly speaking, **symbols** are observable, physical realities that represent invisible qualities or elements. The word *symbol* comes from the Greek root *symballein*, which means "to throw together." So to think symbolically means to take something tangible (something that we can perceive with our senses), like fire, and throw it together with something that has no material, physical form—like an emotion or a concept or an idea. Smells can be symbols. For instance, the smoke and flames of burning sulfur were traditionally associated with the Christian idea of hell. Actions can be symbols as well, but these are usually connected with rituals—the topic of chapter 3.

Symbols help us to see beyond the surface of things, to search for the deeper significance and levels of meaning in things, to take that "second look" mentioned in chapter 1. In a sense, symbols are "meaning pictures" that serve as doorways to the sacred.

*Student art:* Colored pencil by Ryan Martinez, University of San Diego High School, San Diego, California

*a family symbol*

**A** Choose a symbol for your family and write a brief explanation of why you think that symbol is appropriate. For example, if your family does things together, you might pick a paper chain or a mobile. If your family is always on the go, a revolving door may be an accurate symbol for your family.

## Examples of Symbolizing

Take a few minutes now and try doing some symbolizing. Read each of the following exercises once or twice and then do what is suggested:

- Close your eyes, picture a river in your mind's eye, and say the word *river* aloud several times. Try to say the word in the various ways that a river itself might express its different moods. If the river you are imagining were human, what would be its attitude toward life? What qualities of the human spirit does a river represent for you?
- Close your eyes again and say the word *rock* aloud several times. Now picture a rock in your thoughts. Try to imagine the feel of a rock in your hands. Picture a person whom you would describe as rocklike. Imagine yourself as a rock. If you were a rock, what attitude toward life would you have? What human emotions do you associate with a rock?

- Now close your eyes and picture a cat. In your imagination follow the cat around for a while. What is it doing? How is it acting? How does it deal with things that cross its path? How does it view the world? What are catlike characteristics? If you told someone, "You remind me of a cat," what would you mean?
- Picture a dot, a straight line, a wavy line, and a spiral. If these figures could make noise, what sound would each one make? If you were to describe your life as one of these figures, which would you choose? Why?

When we look at some physical object like a river, a rock, or a cat and say, "There's more to this than meets the eye," then we are starting to see the object as a symbol. A river might remind us of the constant passing of time or conjure up images of things dark and mysterious. A rock might summon up positive images of someone who is strong and steady, or it might evoke negative images of someone who is cold and

*more than meets the eye*

unfeeling. A cat might be used to symbolize sleekness, quickness, or a sense of independence. Ⓐ

# Simple Signs and Symbolic Signs

The words *sign* and *symbol* are often used interchangeably, a practice that confuses the precise meaning of both. For instance, we usually think of a stop sign as a symbol. Often, the insignia of a sports team is considered a symbol for that team. The images %, <, >, ÷, +, and = are math symbols, and the sequenced letters *t-r-e-e* are said to symbolize a tree. In each case, however, the word *symbol* is used too loosely to fit the concept as described so far in this chapter. The word *sign* is more accurately used in these examples.

A few distinctions between symbols and signs will help us arrive at the richer appreciation of symbols needed for seeing how symbols relate to sacraments.

### What Makes a Sign a Sign?

*Sign*, as a general term, refers to any object that represents something else. Thus there are symbolic signs and signs that are less than symbolic. Simple, nonsymbolic signs are objects that have only one meaning: A yellow light at an intersection is a simple sign meaning "proceed with caution." A sign in a store window that reads "SALE" also has only one simple meaning. And a five-dollar bill is a sign of one particular monetary amount.

### What Makes a Symbol a Symbol?

Although symbols, like all signs, represent something other than their physical realities, they have three main characteristics that distinguish them from simple signs.

Simple objects in our life can be rich with personal meaning.
✳ *Student art (above):* Colored pencil by Virginia Bernard, Saint Joseph's Academy, Baton Rouge, Louisiana

✳ *Student art (facing page):* Photo by Lisa Hensley, Seton Keough High School, Baltimore, Maryland

**B** List five symbols that you would use at your ten-year high school class reunion to remind your class members of their high school days.

**C** Symbols often have emotional significance—the sound of a siren might summon the memory of a car accident. Recall an emotionally intense moment in your life. In writing, describe any symbols you associate with that moment.

**Symbols may have more than one meaning.** Symbolic signs are much richer types of signs than simple signs. Recall the symbolizing exercises you did earlier with the river, the rock, and the cat. You probably came up with a number of different meanings for each of these images. Unlike simple signs, symbols may have more than one meaning.

**What symbols stand for is connected to what they are.** Symbols have certain meanings associated with them by their very nature. For instance, a rock, because of what it is, has many symbolic meanings that are very different from those of a cat. It is unlikely that we would choose a rock as a symbol for softness or quickness. In the same way, a cat, as a symbol, would not serve well as a sign of either unchangeableness or lifelessness. **B**

In other words, we do not impose meanings on symbols. Rather, we discover meanings in symbols. To be precise, what we discover is a vital connection between the visible object and the invisible reality that it represents. So a rock actually helps us to define our ideas of strength, steadfastness, and other qualities. The same is true for other symbols. What meanings do you connect, for example, with sunshine? mountains? food and drink?

Discovering the appropriate symbols for our experiences can help us express the true significance of those experiences—a significance that might otherwise remain hidden. To say "Jesus is the light of the world," for instance, captures an aspect of the Christian experience of Jesus that cannot be reduced to a one-dimensional, factual description.

**Symbols evoke more than one kind of response from us.** Symbols speak to us in a more powerful and personal way than do other, simpler signs. When a sign speaks to only one dimension of our being, it cannot evoke a variety of responses from our many human dimensions—that is, from our mind, body, emotions, memories, senses, and spirit. Symbols, on the other hand, can touch us on many levels and dimensions. Symbols get us more totally involved; they spark a deep response. They touch our heart as well as our head. **C**

Thus "light" can be viewed either as a simple sign or as a symbol. We generally treat a traffic light at an intersection as a sign with one narrow meaning. Yet we understand lights on a Christmas tree or Christmas candles as symbols with many meanings—perhaps as symbols of the brightness of the holiday season with its good cheer, perhaps as symbols of the coming of Jesus as the light of the world. And if we allow Christmas lights to speak to us symbolically, we may be touched by the memory of past Christmases, by the recognition of the many friends who act as "lights" brightening up our life, or by the light and warmth symbolized by the Christ Child in the stable. Indeed, lights are an essential part of what we think of as Christmas.

Symbols can never be confined or reduced to narrow, one-dimensional meanings. What symbols are is intimately linked with what they represent. Symbols are thought-provoking and stimulating and soul-stirring all at once. These characteristics contribute to their power as a means of communicating the sacred in our life.

# communicating
## through symbols

## For Review

1. What does *symballein*, the Greek root word for *symbol*, mean? How does this meaning relate to our present-day understanding of what it means to think symbolically?

2. Name three characteristics that distinguish symbols from signs.

# Different Kinds of Symbols

Although communicating through symbols is something every human being does, not all symbols communicate meanings that will be the same for everyone in all places or times. Symbols that are closely dependent on a specific situation, place, or group might be called **cultural symbols.** Symbols that are clearly recognized throughout the world are called **universal symbols.** Let's take a closer look at the distinction between these two kinds of symbols.

## Cultural Symbols

Simply put, the meaning of a cultural symbol is tied to the situation the symbol is used in. Outside of that situation, a cultural symbol loses or changes its meaning, as the following story illustrates:

> We invited a newly arrived Chinese exchange student to dinner at a Chinese restaurant. At the end of the meal, we passed around the fortune cookies. When the plate reached her, she plainly blanked. We asked if fortune cookies weren't a custom in her country. She looked carefully at the cookies and replied, "I've never seen such a thing before."
>
> We all laughed at our presumption—not the first one we had made about her culture. We then showed the student the fortunes inside the cookies and read them all out loud. The student laughed with us but then leaned over to the person next to her and asked, "Does this have religious significance for you?"

As the Chinese student in the preceding story experienced, one of the frustrating things about moving to a different community or culture is that many of the symbols that are shared in the new community may not be familiar to us. Some North Americans who travel to southern Europe, for example, are taken aback when they first encounter men kissing each other—a common symbolic gesture of greeting in southern European countries. E

Cultural symbols also change in their meaning, or lose their meaning and die altogether. Did you know, for instance, that sixty years ago, shoulder-length hair on men was associated with classical musicians and conductors? "Long-hair" music was classical music. Later, in the 1960s, long hair on men symbolized rebelliousness. Nowadays long hair on men is perhaps more a matter of personal style than a cultural, symbolic style with a particular meaning.

## Universal Symbols

Universal symbols are unlike cultural symbols in that they are not tied to a specific situation, group, or place. The meaning of universal symbols can be understood by people of many different cultures.

Consider that although people in the Sahara Desert have a greatly different experience of water from people in the Samoan islands, water probably signifies life for both groups. A tree is a symbol for life in many different cultures.

Sign, symbol, or what?
*Student art:* Photo by Megan Rulli, Oak Knoll School, Summit, New Jersey

D Imagine you are conducting a class in which you want to explain five important Catholic symbols. Pretend that your audience knows nothing about Catholicism. Write down which symbols you would choose, and relate how you would explain them.

E In writing, compare a symbol representative of today's teenage generation with a symbol representative of your parents' teenage generation. Explain how each symbol's meaning is tied to its cultural situation.

F Imagine you are part of a study group made up of people from the seven continents. You have been chosen to present to the group three symbols whose meaning you think all the members of the group will be able to understand. List these symbols and explain why you think they are universal symbols.

Another universal symbol might be fire, which people of many cultures could also understand as symbolizing spiritedness or destructiveness. F

Sometimes, universal symbols convey complex or even contradictory meanings. Wind, for example, can be refreshing—a bringer of life-giving rain and relief from heat. Hurricane-like winds, however, can be a terribly destructive force. Likewise, hands can be seen as both creative and destructive. The heart is powerful yet vulnerable. Explosives are used in fireworks for celebrating and in bombs for killing.

Generally symbols like water and wind are so rich in meaning and so much a part of human existence that they can be said to be universal.

God's loving presence is communicated to us through symbols. ▓ *Student art:* Watercolor and colored pencil by Elise Schweitzer, Cor Jesu Academy, Saint Louis, Missouri

like water & wind

For Review

3. Describe the differences between a universal symbol and a cultural symbol. Give an example of each symbol.

## Symbols and the Natural World

Frequently, universal symbols come to us from the natural world. But in today's more urban and industrial culture, how many of us are in touch with the natural world enough to be able to appreciate the significance of nature-based universal symbols?

When most of the objects that surround our life come ready-made by machines, for instance, can we appreciate hands as symbols of creativity? When curative, medicinal oils come in spray containers, can we recognize oil as a symbol of healing? When microwave ovens cook our food, can we understand a hearthfire as a symbol of warmth and nourishment?

The natural world is one of God's primary means of communicating with us (the other way being our relationships with people). When we cut ourselves off from the natural world or do not cultivate a relationship with it, we are cutting ourselves off from God and from life itself.

# Literal Thinking Versus Symbolic Thinking

Communication by way of symbols is based on the human ability to think symbolically. But for a variety of reasons, modern Western people often have a hard time thinking symbolically. So when we think of the moon today, we often think of rocks in a museum or of lunar landings and robotic equipment collecting specimens from the barren terrain. We tend not to connect the moon with the mystery of the night anymore—or even with romance.

Instead of seeing the moon in terms of symbols, we tend to think about it in more literal, obvious terms. When we see things only at their literal level, we endanger our ability to recognize the deeper meanings they can convey to us. We endanger our ability to recognize the sacred.

## Literal Thinking: "That's All There Is"

Literal thinking involves considering something only at face value or just being concerned with the "facts." The attitude behind literal thinking reduces all of life to just the observable, measurable things and says, "That's all there is." It is as if visible, measurable facts are the only valid foundation of knowledge. This attitude closes the door to the possibility of there being a deeper significance to something than just what our limited senses can detect.

Of course, literal thinking is often necessary. An airplane pilot must be more concerned about the speed and direction of wind currents than about the wind as a symbol of the Spirit touching human lives. Still there is something very natural, human, and necessary about symbolic thinking. Just think, without the willingness to communicate in symbols, we

Ⓖ Using only literal language (that is, writing about measurable, physical realities), start a one-page essay that describes a close friend. Be as precise as you can. After a couple paragraphs, ask yourself if this description does justice to your friend's qualities. Finish your essay by explaining why such a description seems satisfactory or unsatisfactory to you.

Ⓗ Things can be viewed both symbolically and literally. Choose three of the following four objects and write a literal description and a symbolic interpretation for each:

- a rocky road
- a lightning bolt
- a seed
- a roller coaster

could not talk about our emotional, intellectual, moral, and spiritual experiences—all of which defy description in literal terms.

For instance, consider for a moment the invisible realities we call love, hope, and faith. Would a person in love say, "She raises my heart rate five beats per minute, she increases my oxygen intake by 25 percent, and she and I scored 'compatible' on personality tests"? These statements may be literally correct, but they are lifeless. They certainly do not appeal to our emotions or spirit. Ⓖ

More likely someone would use symbolic language to express his or her love, saying something like, "She's special—like one song is different from any other." Or, "He's pure treasure to me." Or, "She brings light to the darkness of my life." Only a symbolic language can help us to explain and fully experience these powerful realities.

## Symbolic Thinking: "There's More Here than Meets the Eye"

The following story further illustrates the differences between literal thinking and symbolic thinking:

One day the English poet William Blake was looking up at the sun. One of his companions challenged him: "Surely when you look at the sun you see a round, golden globe shining in the sky." Blake responded, "When I look at the sun, I see choirs of angels singing 'alleluia,' and who are you to say that you are right and I am wrong?"

Blake's friend tried to describe the sun in a simple, one-dimensional statement. Literalists generally look at things as objects isolated from everything else. They stick to the dictionary definitions of things. The symbolic thinker, on the other hand, sees things in relationship to all other things and as having meaning at many levels.

Some more examples might help to clarify this distinction. As you read the following statements, think about what they mean literally; then think about what they mean symbolically:

- It's raining cats and dogs.
- He has a fiery temper.
- The movie is a watered-down version of the book.
- He was a cold shooter in the basketball game tonight.
- He's a real down-to-earth person.

Obviously these statements are meant to be understood symbolically. Intepreted literally, they are silly or meaningless. Yet something about each of these images makes them work as symbols. Ⓗ

Symbolic thinking helps us discover the many meanings that the things of our world can have. And because symbolic thinking helps us see the specialness of all things, it is a skill necessary for celebrating sacraments.

# a necessary skill

## For Review

4. What is literal thinking? When is literal thinking appropriate and when is it not?

5. What is symbolic thinking? Why is symbolic thinking a necessary skill for celebrating sacraments?

6. Explain why symbols can be thought of as the language of faith.

7. When does symbolic thinking become sacramental awareness?

# Symbols and the Sacraments

## The Language of Faith

As powerful conveyors of meaning, symbols are well suited for communicating experiences of faith. A quick look at the way Jesus preached his message testifies to the appropriateness of symbols as the language of faith:

- In the story of the prodigal son, Jesus described God as a forgiving father who rushes out to greet his wayward son.
- Jesus called himself the Good Shepherd.
- Jesus likened God's Kingdom to the lowly mustard seed that becomes a tree with many branches, to a treasure hidden in a field, and to a wedding feast.

The Christian church throughout its history has built upon and added to the symbols present in the Scriptures. Walk into any church building and you will be surrounded by symbols. The crucifix, candles, altar, tabernacle, assembly of people—all have symbolic meanings. Even the way a church is laid out, whether as a circle, a semicircle, or a long rectangle, communicates a certain message symbolically. ☐

## Sacraments as Symbols

The most important symbols of the Catholic church, of course, are the seven sacraments, which contain both universal symbols and symbols that are unique to the Christian community. Indeed, symbols are so commonly used in our attempts to recognize the sacred that it is almost impossible to talk about sacraments apart from symbols.

When the experiences we are trying to describe are our experiences of God's presence, then symbolic thinking becomes sacramental awareness and our symbols may become sacraments for us. To get a clearer idea of how sacraments are expressed through symbols, consider the following example:

> Suppose you fall in love. Imagine, too, that your love is so powerful that it seems to you to reflect an infinitely greater love—that is, God's love that lights the whole world. Then any symbol of your love—a gift, a ring perhaps—might take on a genuine sacramental meaning because to you it would symbolize God's love.

The church's sacrament of marriage is based on just this sacramental understanding enhanced by Jesus' vision.

Earlier, sacraments were defined in the broadest sense as God's loving presence made visible and tangible in our life here and now. Now, with an understanding of what symbols are, we can say that sacraments are symbols of God's grace. ☐

☐ Spend some time in a church observing its art and architecture. Sit down in a pew and write about the symbols and the meanings that you perceive from those symbols. Consider visiting a church of a different denomination, a mosque, a temple, or a synagogue for comparison.

☐ Draw or describe in writing a symbol of grace, God's loving, transforming presence in the world.

picture grace

# From Symbols to Rituals

Like the skills of listening and responding, symbolic thinking opens us up to the world of the sacred, helping us look deeper at objects and discover their different meanings. An appreciation of symbols also enables us to experience the sacraments of the church as fresh and alive, as avenues to deeper realities and meanings, and as places where God meets and moves us. Rituals, the topic of chapter 3, take symbols one step further by adding movement and gestures.

# 3
# Rituals
## meaning in symbolic actions

God of our joy, God of our joy,

know who we are

God of our joy, we celebrate you
and we sing your praises.
We join in the dance of life,
confident that you are with us.
May we joyfully and playfully
treasure special moments, sacred places,
and saintly people in our life.

**Amen.**

Chapter 2 described symbols as "meaning pictures" that help us see beyond the surface of things. Rituals, or symbolic actions, take the notion of symbols one step further by adding movement and gestures to these pictures. The role of rituals in life and their relationship to worship and sacraments are the subjects of this chapter.

Like symbols, rituals are part of human culture and communication. They help us express what is important to us, as the following story illustrates:

# adding
# movement & gestures

**Carmen sits nervously,** waiting to give her presentation on the culture of her home country, Mexico, to Ms. Halling's first-semester Spanish class. As an exchange student, Carmen knew that she would be asked to do this kind of thing once in a while—she just never expected to be doing it within the first two weeks of being at her host school. Fortunately choosing what to talk about was easy; fiestas are such a common part of the life of her people that Carmen figured that describing one would give the class a good introduction to her country's culture.

Carmen begins her presentation: "Celebrations, or fiestas, are an important part of my culture. Today I want to describe a typical fiesta, a Mexican-style birthday party.

"Every year parents try to have one big party for each child in their family. Up until the child becomes a teenager, the party usually celebrates the child's birthday—though sometimes the party is held on the feast day of the child's patron saint. Either way, the party is a major event that lasts for five or six hours. A birthday fiesta like this requires a lot of preparation.

"Many people are invited to a birthday fiesta: all of the extended family—grandparents, cousins, aunts and uncles; parents' friends and their children; and the child's own classmates and friends. Each family brings a gift for the child whose birthday is being celebrated.

"About an hour after the guests have arrived, everyone gathers for the breaking of the piñatas. A piñata is a decorated, breakable container filled with candy, fruits, toys, or other small gifts. It hangs from the ceiling, and blindfolded children take turns striking at it with a stick until it breaks. Then the children scramble to collect all its fallen contents.

"At a party like this, everyone has a chance to get involved with the fun. Usually there are several piñatas for the different age-groups of children. The teenage boys get to move the piñata to a different spot once in a while, and the teenage girls are in charge of the blindfolding. The adults stand around the center of activity, throwing confetti and cheering for the children. In my culture a birthday party—or any fiesta—would not be complete without a piñata.

"A large dinner follows the breaking of the piñatas and includes a birthday cake traditionally made by the child's grandmother. After dinner the kids go off to play and the adults socialize. Or, if someone has a guitar, there is singing and dancing. The partying usually lasts until about midnight, and then everyone thanks their hosts and goes home.

"Fiestas like this are important to my culture because they bring all the different age-groups together. My culture stresses interaction between the generations very much. Fiestas often bring different social classes together as well, and give families and friends a chance to stay in touch with **each other.**"

# Rituals: Actions Serving as Symbols

Unless you are Mexican, the birthday party described in the opening story of this chapter is probably quite different from what you are familiar with. One striking difference may be the presence of so many people of all ages. When we put the differences aside, however, some common characteristics can be seen. Most obviously both the birthday fiesta and a typical birthday party in the United States are celebrations of the life of the person whose birth is being remembered.

In many respects a celebration like a birthday party serves no practical purpose. It is not necessary for human survival, nor does it produce something useful. Yet such an event is likely to be important to the people involved, no matter what culture. Why? Because a birthday celebration (or a pep rally, a graduation ceremony, and so forth) binds its participants together and gives expression to their identity as a family, a community, or a people.

Whether it takes place in a North American or a Mexican culture, a birthday celebration is an out-of-the-ordinary event. A celebration leads people out of their daily business and their mundane concerns into a special time and a special way of being together—a ritual.

Simply put, **rituals** are symbolic actions that help us concretely, or physically, express our beliefs, values, and deepest concerns. So like other symbols, rituals have deeper meaning than what immediately meets the eye. Rituals can be as simple as a handshake, a wave, or the sign of the cross; or they can be as complex as the Olympic Games, the celebration of a nation's founding, or the consecration of a pope. All rituals serve as ways of communicating what is important to us, what has meaning for us.

Oftentimes, rituals help us express those things that are hard to express any other way but through symbolic action— like the bonding of two people who love each other (as in the sacrament of Matrimony) or the consecration of a person for special ministry within the church (as in the sacrament of Holy Orders). In the church's sacraments, ritual expresses the deeper meaning of the sacraments to

*Student art:* Photo by Cara A. Brown, Bishop O'Dowd High School, Oakland, California

those who participate in them and to the whole community of faith. Ⓐ

# Practical Actions Versus Symbolic Actions

### Distinguishing the Practical from the Symbolic

By definition all rituals involve actions. Obviously, however, not all actions are rituals, or symbolic actions. Actions that are performed only for specific, practical purposes are not rituals. Simply walking down the street to get to school is not symbolic and therefore would not be a ritual. On the other hand, walking down the street in a parade, a procession, or a protest march would be a ritual. Such activities symbolize some important reality—things like community pride, the solemnity of an occasion, or the right to free speech and participation in choosing the policies and practices that affect people's lives.

### Combining the Practical and the Symbolic

Fortunately practical actions and symbolic actions do not necessarily exclude each other. They can be intertwined, and to good advantage. In China some people do not just walk down the street on their way to work. They dance along the way, taking time to slay imaginary monsters in intricate, ritual movements that provide entertainment and exercise for themselves and a free theatrical performance for onlookers. Ⓑ

Like walking, waking up and going to sleep are strictly practical activities; all creatures need rest. Morning and evening prayers, though, are symbolic actions that can bring deeper significance to our waking and sleeping. Saying grace before meals serves the same purpose for the practical business of eating. This brief ritual reminds us of the giftedness and beauty of sharing food—a significance that might not be called to mind if we just start eating.

### Realizing the Practical Implications of Rituals

Although rituals are not practical actions in themselves, they can lead to practical action. For example, the people whom we honor in special ceremonies—sports heroes, Nobel Prize winners, or civil rights leaders—tell us about our values and serve as models for young people to imitate. Participating in such rituals may eventually result in practical actions like choosing a career in sports or education, voting in elections, or even running for public office. Praying before class or a game, if done attentively, can lead to a deeper, more genuine faith. Later this course will discuss how the seven sacraments, as rituals, also have practical applications.

# Rituals and Routines: A Popular Confusion

Confusion over what constitutes a ritual may come about because in popular jargon an action that is repeated often or routinely is called a ritual: we talk about the "ritual" of brushing our teeth every morning or the "ritual" of riding the school bus every day. These are routines, however, not rituals, because they are not symbolic actions.

### Rituals: Meanings at Many Levels

The distinction between a routine and a ritual is similar to the distinction made earlier between a sign and a symbol. Routines, like signs, are one-dimensional in meaning, whereas rituals have deeper, multilevel meanings.

The contrast between a blink and a wink serves as a good illustration of the difference between a ritual and a routine:

Ⓐ In one page, tell about a celebration you know of or have participated in that involved rituals. Include a discussion of the meaning behind the rituals—why were they part of the celebration?

Ⓑ Write down three practical actions you do regularly. Then explain how a symbolic action could be intertwined with each of them.

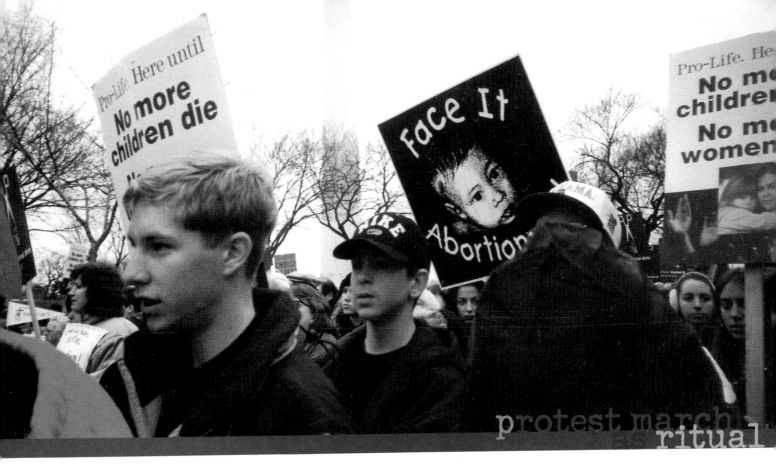

protest march as ritual

As humans we blink regularly and routinely to keep our eyes moist. In contrast, a wink has public and symbolic significance. Although a wink is physically almost the same action as a blink, it possesses any number of symbolic meanings in a community. The next time you walk through the halls between classes, try winking at a few people to see how they react!

### Keeping Rituals from Becoming Routine

Unfortunately many gestures and actions that people perform regularly as rituals become so familiar that the distinction between the practical (routine) and the symbolic (ritual) can be blurred. We can forget what the ritual actions symbolize. Saying grace before meals can become simply another part of eating—rushed and hurried through without much thought about why we do it. Even potent rituals like the Mass can be experienced as lifeless routines if they are repeated continually without any sense of their deeper significance. Ⓒ

Oddly enough, often it is when our rituals are disrupted or taken away from us that we realize what special significance they have. Imagine being at the funeral service of a person who was close to you and then suddenly hearing someone start to laugh. Imagine a group of noisy, enthusiastic basketball players chasing a loose ball into a church during the consecration of the Eucharist. Or imagine if Christians were denied celebration of Christmas for a year.

## Rituals and Play

Rituals can also be distinguished from routines in that rituals are often playful activities. Connecting play with ritual does not mean that rituals are not serious. Rather, it means that they are not work: they are not done solely to provide physical, practical results. They are done

✳ *Student art:* Photo by Leah Deeg, Shawe Memorial High School, Madison, Indiana

express what you get

Ⓒ Write a brief description of a ritual in which you have often participated. Express what you get out of that ritual. Does it still have meaning for you, or has it become routine? Why?

◫ Holidays, club meetings, induction ceremonies, and sporting events like the Olympics are filled with symbols and rituals. Choose a holiday, an induction ceremony, a club meeting, or a sporting event and jot down all the rituals and symbols associated with it.

▨ *Student art:* Photo by Cara A. Brown, Bishop O'Dowd High School, Oakland, California

for enjoyment. As playful activities, rituals enable us to pause from our daily routine. They free us to pursue aspects of life that might otherwise be neglected—friendships, family relationships, physical and spiritual renewal, creative hobbies, and so forth. Birthday parties, fiestas, pep rallies, and graduation ceremonies, as well as drama, dance, and athletics, are all forms of play in this sense.

Think about the people who put on school plays. They invest enormous amounts of energy in creating sets, acquiring costumes, and memorizing lines. Then the play is performed only four or five times. So why do they do it? For money? For experience? For fame and glory? For fun? The last reason is probably the most common answer. Leaving our everyday life and playfully entering another world is exciting. This kind of fun also expresses something profound: Life is meant to be enjoyed. Through rituals we can play at being bigger and better characters than the ones we usually are in real life.

Athletic activities are another case in point. Sports are popular throughout the world. Many people, young and old alike, spend Saturday or Sunday afternoons playing or watching sports of one kind or another. We enjoy celebrating life in a way that involves friends, nature, exertion, and resourcefulness in a nonworking, playful atmosphere. ◫

Margaret Mead, a famous American anthropologist, claimed that every culture develops rituals. Like symbols, rituals seem to be at the core of what it means to be human. Ritual celebrations open people up to the life-giving Spirit of God. They help people break through the barriers of isolation and boredom. When rituals are public, community cermonies, they symbolize in word and action people's deepest hopes and dreams. Through rituals people can re-establish their connection with the Earth, the cosmos, and their Creator. In other words, rituals are symbolic actions that speak to and for people.

# celebrate life through play

2. Describe the difference between symbolic actions and practical actions. Give an example of each type of action.

3. How are rituals different from routines?

4. What similarities exist between rituals and play?

# Characteristics of Rituals

Many of the following characteristics of rituals have been referred to in one way or another in the previous discussion. Here we will describe them a bit more. Of course, not all these characteristics are found in every ritual. Complex rituals, like weddings and Fourth of July parades, include more traits than simpler ones. And some rituals stress certain of these traits more than others do. When these traits are all viewed together, however, they make a powerful statement, not just about rituals but about what it means to be human.

### Movements and Gestures with Meaning

The most basic characteristic of all rituals has already been mentioned in this chapter: rituals involve movements and gestures that convey meaning. Shaking hands, kissing someone, waving good-bye, and clapping hands at a performance are all examples of simple rituals. They are acted out, and they have meaning beyond what they express as literal actions. Applause does not just make a lot of noise; it celebrates a performance. In religious language we might say that applause "blesses" the performer just as a priest blesses the congregation at

Mass by raising his hands over them.

### Repeated Actions

Ritual actions are often repeated—mostly because, as symbolic actions rich in meaning for us, they are worth doing more than once.

Sometimes the meaning of a ritual is in the repetition itself. Consider this example: Each year near the anniversary of their mother's death, Ron and his brothers and sisters join their father in attending Mass and visiting the grave site. Afterward, Ron, his father, his brothers and sisters, and all the grandchildren gather to picnic, play games, and reminisce.

By repeating this ritual every year, Ron and his family are reassured that their wife, mother, and grandmother continues to watch over and be present to her family. In turn Ron and his family keep alive her memory in the way she would have wanted—by eating together, playing together, and enjoying one another's company.

# The Fox Explains Rituals

In Antoine de Saint Exupéry's story *The Little Prince*, there is a classic passage in which a fox describes the value of repeating rituals to the little prince, a boy from another planet. As the fox explains, the repetition of a ritual does not necessarily make it routine:

The fox gazed at the little prince, for a long time.

"Please—tame me!" he said.

"I want to, very much," the little prince replied. "But I have not much time. I have friends to discover, and a great many things to understand."

"One only understands the things that one tames," said the fox. "Men have no more time to understand anything. They buy things all ready made at the shops. But there is no shop anywhere where one can buy friendship, and so men have no friends anymore. If you want a friend, tame me . . ."

"What must I do, to tame you?" asked the little prince.

"You must be very patient," replied the fox. "First you will sit down at a little distance from me—like that—in the grass. I shall look at you out of the corner of my eye, and you will say nothing. Words are the source of misunderstandings. But you will sit a little closer to me, every day . . ."

The next day the little prince came back.

"It would have been better to come back at the same hour," said the fox. "If, for example, you come at four o'clock in the afternoon, then at three o'clock I shall begin to be happy. I shall feel happier and happier as the hour advances. At four o'clock, I shall already be worrying and jumping about. I shall show you how happy I am! But if you come at just any time, I shall never know at what hour my heart is to be ready to greet you. . . . One must observe the proper rites . . ."

"What is a rite?" asked the little prince.

"Those also are actions too often neglected," said the fox. "They are what make one day different from other days, one hour from other hours. There is a rite, for example, among my hunters. Every Thursday they dance with the village girls. So Thursday is a wonderful day for me! I can take a walk as far as the vineyards. But if the hunters danced at just any time, every day would be like every other day, and I should never have any vacation at all." (Pages 83–86)

### Symbolic Celebrations

As the description of the birthday fiesta at the beginning of this chapter suggests, rituals are often closely tied to playful, lively celebrations. In this way many rituals become more than just symbolic actions; they become symbolic celebrations that break us out of life's routines. Even simple rituals, such as prayer, can be seen as celebrations. In prayer we are taking time out to rejoice in God's presence in our life.

When we talk about celebration, we often think only about laughter, partying, and general fun. Most celebrations, however, have their serious side. For example, the modern-day Olympic Games, with their opening and closing ceremonies paying tribute to all the participating athletes from around the world, bring a solemn purpose to sports. Embodied by the Olympic Games are values such as striving for excellence, commitment to a goal, respect for other cultures, and world unity. The Olympic Games would become mere routines if they did not possess meanings somehow related to human beliefs and concerns.

### Important Events

Rituals are usually connected to important events in people's lives. Many rituals formalize our "firsts": The first ball of the baseball season is always thrown out by someone special. Turning the first spade of dirt on a building project, driving the first vehicle across a bridge, and cutting the ribbon during an opening ceremony—these are new-beginning rituals. E

Anniversaries, graduations, award ceremonies, or ceremonies to induct someone into a community illustrate some other types of important events that call for symbolic celebration. Did you celebrate your thirteenth birthday—your first day as a teenager? Have you celebrated a baptism in your family? Life would be pretty boring if we did not take time out to mark certain occasions for what they are—special!

your special celebrations

E Rituals celebrate special occasions. List five special events (either personal or communal) in your life, along with the rituals associated with each event.

*Student art:* Colored pencil by Michelle Barrack, University of San Diego High School, San Diego, California

embodying our values

# The Power of Words and Deeds

Although words are not essential to ritual, using the right words can lend a powerful boost to one's actions. Even more striking is how the right actions can give life to what would otherwise seem like empty words, as the following true story demonstrates:

Chris froze as he opened the door to his cabin. It was a disaster. Clothes covered the floor, blankets were balled up in a heap, and a deck of cards was scattered across the table, along with the remains of a light bulb from the overhead fixture. Chris looked around the room at the ten junior high boys who had also frozen when Chris opened the door.

"Guys," Chris said sharply. "I leave for two minutes and the cabin is a complete mess." He shook his head.

Danny, a kid taller than Chris, stepped forward. He was the self-appointed leader of the group at the church Bible camp, and he stood looking boldly down at his counselor.

"We were only playing baseball," Danny said, turning and pointing to Bill. Bill nodded and picked up a sock and Chris's fishing rod, threw the sock into the air, and smacked it across the room with the rod.

"Enough!" scolded Chris. "Let's get this place straightened up."

Chris, a college freshman, sat down on his bunk and began chewing his fingernails. He watched the campers' shoddy efforts at decluttering. They bickered among themselves, and punches were close to flying over who would scrub the bathroom toilets. Chris glanced at the clock. It was 10:00 a.m.

Camp rules said that Chris had to lead Bible study at 10:15 a.m. every day. This was the one time in the day when all the boys became united: They hated Bible study. In truth Chris was not that keen on it himself. He had signed up as a counselor hoping that he could spend the summer taking kids canoeing on the white-water rivers that he loved. Teaching religion was an unfamiliar and uncomfortable experience.

Yesterday had been the worst. Chris had started by reading the story of Noah and his ark. Then each kid had taken a chunk of clay and molded his own animal. Chris had looked at their creations; none of them resembled any animal he had ever seen, except one fierce-looking dinosaur.

Each kid had then put his sculpture on the wooden boat that Chris had fashioned. The whole group had walked down to the lake and launched the ark, which promptly capsized, with all the monsters lost. Still, Chris had tried to close the lesson with prayer, but the kids just shook their heads and refused to contribute. . . .

Chris's daydreams were interrupted by a pillow fight between Bill and Danny. He broke it up and glanced at the clock: 10:13 a.m. Chris had no idea what to do. He was all out of gimmicks. Not that good ideas would necessarily work with these kids, most of whom came from rough, inner-city neighborhoods. They found hiking in the woods and canoeing scary, and spent most of their time doing more familiar things, like bullying and hassling one another. Chris knew that some kept knives.

Chris had the boys drag their chairs into a circle, but when he finally got their attention, he still did not know how to get through to them. His silence grated on the boys, who had had a late night. "What?" "Speak up, Chris!" "We're being quiet," they whined.

Finally, Chris asked, "Did Jesus rule by force or love?"

That was easy enough. "Love," a couple answered.

"If Jesus ruled by love, was he a king or a servant?"

The boys gave both answers. Then, unsure, they looked to Chris for the right one. Instead of saying anything, Chris walked to his bed and grabbed a clean washcloth and towel from his bag. Next, he got a bucket from a nearby closet and filled the bucket with warm water. He then proceeded to kneel before the nearest boy and pull off his shoes. Wetting the clean washcloth, Chris carefully washed the boy's feet. After patting them dry with the towel, he looked up at the boy and said, "I am your servant." The boys were silent as Chris went around the circle, doing the same for each kid.

When Chris led the closing prayer and asked for contributions from around the circle, there were a few comments. Bill just said thanks, but Danny had more:

"Yeah, I've got something," he said. "Dear God, thanks for this Bible study and thanks for my servant. He's better than my own dad."

The prayer came back to Chris and he closed it, "Amen."

### Significant Words

Rituals often include words that underscore the significance of the action. Drinking a toast is a good example of words combining with a gesture to make a symbolic statement: "May the best of the past be the worst of the future." Standing and reciting the pledge of allegiance, taking an oath of office, and making the sign of the cross also combine verbal with nonverbal actions.

Though rituals always involve actions, they do not always incorporate words. In rituals, words are typically secondary and supportive to the actions. Because a ritual is a physical, sensual activity, its power can be diminished by wordiness or excessive explanation. For example, to continually prompt the audience at an awards banquet by saying, "You may now applaud for this year's winners," would be unnecessary and even distracting, because spontaneous, heartfelt applause is normal and appropriate at such a

ceremony. Choosing which words to use or not use in a ritual can determine how effective the ritual is at conveying its intended message.

### Linkages to the Past

Rituals link people with their past. Fourth of July parades and fireworks displays are meaningful celebrations in the United States. Festivities like these speak to people about their past, reminding them of who they are.

As a more elaborate instance: In colonial times in South America, a group of African slaves defeated their Dutch masters. The slaves fled into the jungle, where to this day they have preserved their African heritage. The present community regularly re-enacts the revolt and victory of their ancestors. The ritual lasts for hours, until all the participants are exhausted. By the end of the celebration, everyone in the group not only knows the story—their history—but has ritually

The ritual feast of Thanksgiving reminds us of our country's past, of the first meal of gratitude shared by Pilgrims and Native Americans hundreds of years ago.

For Hindus in India, the ritual of bathing in their sacred Ganges River has deep religious significance.

relived it. Through the ritual experience, they remember that their ancestors were a powerful and free people, and that they today are a powerful and free people. By partaking in the ritual, they seek to keep alive the inspiration and ideals handed down to them.

## Communal Actions

Rituals are often communal actions; that is, they may involve a whole group of people at once. Christmas, New Year's Day, and graduations are just a few examples of events celebrated within a community setting.

In rituals people come together to celebrate being a community with a common identity. For example, if U.S. citizens were in a foreign country during Thanksgiving, they would find it strange that no one around them celebrated the day. They might seek out other individuals from their homeland with whom to commemorate Thanksgiving. Even a simple religious ritual like private prayer can connect individual persons to a community when the ritual employs traditional prayers developed within that community. F

### Participation, Not Observation

People make rituals "happen" by participating in them. In other words, it is not enough merely to observe rituals. Nothing is more boring than being at a ritual and not understanding or being part of it. For example, an American once went to a Japanese tea ceremony, an ancient ritual founded upon appreciating the beauty in life's daily routines. From the visitor's perspective, the ceremony was a long, drawn-out way to brew a cup of tea. The Japanese attending it, however, were completely captivated during the hours that the ceremony lasted.

Even fans at a sporting event are not just spectators; they are actual participants. Sports analysts talk about a home-crowd advantage in most sports. What they mean is that an enthusiastic, supportive crowd can actually improve a team's performance.

When participating in rituals, we need not know all that they mean intellectually. But if rituals are to have any kind of meaning for us, we must be able to enter into them wholeheartedly. They do not affect us "magically"; that is, they can affect us and transform us, but not without our own engagement in them. Simply going through the motions is not enough.

In summary, rituals involve these characteristics:
- They consist of movements and gestures that convey meaning.
- They are often repeated.
- They can be called symbolic celebrations because they break us out of life's routines.
- They are usually connected to important events in people's lives.
- They often include significant words that support the actions.
- They link people with their past.
- They are often communal actions.
- They require people's wholehearted participation.

F Using examples from your own experience, explain and critique the following statement in writing:
- "All true rituals are memory-makers and memory-shakers. Good ritual is how we remember who we are and celebrate who we shall become" (Hixon, *RCIA Ministry,* page 35).

characteristics
of rituals

## For Review

5. List the eight characteristics of rituals described in this book. Give a short example of each.

# Rituals and Worship

As you probably know from experience or have gathered from earlier discussion in this course, each of the seven sacraments of the Catholic church is celebrated in a ritual. In fact rituals in general have deep roots in prehistoric religion and worship.

## The Roots of Rituals in Worship

The historical roots of rituals go back to the prehistoric era. From cave paintings and remains from early human communities, anthropologists (researchers who study ancient civilizations) have learned that after a hunt, not all of an animal was eaten. Apparently, early humans would save or burn certain parts, such as the brain. In many early farming cultures, the firstfruits (that is, the earliest portion of the harvest) would also be burned, not eaten. Anthropologists interpret these early practices as ritual acts, and they feel that human society was performing religious rituals at its earliest stages of development.

### "Doing the Holy"

For most ancient cultures, life necessarily centered on nature, and in these cultures, nature was believed to be controlled by both supportive and threatening spirits. Rituals functioned as the primary means of communicating with these spirits. Through rituals people thanked the spirits of nature and attempted to keep them friendly.

From the beginning, then, rituals and ritual sacrifices were linked with worship. The word *sacrifice* comes from the Latin *sacrum facere*, which means "to make

Rituals have been central to human communities through every age and across every culture.
*Student art:* Watercolor by Elise Schweitzer, Cor Jesu Academy, Saint Louis, Missouri

holy" or "to do the holy." Thus when the early Israelites sacrificed the best young lambs of their flocks, they were doing the holy; they were performing acts of worship expressing their grateful acknowledgment of God's gifts to them. Likewise, Native Americans shared their peace pipe and lifted it up to the four corners of the Earth in a gesture of gratitude—a ritual that is still practiced today. Ⓖ

### Ritual Worship or Magic?

In discussions about the ritual practices of ancient cultures or contemporary cultures different from our own, the distinction between worship and superstition, or magic, sometimes becomes blurred. In actuality a clear distinction can be made: Ritual worship is an attempt to get in touch with the spirit world, to put oneself in harmony with spiritual powers. Magic, on the other hand, is an attempt to manipulate spiritual powers. Magical actions and objects are believed to produce their effects on a person regardless of his or her motives or intentions. (If I stick a pin in this woman's picture, harmful supernatural powers will be unleashed toward her. If a black cat crosses my path, evil forces will work against me.)

Magic, in which humans try to control the world of the spirit by words or actions, is the total opposite of genuine ritual worship, in which humans bow down in gratitude and humility before the Divine Mystery.

*cycles of nature*

Ⓖ Some rituals celebrate the cycles of nature. For example, flying kites is a way of celebrating spring. Describe in writing two nature-related rituals you have participated in.

A magic cultic symbol is carved out of a grain field.

magic & manipulation

# Christianity and Rituals

The New Testament shows us that rituals have been a part of Christianity from its very beginning. In the Acts of the Apostles and in Saint Paul's epistles, we read that the early Christians gathered together for meals and broke bread and shared the cup as Jesus had instructed them to do. We read about converts to Christianity undergoing a ritual washing that symbolized the change they felt inside. We also read about the laying on of hands, a practice that developed out of the Apostles' experience of receiving the Holy Spirit at Pentecost. Each of these rituals in the early church was closely tied to things that Jesus had said or done. This association, along with people's experiences, gave the rituals their meaning. H

As the church grew and became a more complex community, rituals became more important to the life and identity of the church. And as the church became more complex, so did its rituals and the explanations of their meaning. Over time the church also acquired more and more rituals, and many of these were called sacraments. Eventually, though, the church came to understand that the **sacraments** were not just *any* Christian rituals but were those specially privileged moments in which Christ communicates his grace through certain words and actions. By the end of the thirteenth century, the term *sacrament* was identified only with the rituals of Baptism, Confirmation, the Eucharist, Reconciliation (also known as Penance), Extreme Unction (now the Anointing of the Sick), Matrimony, and Holy Orders—the seven

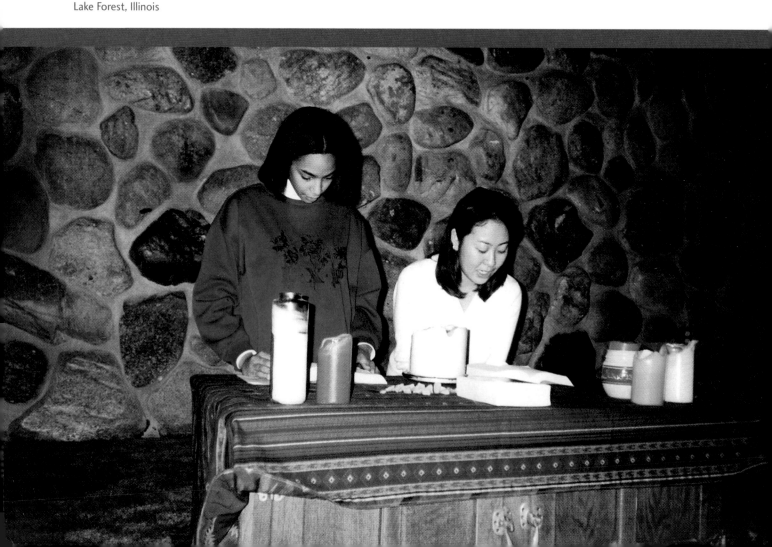

sacraments still recognized by Catholic Christians today.

Chapter 6 will take a closer look at the historical development of the sacraments in the church, including why Catholicism has a more extensive ritual system than most of the other Christian churches. Also, the chapters on the specific sacraments cover each sacrament's particular history. For now, however, simply note the following points:

• Rituals, whether formalized into sacraments or just into simple actions such as the kiss of peace, have been an important part of expressing Christian faith and community from Christianity's very beginning.

• Someday you may help plan a class or graduation liturgy, your own wedding service, or the funeral arrangements for someone close to you. By studying and knowing more about rituals, you can become a more creative participant both in your life generally and in your religion. ⊡

create a new way

⊡ Imagine that you have been chosen to create a new way of celebrating an important event. Describe two symbols and two rituals to accompany the celebration. Choose one of the following events to work with: a basketball championship, a family reunion, a sixteenth birthday, a high school graduation, or a marriage engagement.

**ritual & worship**

## For Review

6. Describe the connection between ritual and worship.

7. What is the difference between ritual worship and magic?

8. Give three examples of rituals in the early church that are described in the New Testament.

# Rituals, Sacraments, and the Christian Community

Rituals help us keep alive our history, our values, our ideals—in fact our very identity. As rituals of worship, the sacraments play a vital role in the life of the church as a community of believers.

Sacraments help Christians come in touch, and stay in touch, with Jesus Christ through his grace. They bring people into and keep them connected to the Body of Christ, the church, whose mission it is to carry on the work of Christ in the world. Thus the sacraments are the means through which God's love, poured out in Jesus' life, death, and Resurrection, is saving the world.

Sacramental awareness and an appreciation of symbols and rituals are two important elements in any celebration of the sacraments. A full experience of the sacraments is further enhanced by another element: an appreciation of prayer. In chapter 4 we will turn our attention to the role of prayer in celebrating the sacraments.

*Student art:* Tempera paint by Matt Carroll, Saint Peter–Marian High School, Worcester, Massachusetts

# Prayer
### worshiping in word, in act, and in silence

... your presence brings peace

... show me the way

Word of God, teach me silence.
Lead me to that inner place
        where your presence brings peace.
From there, make all of my life a prayer—
        my thinking, feeling, sharing;
        even my hesitating, doubting, and fearing.
May the spirit of prayer
        always find a home
        in my heart.

                        Amen.

As we discussed in chapter 3, not all rituals are forms of worship. As simple religious rituals, however, prayers clearly are worship. This chapter offers information both on prayer itself and on specific ways of praying. Using a variety of prayer forms can give us much-needed islands in the swirling river of daily life—time-outs to appreciate the mystery of God's presence in our life.

To get an idea of the different ways some young people pray, reflect on the following personal sketches:

# islands in the
# river of life

**Steve is sixteen** years old. His main interest right now is getting a license to drive. He receives average grades in school, which is fine with him. He has a nice family, a crowd to do things with, and no particular plans for the future.

If Steve was asked about his prayer life, he would probably roll his eyes and look embarrassed. Steve was an altar boy for a number of years, a service he enjoyed. He believes that was prayer for him. He also appreciates the occasional times when classes stop and the school day is given over to prayer; these are times for a breather, and he enjoys the peace they bring in a hectic day.

When Steve does stop and look inside himself, he often finds that he is carrying around many worries that burden him. At those times he usually thinks of God and says a simple "Help!" as a prayer. On other occasions he feels very grateful for his life, his family, and his friends. The words "Thank you, God" sometimes come to his mind. For the most part, though, Steve would have to say that prayer doesn't much fit into his life. He's all for it, but somehow it has gotten lost in other concerns.

*   *   *

Since she was eleven years old, Rachel, now fifteen, has kept a diary. When she was younger, she filled it with accounts of what she had done all day, which friends she had walked home from school with, whether she had passed a test, and so on. As she has grown older, her diary entries have become more reflective. Now Rachel does more than just describe things that happened; she finds herself pouring out her feelings in her diary, which she now calls her journal. Whether she is hurt by a friend's remark, thrilled at a favorite team's victory, or torn in two directions by a difficult choice, Rachel spills out her experiences on paper every night. It's remarkable how this process has helped her sort out some dilemmas, and it even seems to help her communicate better with her friends.

One night Rachel has an argument with her mother. She feels awful about it, and she's mad at her mother and herself and confused about what she should do next. She sits down to pour out her troubles on paper. Ordinarily, she doesn't think of herself as a praying person, but to her surprise, she finds herself beginning the entry, "Dear God . . ."

*   *   *

Joshua feels a lot of stress trying to balance the pressures of tough courses, basketball practices, and a part-time job. When Joshua feels really hassled, sometimes he just has to get away from it all and take a long walk by himself. These times alone help him clear his head and take away the sense of being overwhelmed by **pressures.**

Do these sketches remind you of yourself at times, or of how you pray? Almost all teenagers pray at least occasionally, but many may not recognize what they are doing as prayer. Like Steve they may have had some positive experiences with prayer but seldom take the time to pray intentionally, except in a pinch. Or, as happened with Rachel, they may discover that what they had been doing all along —writing out their thoughts and feelings to themselves—was really a way of talking to God. Joshua is like a great many teenagers who may not recognize that taking time and space for solitude that renews them is actually a form of praying.

Thirty or more years ago, most Catholics had a fairly restricted notion of prayer. They believed they were praying only when they were at Mass, when they recited formal prayers such as the rosary, or when they simply talked to God during quiet moments. Today Catholics understand prayer in a broader sense, recognizing that it occurs in many diverse ways of responding to God's gift of love. Ⓐ

**Prayer** is a wholehearted faith response to God, who loves us without conditions and is with us in every moment of our life. Because God is in every aspect of our life, we could offer our very living as a prayer, as a response to God. But there is something more intentional and conscious about the kind of wholehearted response that can be termed prayer. Suppose you had a friend whom you considered very important to you. Certainly you would not always need to be talking with or thinking of that friend in order for the friendship to be real. But if you never made contact with your friend or thought of him or her, the relationship would eventually wither. You need to intentionally nurture a relationship if it is to become a real friendship.

The same is true about our relationship with God. Although all living can be praying, moments of praying—intentional, conscious moments—give substance to prayer as a wholehearted faith response to God.

Ⓐ **Write a one-page essay using either of the following titles as your topic: "The** History of My Prayer Life" or "The Importance of Prayer in My Life Today."

*Student art:* Photo by Vanessa Navarro, Talent Unlimited High School, New York, New York

# Finding Sacred Time and Space

## Reminded of God's Presence

Certain prayer rituals may be quite familiar to us:

- Classes in Catholic schools often begin with a prayer.
- Many people and families say grace before meals.
- Athletic contests, meetings, or ceremonial events often begin with a prayer.

What is the purpose of such ritual prayers? Even though everyone's attention is not necessarily focused on the words of the prayer, these little rituals can remind us of God's constant presence with us. All of life is holy, and God is never truly absent from us. But we need to carve out the time and space to make ourselves conscious of God-with-us, or we are like friends who never take the time to notice each other.

Just as the innings and the playing field remind us when and where we are in a softball game, so prayer reminds us that we are living in God's time and space—that is, all of time and all of creation. Even our briefest prayers, then, can enhance our sense of being in a sacred place at a sacred time.

Friends take time to be together.
*Student art:* Photo by Colleen Hagan, Saint Patrick High School, Maysville, Kentucky

## A Time and a Place for Prayer: Essential to a Life of Love

A number of modern-day Catholics known for their commitment to justice for poor people have emphasized the need to have sacred time and space.

Dorothy Day, the cofounder of the Catholic Worker Movement, often gave this advice to anyone who wanted to help provide shelter for poor people: Always leave room in the house for a place of prayer. Dorothy Day's houses of hospitality continue to provide shelter, food, and care to homeless people in many cities. And those who run Catholic Worker houses still see to it that prayer remains a vital part of their life together.

The L'Arche communities, founded by Jean Vanier and dedicated to caring for mentally handicapped adults, find their inspiration and strength in a life of prayer together. From his experience with these communities, Vanier writes:

Community life demands that we constantly go beyond our own resources. If we do not have the spiritual nourishment we need, we will close in on ourselves and on our own comfort and security, or throw ourselves into work as an escape. (*Community and Growth*, page 104)

Mother Teresa of Calcutta, India, always had her Missionaries of Charity begin their day with Mass and end it with adoration before the Blessed Sacrament. They have continued this practice since her death. During the day the sisters care for destitute poor and dying people, hoping to communicate God's love to them through their own tender concern. Mother Teresa knew that beginning and ending the day in prayer creates the sense of sacred time by which the whole day becomes prayer.

In each of these examples, a certain time and place are designated as sacred, creating the awareness that other times and places are also sacred. Mother Teresa would not have said, "I take time out to pray and then I go to work." To her, taking time out allowed the rest of her day to be prayer as well as work. Ⓑ

In the same way, morning prayer can be taking time out to welcome the day, the entire day. And it can help us be more welcoming throughout the day. Saying grace before a meal reminds us of God's presence during the entire meal. Praying before a game is taking time out to ask God to be with us for the entire game. Taking time out to pray in specific situations can create a sense of prayer in all aspects of our life.

## Silence as Inner Space

Besides needing actual time and physical space in which to pray, people need another kind of space—inner space, or the space within a person's consciousness that makes room for God. Such inner space can be cultivated by allowing silence into one's life.

### Filling Up with Noise

We live in a world in which silence is a stranger. Our human habitat is filled

A prayerful heart is essential for the Missionaries of Charity, who care for destitute people who are sick and dying.

*the difference prayer makes*

Ⓑ Write a brief essay about someone—either a public figure or a person in your life—who is a prayerful person. Explain what difference prayer seems to make in the life of that person.

listen to God

© Spend five minutes in silence trying to listen actively to God. Describe the experience in a brief written report.

with noise; silence can be a rarity in our life. And though we may complain about a noisy environment, the truth is that given a choice, we often seek out the noise. Rather than enjoy a bit of silence when we have it, we may turn on the television, call a friend, or busy ourselves with activities that fill up our awareness.

Unfortunately by running from silence and solitude, we deprive ourselves of the inner space needed for God to enter our awareness. It is important to ask ourselves, "Am I running away from myself, or am I moving toward greater intimacy with myself?" Because God is at the core of our true self, in the depths of our being, running away from ourselves through constant noise or activity is really running away from God.

### A Way of Listening to God

Silence draws us inward. It enables us to listen to God, that is, to be attuned to what is going on inside us so that we can discover how God is present in our life at any given moment. "Listening to God" does not mean that we hear God speaking, as a voice, directing us to do this or do that. Instead, it means that we are quiet, receptive, and able to reflect on our own experiences in such a way that we can sense how God is present with us, even in troubling times.

Although we may go on a retreat for a day or two during which we encounter silence, few of us will ever experience the life of solitude and silence found in a monastery. Nevertheless, we can seek to spend time daily alone with ourselves and with God. ©

### Both Peaceful and Disturbing

Silence will not always be peaceful. Sometimes when we become quiet, we will be uncomfortable with our memories and emotions, or we will be just plain restless. No wonder we often want to flee from silence; it can be disturbing to us.

Yet God is present with us in disturbing encounters with ourselves as well as in peaceful times. An uncomfortable solitary silence signals us to pay closer attention to what is going on inside us, to feelings and fears that deserve to be taken seriously by us, just as God takes them seriously.

## silence & solitude

## For Review

1. How does the textbook define prayer?

2. Why is taking time out to pray important to Jean Vanier? to Mother Teresa?

3. What other element besides time and a physical space do people need in order to pray? How can this other element be cultivated?

4. Explain how silence can be both peaceful and disturbing.

# Paths to Intimacy with God

Three paths that Christians have traditionally taken to intimacy with God are vocal prayer, meditation, and contemplation (the prayer of simply being with God).

## Vocal Prayer: Finding Your Voice with God

Talking to God, which is termed **vocal prayer,** is an ancient prayer form. For Christians it often involves talking directly to Jesus. This sort of conversation is usually an interior kind of talk, something that anyone can do. Many believers over the centuries, whether educated in theological matters or not, have felt at home simply expressing their needs and hopes to God, through Jesus, in their own plain words.

A spiritual writer tells a story of a priest who went to visit a sick man in his home:

> [The priest] noticed an empty chair at the patient's bedside and asked what it was doing there. The patient said, "I had placed Jesus on that chair and was talking to him before you arrived. . . . For years I found it extremely difficult to pray until a friend explained to me that prayer was a matter of talking to Jesus. He told me to place an empty chair nearby, to imagine Jesus sitting on that chair, and to speak with him and listen to what he says to me in reply. I've had no difficulty praying ever since."

Some days later, so the story goes, the daughter of the patient came to the rectory to inform the priest that her father had died. She said, "I left him alone for a couple of hours. He seemed so peaceful. When I got back

*Student art:* Photo by Jason W. Chan, La Salle High School, Pasadena, California

Ⓓ Think of a situation, issue, or person in your life that you would like to talk with God about. Dialogue with God and write down the conversation between you two.

*Student art:* Photo by Clare Major, Saint Joseph's Academy, Baton Rouge, Louisiana

to the room I found him dead. I noticed a strange thing, though: his head was resting not on the bed but on a chair that was beside his bed." (De Mello, *Sadhana,* page 78)

Relating to Jesus or God as a real person who hears us, and not as an abstraction or an impersonal force, is the key to genuine vocal prayer. Ⓓ

Vocal prayer takes numerous forms. You may be familiar with the prayer of petition, calling on God's help in time of need, because this type of prayer is part of the Mass. Prayers of praise, thanksgiving, contrition, and blessing are types of vocal prayer also found in the Mass.

The fundamental form of vocal prayer is spontaneous prayer, in which we pour out our honest feelings and deepest concerns. Sharing the most personal part of ourselves in intimate conversation with Jesus means placing our concerns in his

hands. Talking to Jesus opens the door to his saying to us, "In all things, I am with you. Do not be afraid."

## Meditation: Focusing Your Mind

The form of prayer that involves focusing your attention on an idea, a story, or a particular object is termed **meditation.** Focusing on something takes energy and concentration, so meditation does not come easily to most of us, but it can be learned. It helps to begin a time of meditation by trying to quiet the mind and the body, to become relaxed but alert. In this way the noise that tends to fill us up and scatter our attention in everyday life will recede into the background, and we can be better attuned to God's presence.

quieting
mind & body

The Christian tradition has a great history of experience with meditative prayer. Many saints, such as Teresa of Ávila and Ignatius of Loyola, have written extensively about meditation in works that have become spiritual classics. In recent decades Christianity has also learned much from other religious traditions that emphasize meditation, such as Hinduism, Buddhism, Sufi mysticism, and Native American spirituality. Techniques like deep breathing, meditative postures, and repetitive chanting, which quiet the body and mind and thus lead to an inner experience of peace, have been integrated into Christian methods of meditation to enrich the prayer life of many Christians. E

## Contemplation: The Prayer of "Being With"

There are times in a friendship between two persons when words, and even focused thoughts, are not all that necessary. Words may just get in the way. The two persons may be happy just being in each other's presence, neither one talking and neither one thinking ahead to what either will do or say next. This is like the prayer of just being with God—**contemplation,** as it is known in the Christian tradition.

A brief story illustrates this kind of prayer:

An old man would sit motionless in church for hours on end. One day a priest asked him what God talked to him about.

"God doesn't talk. He just listens," was his reply.

"Well, then what do you talk to him about?"

"I don't talk either. I just listen." (De Mello, *Taking Flight,* page 29)

This simple, mutual presence can be an extremely nourishing form of prayer, but it relies on a person's being receptive and open, able to quietly perceive and appreciate God's presence. For that reason, meditation, which quiets a person and allows his or her attention to be focused, can lead to the prayer of contemplation. In fact meditation and contemplation often overlap and cannot really be separated, just as vocal prayer often overlaps with meditative prayer.

The habit of engaging in contemplation tends to spill over into finding God's presence in the ordinary—in a tree, in a breeze passing over on a warm day, in a delightful time with friends, or in the hurt and loneliness of a classmate who feels like an outsider. This ability to be attuned to God's presence in all of reality is the sacramental awareness that was first discussed in chapter 1. So contemplative prayer and sacramental awareness are very much related.

The three paths to intimacy with God discussed in this chapter—vocal prayer, meditation, and contemplation—can take many different forms. The next section will look at a few possibilities.

E Research and write a brief report on the prayer traditions of a non-Christian religion or religious group.

*others' traditions*

## For Review

5. **Identify and briefly describe three ways of praying traditionally used by Christians.**

# Praying "All Ways"

Saint Paul, in the Letter to the Ephesians, urges Christians to "pray in the Spirit at all times" (6:18). Of course, Paul, and Jesus before him, did not expect us to sit in silence all day. Nor did he expect us to use vocal prayer incessantly. What he did mean was that we are to pray in all the ways that we live our life: in our caring for pets, our visiting with relatives, our talking with friends and strangers, our attitude toward everything that comes our way. To pray "all ways" means to use all of ourselves—our senses and abilities—in prayer. If we limit prayer to an internal activity only, we risk missing out on the intimacy and vitality that come from seeing and celebrating God's presence in other people or in creation. A sacramental vision that sees God present not just within ourselves but outside as well opens up many worlds and many ways of praying. The following are some prayer forms that reflect the strong sacramental character of Christianity.

## Praying with Our Imagination

One popular form of meditation is the method of praying with our imagination. This kind of prayer form is also known as guided meditation, in which one's mind is led through a scene or an incident in order to imagine an encounter with God or a similarly significant experience. The person reads the meditation quietly or listens as the meditation is read aloud to her or him, filling in the details mentally at the pauses.

Here is a guided meditation to try (the pauses are indicated by ellipses, or series of periods):

Even caring for pets can be a way of praying.
*Student art:* Photo by Andrea Kohler, Lehman Catholic High School, Sidney, Ohio

Picture yourself walking in a beautiful garden. . . . As you slowly move along the path, you take time to enjoy the many flowers, berry plants, and trees in the garden. . . . You savor each one and move on to other parts of the garden. . . . Eventually, you come to another section of the garden that has clearly been neglected. It is overgrown and tangled. You decide to walk through this section of the garden anyway, spending time with the weeds, bushes, and foliage found here, just as you did with the other, well-kept area. . . .

Imagine that this garden is you. . . . How is this garden like you and your life? . . . What are the well-kept, beautiful flowers in the garden of your life? . . . What are the weeds hidden in the out-of-the-way reaches of your life? . . .

Now you see a gardener across from you, in the nice section, wanting to join you but separated by the tangled weeds. As you see the tenderness in the gardener's eyes, you realize the gardener is God. . . . What does God have to say to you about the garden of your life, both the beautiful sections and the overgrown sections?

Guided meditation works best in a silent and calm setting, which enables us to relax enough to put imagination into the service of prayer. This activity is helpful in allowing God to touch us through the images that we create in our imagination. F

## Praying with the Scriptures or Other Spiritual Writings

Another form of meditation uses the Scriptures or other spiritual writings as the stimulus for reflection. After reading a passage, the person can ask self-directed questions that relate the passage to his or her own life.

For instance, you might read this passage from the Gospel of Matthew:

[Jesus said:] "The kingdom of heaven is like treasure hidden in a field, which someone found and hid; then in his joy he goes and sells all that he has and buys that field.

F Using an image other than a garden, write a guided meditation that could help you pray. If you like, draw a picture to accompany your narrative.

*write your own*

reflect on a passage

ⓖ **Search through the Scriptures and select a passage that you find insightful. Identify the passage and** give it an appropriate title. Then write three questions to help you reflect on the passage. Finally, compose a prayer based on its message.

"Again, the kingdom of heaven is like a merchant in search of fine pearls; on finding one pearl of great value, he went and sold all that he had and bought it." (13:44–46)

Then you might pose questions such as these to yourself for reflection:

- Is there a treasure hidden in my life that is worth the price of everything else in my life?
- What is the fine pearl in my experience, and what am I willing to give up for it?
- What is the treasure or the fine pearl that Jesus is talking about? Is it similar to what I consider to be a treasure, or is it different?
- How does Jesus' message apply to my life here and now?

Reading and reflecting on the Scriptures allows God to speak to us through the words of the Bible, helping us understand the Bible's meaning in our own life.

God can also speak to us through other writings, such as spiritual books written specifically for aiding prayer. Some people have found biographies, essays, poems, and fictional works to be pathways to prayer. ⓖ

## Praying with a Pen

Recall Rachel's use of a journal in one of the brief sketches that opened this chapter. When she wrote "Dear God" at the beginning of a journal entry, she discovered that what she had been doing all along—expressing her thoughts and feelings to herself on paper—was actually a kind of prayer. She had been engaging in vocal prayer in a written form.

If you have never kept a journal for writing down personal thoughts and reflections, try keeping one. You may notice something exciting. In the very process of writing, insights will come to you. Writing is not just a record of inner thoughts and prayers. It is an activity that helps bring forth hidden thoughts and ideas. Taking time to write honestly and openly to ourselves is a way of entering that sacred place where we talk with God.

## Praying with Our Body

Our mind and heart in particular are engaged during meditation and vocal prayer. But even more of ourselves can be engaged when we pray. Our senses and our limbs, even our whole body, can be involved in prayer. In fact contemplation—the prayer of "being with"—often happens when we get "out of our head" (in the sense of analyzing and questioning) and simply experience God present around us.

Contemplation has been called by one theologian "a long loving look at the real." "Look" means more than simply gazing; it means taking in reality with all our senses so that, in a way, we become united with that reality. We do not look at the real as something to be analyzed but as something to be appreciated and loved:

This real I *look* at. I do not analyze or argue it, describe it or define it; I am one with it. I do not move around it; I enter into it. Lounging by a stream, I do not exclaim "Ah, $H_2O$!" I let the water trickle gently through my fingers. (Burghardt, "Contemplation")

Let's consider some ways we can pray with our body, in order to bring our whole self to God.

### Our Eyes

For meditation and for inner vocal prayer, we may be accustomed to closing our eyes to quiet our mind and prevent all kinds of distractions from entering into our attempts to focus. However, some of our most profound prayer can come through our eyes. Eyes are great

# "Dear Diary": Journal Writing as Prayer

This journal entry of a sixteen-year-old girl gives a sense of how important an activity reflective writing can be for us:

I had an awfully strange dream last night—that Mom and I were fighting. We weren't just yelling, but actually hitting each other too. We were outside in the backyard at high noon (like in one of those old Westerns); she would scream something mean, and then I would scream back. Then came the hitting. The really strange part was that the sky was clear, the birds were singing, and there was Muzak playing from somewhere. I woke up crying and went into Mom's bedroom and crawled into bed next to her.

In school today Beth told me that she had a fight with her mom. I told her that I never fight with mine and that she lets me do whatever I want. Beth said that's because I don't have a dad around to make my mom miserable and crabby. I feel sorry for Beth because she just doesn't understand.

Last weekend at Grandma's house, during Sunday dinner, Grandpa said his son married my mom only because he had to and they'd still be married if she wasn't so immoral. I was so mad I wouldn't finish my dinner or help with the dishes. He acts as if Dad is a saint. Truth is, they don't understand either, and even if I am mad at Mom, I'll never tell them. I don't know who I'll tell. I'll probably just write it down.

The thing is, I don't know why I told Beth what I did, because I do fight with Mom. The things she does make me mad; the guys she dates are losers, and she's always down at the bar. I don't know why she lowers herself that way. I think it's disgusting, and I never want to be like that. Sometimes I think I'd like her more if I didn't live with her. I told Beth's mom that, but she said I'd miss my mother, the way I miss my dad and don't really know it.

The whole thing just confuses me, which makes me angry, because I want to understand everything, and I don't want anyone to think I'm wrong. I just think the more confused I am, the more I keep writing.

In what ways can this young woman's journal entry be thought of as a prayer?

gifts of God that are meant to be instruments of prayer. We can pray by closing our eyes to gaze inward, but we can also pray by seeing God's splendor in the world around us. Try praying with your eyes:

Visit a church—if possible, an old church. Look around at the statues, paintings, crucifix, stained-glass windows, candles. These objects can provide a rich feast for your eyes and mind, in what they communicate about the artist, about the world, and about divine realities and mysteries.

Go to one of your favorite natural spots—perhaps a park, a beach, or a wide-open field. Take in the beauty and unite yourself to it in gratitude. Realize that you are praying with your eyes there as well as you do in the church.

### Our Ears

Although silence is an important dimension of prayer, prayer sometimes involves paying attention to the sounds around us, whether the sounds are natural ones like rain beating on the ground or human-made ones like music. Attending to sounds can be a meditative and even contemplative experience, as the following story demonstrates:

When Brother Bruno was at prayer one night he was disturbed by the croaking of a bullfrog. All his attempts to disregard the sound were unsuccess-

ful so he shouted from his window, "Quiet! I'm at my prayers."

Now Brother Bruno was a saint so his command was instantly obeyed. Every living creature held its voice so as to create a silence that would be favorable to prayer.

But now another sound intruded on Bruno's worship—an inner voice that said, "Maybe God is as pleased with the croaking of that frog as with the chanting of your psalms." "What can please the ears of God in the croak of a frog?" was Bruno's scornful rejoinder. But the voice refused to give up. "Why would you think God invented the sound?"

Bruno decided to find out why. He leaned out of his window and gave the order, "Sing!" The bullfrog's measured croaking filled the air to the ludi-

attending
to sound

crous accompaniment of all the frogs in the vicinity. And as Bruno attended to the sound, their voices ceased to jar for he discovered that, if he stopped resisting them, they actually enriched the silence of the night.

With that discovery Bruno's heart became harmonious with the universe and, for the first time in his life, he understood what it means to pray. (De Mello, *Taking Flight,* page 17)

To his amazement and delight, the monk had discovered the music of the universe.

Music is one of the most ancient prayer forms. Indeed, Hindus believe that creation began with the music of a drum. In the Christian tradition, we have the story of the Nativity, in which Jesus' birth is accompanied by the music of angels. We also have the Book of Revelation's portrayal of the Second Coming of Jesus, in which Jesus' future return is announced by the sound of trumpets. Music can keep us in tune with the Earth—even plants, it seems, grow better to the sounds of certain music.

Perhaps you have already had some meditative experiences through listening to music, though you may not have thought of your experiences as meditation at the time. Have you ever felt an emotional release from listening to a stirring, popular song that expressed a simple truth for you? Have you ever felt uplifted from listening to one of the great classical works? Try listening to a piece of reflective music or a song with strong, positive lyrics that expresses significant values for you, and think of your listening as a way of communicating with your inner self and with God. Ⓗ

### Our Feet

"Remove the sandals from your feet, for the place on which you are standing is holy ground" (Exodus 3:5). With these words the Exodus account of Moses' first encounter with God reminds us that the ancient Israelites had a sense that certain places were meant to be savored as sacred —places where God was especially present.

We people in modern, Western societies are always on the go. In our comings and goings, however, we should try to be involved travelers, or pilgrims, not simply detached tourists. When we savor special places, we can allow God to speak to us through them.

The church teaches that all Christians are pilgrims on Earth, in the sense of being people on a journey toward a destiny—both as individuals and as a community. Even in our everyday physical travels, we can think of ourselves as pilgrims searching for God. We can be somewhat like the pilgrims to the Holy Land or the people who visit shrines where Jesus' mother, Mary, is believed to have appeared. Travelers go to such places expecting to encounter God in a special way. God is present not only in the "official" holy places but everywhere in life. Our awareness of God in a certain place makes that place holy ground for us and reminds us that all the world is holy ground.

Here are some questions to consider about how you might pray "with your feet":
- Do you have any special places that you consider holy ground?
- Can you go to certain places in your neighborhood that bring back special memories?
- Do you connect certain places with people or events that you treasure?
- Are there places that hold spiritual significance for you or for your community?

If you thought of certain places in answer to any of these questions, visiting one of them could be a pilgrimage—a way of praying with your feet.

*compose for sounds*

Ⓗ Compose a song, poem, or prayer that illustrates praying with our ears.

*body in spirit*

Reflect on ways you use your body —in athletics, in creative activities and hobbies, in helping others, or simply in communicating with body language. Try doing one of these activities in a spirit of prayer. Write down your reflections about the experience.

Our special places can be holy ground. *Student art:* Pastel by Maureen O'Mara, Coyle-Cassidy High School, Taunton, Massachusetts

## Our Whole Body

Incense, flowers, dance, and song— all of these suggest further ways of praying with the body. Our body itself is a sacrament of God's presence. Nothing could be more natural than using the sacrament we are born with to communicate with God in prayer.

The Old and New Testaments present us with wonderful images of praying with the whole body through dance and song. In one account King David, bringing the precious ark of the covenant back into Jerusalem, leads the crowd in rejoicing in worship:

David danced before the Lord with all his might; David was girded with a linen ephod [apron]. So David and all the house of Israel brought up the ark of the Lord with shouting, and with the sound of the trumpet. (2 Samuel 6:14–15)

The Psalms of the Old Testament, too, give a sense of the joy, expressed through their whole bodies, with which the people of God worshiped:

Praise the Lord!
Sing to the Lord a new song,
   his praise in the assembly of the
   faithful.
. . . . .

Let them praise his name with
   dancing,
   making melody to him with
   tambourine and lyre.
. . . . . . . . .
Let the faithful exult in glory;
   let them sing for joy on their
   couches.

(149:1–5)

Writing to the early Christian community at Ephesus, Saint Paul remarks on how good it is for the people to express the Spirit of God in them through their singing:

Do not get drunk with wine, for that is debauchery; but be filled with the Spirit, as you sing psalms and hymns and spiritual songs among yourselves, singing and making melody to the Lord. (Ephesians 5:18–19)

Until the last couple of centuries, the arts were closely associated with praising God. So it made perfect sense to the ancient Israelites that David was praying when he "danced before the Lord with all his might." The bodily expressions of drama and music making were used by Christians to pray since early on; these expressions were likewise part of Greek, Roman, Hindu, and Buddhist worship. Even the Oriental martial arts, often cheapened into a form of violence, traditionally were forms of bodily meditation.

If quieting our body through silence and solitude can lead to internal meditation, then using our body creatively and expressively can be thought of as external meditation. Have you ever felt especially alive and in union with your surroundings while dancing, playing music, skiing, running, painting, or creating sculpture or pottery? Activities like these, done in the right spirit, possess a meditative quality. As such they foster prayer and can themselves be prayer.

pray
all ways

Student art:
Charcoal and
pastel by
Margaret
Ferguson, Sacred
Heart High
School, Kingston,
Massachusetts

## For Review

6. What does Saint Paul mean when he urges Christians to "pray in the Spirit at all times"?

7. Explain how we can put our imagination to use in prayer. Why might this activity be helpful?

8. Explain a common way of using the Scriptures or other writings in prayer.

9. Summarize four ways that we can pray with our body. Give an example of each.

# Being Rooted and Uprooted by Prayer

*your impressions*

▢ Find out more about Malcolm X or Dorothy Day and summarize your findings in a brief essay. Conclude the essay with your impressions of the person.

Malcolm X was an African American who converted to Islam as a Black Muslim. In the 1960s, he became a leading figure for racial justice. A few words from him serve to illustrate prayer's ability to both root us and uproot us:

> The hardest test
> I ever faced in my life
> was praying. . . .
> Bending my knees to pray—
> that *act*—well, that took me a week.
> (*The Autobiography of Malcolm X,*
> page 170)

## Prayer as Changing Us

What could Malcolm X have found so difficult about praying? Isn't praying something one either does or doesn't do? It appears that Malcolm X knew that real prayer changes a person. Through prayer Malcolm X was letting God into his life. Once that happened he found he had to live life differently. He was uprooted from his everyday security and mind-set by prayer at the same time that he became more rooted in God's presence.

Paradoxically, prayer roots us more firmly into life and yet uproots us. It can fill us with confidence and humble us at the same time—as Malcolm X experienced. Prayer makes us more clearly aware of God's presence in all of life. Once we are rooted in that awareness, we observe the world with a sense of its sacredness. That very likely will call for changing our personal life— perhaps by simply growing out of bad habits, perhaps by taking a risky stand against injustice, or perhaps by committing our own time, energy, or even our life for a particular cause.

## Toward a Deeper Security

This challenging, uprooting quality of prayer is exemplified in the life of Dorothy Day (see below). In founding the Catholic Worker, she moved from being a single parent and independent journalist to sharing home, meals, and companionship with other volunteers and with homeless people off the streets of New York City. It was a disturbing but ultimately life-giving experience, as she recalled to her friend, the psychiatrist and writer Robert Coles:

"I was frightened in general—the life I left for the new life I was living. I had been a solitary person in certain ways, and now I was a member of a community. I yearned for the change, but I was also scared by the change. I had never known the kind of life I began living once we were running a hospitality house in New York. There were times when I wanted to take my daughter and run, but I didn't want to run, not really. That's what I mean by frightened. I was anxious, I was scared, but I was going to stay there and do the work I needed to do.

"Whenever I became *too* jittery I read the Bible. First the Bible would come to my mind, then I would go get it, then I'd read it. You will probably call me superstitious or childish, but sometimes I would just close my eyes and let my hand stumble to a certain page, and then read what I first saw when my eyes opened. I thought it was God, showing me what I needed to see that day. I knew better, but I loved just accidentally opening the book to this

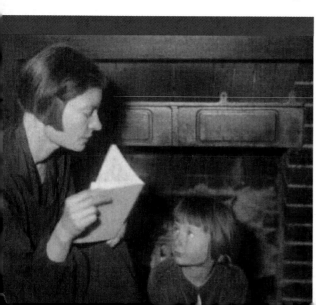

Dorothy Day with her daughter, Tamar Teresa, in the 1930s

page or that page and connecting what I had read to what was happening in my life." (*Dorothy Day*, pages 128–129)

Prayer in Dorothy Day's life both challenged her customary security and gave her the deeper security she needed to live out her calling faithfully. ☐

## For Review

10. With the help of an example from this book, describe the paradox of being both rooted and uprooted by prayer.

# A Sacramental World Made Conscious

The first four chapters of this course have introduced the Catholic Christian vision of a sacramental world—a world alive with God's loving, active presence, or grace.

Sacraments can be broadly understood as God's loving presence made visible in our life here and now through the world around us—through people and the rest of the natural world. We can perceive God's action through symbols—concrete, visible realities that speak to us of deeper, unseen realities. And when symbols of God's activity are combined with rituals, or symbolic actions, the awareness of God's grace can be heightened. When we add prayer (a wholehearted faith response to God) to these rituals, we have a powerful means of celebrating and experiencing God's active love for us. Through the church, seven such rituals have been given to us as special means of God's grace.

Before considering each of the seven sacraments, this course will first reflect on how Jesus and the church can be considered sacraments, on how the seven sacraments of the church are essential to its mission in the world, and on how the sacraments became part of the church's ongoing history.

# 5

# Jesus Christ & the Church

## sacraments of God's love for the world

from death to new life

what it means to be human

Compassionate God,
we thank you for your Word-become-flesh,
Jesus, who walked the earth as one of us,
teaching us about your love
and about what it means to be human.
Grant that we who are your church
may be faithful in bringing Jesus' message
of your gracious love to the world,
through our words, deeds, and sacraments.
Amen.

Christians believe that the clearest, fullest sacrament of God's love to the world is Jesus Christ himself. Through his life and ministry, his death and Resurrection, Jesus showed the world who God is. God came to Earth in the flesh-and-blood reality of Jesus.

The church, the community of Jesus' followers throughout the ages, was founded to carry on the work of Christ in communicating God's love to the world. It does this by proclaiming the Good News, by "giving witness" (publicly affirming its faith) through its teachings and actions, and, in a special way, by celebrating the seven sacraments. The church, then, is to be a sacrament of God's love, as revealed through Jesus Christ, for all of creation.

The mystery that God's love is revealed to the world in Christ is not easy to grasp. The young woman in the following story discovers insight into the meaning of the mystery:

# becoming one of us

## Tracy stretches out,

on the living room couch. She has been waiting all evening for her mom and younger sisters to leave for Christmas Eve Mass. At last she can listen to her new CD on the portable player she just received that evening as a Christmas gift.

Earlier that day Tracy informed her mom that she was not going to Mass on Christmas Eve, as was her family's custom after opening the Christmas presents. Trying the honest approach, Tracy calmly told her Mom, "I just don't buy this business about God becoming human anymore. I'd feel like a hypocrite going to church."

And just in case her mom didn't go for her first reason, Tracy added, "Besides, I heard it's supposed to be below zero tonight and really windy. With my cold, I probably shouldn't be going out."

To Tracy's surprise all her mom said was, "That's fine, honey. I guess you're old enough to make up your own mind. Now why don't you make that salad for dinner tonight?"

Finally, Tracy is alone in the house. As she reaches for her headphones, she can hear the wind howling through the trees near the house. She shivers at the thought of going out into such cold, and promptly covers herself with a blanket and takes a good sip of her hot chocolate.

Then just as she is about to push the CD play button, Tracy hears a loud thumping noise against the picture window on the west end of the living room, followed by tapping and scratching sounds.

Unwrapping herself from her warm nest on the couch, Tracy goes to the window and discovers several small birds huddled outside on the ledge. They are pressing against and pecking at the glass, trying to get in from the frigid cold. An overwhelming desire to help the fragile creatures wells up in Tracy. Her immediate reaction is, "I should try to get them into the house."

First, Tracy tries leaving the door open, hoping the birds will take advantage of the opportunity and fly in. Instead, all that comes in is the wind and some snow; the birds avoid the door and keep tapping at the window. Tracy's next tactic is to place pieces of bread in the snow leading to the open door. When she comes back inside, two of the birds do hop down to eat some bread, but they don't venture near the door.

By now Tracy is getting frustrated. She wants so much to help the birds, to let them know she is their friend and helper. But they are afraid of her. Tracy has never felt so powerless; she wants desperately to help the birds but doesn't know how to reach them.

"What can I do to show them they can trust me?" Tracy's mind races. "If only . . . if only I could show them exactly what I mean, how much I want to help them. . . . If only I could spend some time with them on their own level, become one of them, just for a while. That would do it better than anything else! That would be perfect—if only I could become one of them."

Suddenly Tracy remembers what night it is, and a strange realization comes to her: "Maybe that's what Christmas is all about. I wish I could be a bird so the birds would know I care about them. Maybe God wanted to let us know how much he loves us—by becoming one of us."

For Tracy, Christmas will **never be the same.**

# Jesus: Fullness of Divinity, Fullness of Humanity

## The Incarnation: "God Made Flesh"

Tracy's realization is none other than the Christian belief known as the **Incarnation.** The word *incarnation* comes from the Latin word *incarnare,* which means "to make flesh." Thus the term *incarnation* describes God's embodiment, or "becoming flesh," as a human in Jesus. What Tracy wanted to do in the story—communicate her concern for certain members of creation by becoming one of them—God accomplished in the Incarnation. In the words of John's Gospel:

> In the beginning was the Word, and the Word was with God, and the Word was God. (1:1)
> And the Word became flesh and lived among us, . . . full of grace and truth. (1:14)

The Christian understanding of Jesus as "God in the flesh" underlies the belief that Jesus Christ is *the* fullest, most complete sacrament of God to the world. He is the sacrament out of which all others flow and by which all others are understood. In other words, Christians believe that people meet God most clearly by meeting Jesus Christ.

## Jesus' Life and Ministry

We can see Jesus Christ as the primary sacrament of God most tangibly through his life and ministry, as told in the Gospels of the New Testament.

When we read that Jesus touched and cured ill or outcast people, or dined with despised tax collectors, or protected prostitutes from the scorn and violence of the self-righteous, we see him revealing a God whose love is all-embracing. God's concern, like Jesus', is not limited by the standards and rules of society. Ⓐ

How Jesus treated people is inseparable from the whole purpose of his life and ministry. His mission was to usher in the Reign, or Kingdom, of God, through embodying God's love for all creation in his teaching, his healing, and ultimately in his death on the cross and his Resurrection. Jesus taught about a God whom he called his Father, a passionately caring God whose love is unlimited, healing, tireless, and unreserved.

Jesus also invited people to participate in the Kingdom by loving God and loving their neighbors. More will be said about this aspect of Jesus' teachings on the Reign of God in the following section on the church as a sacrament of Jesus Christ. For now simply note that Jesus embodied the Kingdom of God in a decidedly real sense. He knew that the Kingdom of God was being revealed in his own life and work.

## Jesus' Death and Resurrection

The Christian church's belief that Jesus Christ is the fullest sacrament of God to the world comes out of its understanding of Jesus' death on the cross, and his being raised from the dead.

*an encounter with God*

Ⓐ Read one of the following passages: Luke 8:43–48 (about the woman with the hemorrhage) or Luke 19:1–10 (about Zacchaeus, the tax collector). Go over the story several times, studying it carefully. You may even want to look up the story in a biblical commentary—ask your school librarian for recommendations. Then write a short, reflective essay about why the story is of an encounter with God.

✺ *Student art (facing page):* Watercolor by Virginia Foy, Cor Jesu Academy, Saint Louis, Missouri

### The Paschal Mystery

The early Christians recognized that the events encompassing Jesus Christ's death and Resurrection, his Ascension to the Father, and his sending of the Holy Spirit on his followers were a profound mystery. Throughout Christian history this has been called the **paschal mystery.** The word *paschal* means "Passover." It recalls the Jewish Passover experience recounted in the Old Testament, in which the angel of death "passed over" the homes of the Israelite slaves in Egypt. Consequently, all the firstborn of the Israelites were spared from death, the people of Israel were set free from slavery, and they passed over into new life in the Promised Land.

Starting with Saint Paul, Christians came to see Jesus' dying and rising in terms similar to the Passover: God, through Jesus' death and Resurrection, frees us from the bonds of sin and death, and brings us into a new life with God, given in the outpouring of the Spirit. According to Paul, Jesus Christ is the ultimate sign of God's gracious, saving love. ⓑ

### The Cross

Jesus' death on the cross and his rising from the dead each reveal specific aspects of the God that Jesus embodied while on this Earth. Jesus' death on the cross particularly manifests God's care and concern for those who suffer. Indeed, the

*dying and rising*

ⓑ Ending a friendship, quitting a job, moving to a new town or school, and graduating can be paschal-like events—that is, experiences of dying to one type of life and rising to another. Write about a dying followed by a new life that you have experienced. Describe your feelings about that change.

God in the flesh

God suffers with us

tion. Jesus' rising from the dead by the power of God lets us know that God can turn any kind of suffering—no matter how horrendous—into a grace-filled opportunity for new life. This is the meaning behind many of Jesus' messages about "death":

> "Very truly, I tell you, unless a grain of wheat falls into the earth and dies, it remains just a single grain; but if it dies, it bears much fruit." (John 12:24)

> "If any want to become my followers, let them deny themselves and take up their cross daily and follow me. For those who want to save their life will lose it, and those who lose their life for my sake will save it." (Luke 9:23–24)

That Jesus was raised from the dead shows us the power and victory of God in the world: life, not death, has the last word, goodness is more powerful and pervasive than evil, and God's grace can always transform evil into good, despair into hope, defeat into triumph. Ⓒ

## Jesus as the Model of Full Humanness

Early in the church's history, some Christians denied the mystery of the Incarnation. They wanted an either-or explanation of Jesus—either he is God and not human, or human and not God. The church, however, has always held its ground. In its both/and vision, the Christian church declares that Jesus is both fully God and fully human.

As has been emphasized previously in this chapter, Christians believe that people meet God most clearly in Jesus. At the same time, the Incarnation also teaches that Jesus offers humanity a model of itself at its best, a picture of what we humans can be and what God desires for us—that we faithfully respond to God's offer of grace.

cross is a testimony to the reality that God is present with us in the midst of our suffering and pain. In a very real sense, God suffers with us.

### The Resurrection

God is with us, even in our suffering—as comforting as that message of the cross can be, it is incomplete and makes little sense without the Resurrec-

speak to our world

Ⓒ Draw representations of the cross and the Resurrection that would speak to our contemporary world.

# The Paschal Mystery and Everyday Life

Anyone who ever passes through a time of suffering and comes through it as a stronger, better, more compassionate person experiences the reality of the paschal mystery in everyday life. Jesus' death and Resurrection, then, were not some wild fluke in the history of the world. Instead, they definitively confirm what we can readily see in the world around us—that growth and rebirth can come out of pain and suffering. Consider the example given by a young man named Don:

> When I was twelve, my dad died of lung cancer. It all happened so quick. He first got sick in early May, and by the end of August he was gone. He was supposed to coach my soccer team that summer. At first I was really mad at him for getting sick, for letting me down. Mom had been pleading with him for years to quit smoking. But he always just said, "I'll try after I get finished with this project," or, "I'll quit after the holidays."
>
> After he died I just turned numb. I wouldn't hardly talk to anybody at home or at school. I just wanted to be left alone. By the time I was thirteen, I was drinking a lot—first beer, then harder stuff. The morning of my fourteenth birthday, Mom and Grandpa found me passed out in my room. Right away they got me into the chemical dependency unit at Saint Mary's Hospital.
>
> It's been a long two years. Every day I've had to come up with a list of reasons why I shouldn't drink. Those first lists were pretty short: Mom would hate me. And I'd have to go back to the hospital. But after a while, my lists started to get longer. The clincher just came to me the other day: I want to live. I don't want to kill myself like my dad did.

In our personal life, any time we experience a loss of something only to find new life or new meaning, we enter into the paschal mystery. Every time we witness the cycle of life, death, new life in the natural world, both human and nonhuman, we witness the paschal mystery. Christians can enhance their experience of Jesus as a sacrament if they reflect on and appreciate the dyings and risings, the crosses and the empty tombs, in their own life.

Thus when we hear the story of Jesus' life, ministry, death, and Resurrection, we are always hearing two inseparable messages: First, the story of Jesus is about who God is and what God desires for all people, and all of creation. Second, the story of Jesus is about how human beings are to respond to God—that is, by trusting God completely and by loving their neighbors as they love themselves. In other words, Jesus teaches us how to be fully human. D

*Student art (above):* Scratch board by Francesca Caruso, Cabrini High School, New Orleans, Louisiana

D Imagine you are a member of a panel addressing people who have never heard of Jesus Christ. Their first question is, "What does Jesus' life tell us about God and about being human?" Write a brief response.

## For Review

1. What does the word *incarnation* mean? How does the opening story relate to the Incarnation of Jesus?

2. What is meant by saying Jesus is the primary sacrament of God?

3. Summarize why Jesus' life and ministry are a sacrament of God. Use an example to illustrate your response.

4. What is the paschal mystery? What do Jesus' death on the cross and his Resurrection tell us about God?

5. What does Jesus' humanity model for us human beings?

# The Church: The Sacrament of Christ to the World

To many of the followers he attracted during his lifetime, Jesus was someone who commanded great authority. Of greater importance to his followers, however, was that they felt the presence of God in him. Yet Jesus also constantly challenged his disciples' comfortable images of him. When the disciples heard Jesus speak of God's Kingdom, for example, they envisioned royal robes and awesome power. What they got instead was common bread, talk of tiny mustard seeds, and lessons on being a servant.

Similarly, when Jesus was crucified, his followers felt betrayed and foolish, so they hid. Then the Resurrection brought renewed faith and joy. But soon afterward, Jesus ascended to the Father, and his disciples went back to fear and confusion. They had been offered hope, had it snatched away and then miraculously returned—only to be left alone again. The disciples' frustrations were answered, though, by a key event in the history of the church: Pentecost.

*Facing page:* The coming of the Spirit at Pentecost, depicted in an African village setting

## Pentecost: The "Birthday" of the Church

After his suffering [Jesus] presented himself alive to [the Apostles] by many convincing proofs, appearing to them during forty days and speaking about the kingdom of God. While staying with them, he ordered them not to leave Jerusalem, but to wait there for the promise of the Father. "This," he said, "is what you have heard from me; for John baptized with water, but you will be baptized with the Holy Spirit not many days from now."

. . . "You will receive power when the Holy Spirit has come upon you; and you will be my witnesses in Jerusalem, in all Judea and Samaria, and to the ends of the earth." When he had said this, as [the Apostles] were watching, he was lifted up, and a cloud took him out of their sight. (1:3–9)

When the day of Pentecost had come, they were all together in one place. And suddenly from heaven there came a sound like the rush of a violent wind, and it filled the entire house where they were sitting. Divided tongues, as of fire, appeared among them, and a tongue rested on each of them. All of them were filled with the Holy Spirit and began to speak in other languages, as the Spirit gave them ability. (Acts of the Apostles 2:1–4)

The coming of the Holy Spirit had a powerful impact on the disciples. Suddenly, everything began to make sense: By his leaving, Jesus had not abandoned them. Rather, he had let go of them, like a parent lets go of a child so that the child can become an adult. E

By his Ascension, Jesus had shown that he trusted his disciples. He trusted them to represent him and to continue his mission. Jesus was no longer with the disciples "in the flesh." But as of Pentecost, he was now present with them, and dwelled in them, through the power of the Spirit. ("The Spirit" and "Jesus' Spirit" are other ways of saying the Holy Spirit.)

Just as Jesus had preached, taught, and lived the Kingdom of God while he walked the earth, his disciples were now to follow in his footsteps. Filled with the Holy Spirit, they were empowered to go forth into the world and preach the Good News of Jesus. The church was charged on the day of Pentecost to be a sacrament of Jesus Christ to the world, a sign and an instrument of Christ's—and thus God's—continuing real presence in the world. For that reason Pentecost is often called the birthday of the Christian church.

E Slowly and reflectively read the first two chapters of the Acts of the Apostles. As you read, imagine yourself taking part in the experiences described there. In a brief essay, write about your impressions of the church at its very beginning. Consider what would enable the church of today to be more like the early church.

## filled with the Spirit

"The church" includes the pope (here, John Paul II), but it is a greater, deeper reality than simply the hierarchy.

church primarily in terms of its hierarchy—the pope, bishops, and priests. A few people's notion of "church" extends no further than the building in which Christians worship. But the church is a much richer reality than any of these notions suggest. Three images of the church help us understand that reality: the church as the people of God, the Body of Christ, and the temple of the Holy Spirit.

### The People of God

Catholic church leaders at the Second Vatican Council during the mid-1960s spoke of the church as the **people of God.** Like the Israelites, chosen by God to be an instrument of God's love for the world, the church is God's own beloved people through whom the world is being saved.

The members of this new people of God are brought together by their faith in and love for Jesus Christ, the Son of God, and baptized into his new risen life. The church as the people of God is a community established by Christ to be, as the Evangelist Matthew tells us, "the salt of the earth and the light of the world" (5:13–14). The church as a sacrament is to be a seed of unity, hope, salvation, and transformation for the whole world.

### The Body of Christ

In the First Letter to the Corinthians, Saint Paul "embodies" his understanding of what or who the church is:

> For just as the body is one and has many members, and all the members of the body, though many, are one body, so it is with Christ. For in the one Spirit we were all baptized into one body—Jews or Greeks, slaves or free—and we were all made to drink of one Spirit. (12:12–13)

> Now you are the body of Christ and individually members of it. (12:27)

# Who Is "the Church"?

To grasp how the church is a sacrament of Christ to the world, it is helpful to consider just who the church is; that is, who has the task of carrying on the message and work of Jesus?

All too often, Christians misunderstand the word *church* to mean something other than or outside of themselves. Phrases such as "the church teaches" or "the church says" conjure up the image of an institution that has a life of its own apart from the people in the pews, but whose authority they are under. Similarly, some people mistakenly identify the

# We Took Communion to the Nursing Home, My Friend and I

We took Communion to the nursing home,
my friend and I.

Bodies old, tired, worn out, broken, crippled.
Spirits old, tired, worn out, broken, crippled.
Some spirits very much alive.

We enter a room; he is in bed.
The once-virile body is faded, wasted,
seemingly asleep.
"Shall we pass him by?" we wonder.
But we ask, "Would you like to receive
Communion?"
The eyes open. "Yes," he whispers.
"The Body of Christ."
"Amen." He opens his mouth, receives the host,
has trouble swallowing.
There is a cup of water by the bed.
I put the straw to his lips.
He isn't strong enough to suck.
I hold the cup to his lips and dribble some water
into his mouth. He swallows.
The faded eyes close, open again.
"Thank you," he whispers.

She is in a wheelchair in the hall.
"Would you like to receive Communion?"
"I don't know," she says wistfully.
"I haven't been to Confession lately. I'd like to,
but do you think I should?"
My friend assures her it will be all right,
and she receives gratefully.

She is in a wheelchair, alive, loud.
"Would you like to receive Communion?"
"Come here, let me kiss you." She kisses me.
"And let me kiss you." She kisses my friend.
"Would you like to receive Communion?"
"Yes!" she says loudly. "Amen."
"Come here, let me kiss you."
Her voice follows us down the hall.

We pass several rooms where the residents
are too frail and too weak to respond.
She lies in bed, staring at the ceiling.
"Would you like to receive Communion?"
Her eyes light up.
"Oh, yes," she breathes eagerly, "oh, yes."
"The Body of Christ."
"Amen," she responds, as her aging, wrinkled hand
makes a reverent, slow, deliberate
sign of the cross.
"Oh, thank you, thank you."

We have taken Communion to the residents
of the nursing home,
my friend and I,
and they have shown us illness, senility, sorrow,
suffering, tears, and weakness.

We have taken Communion to the residents
of the nursing home,
my friend and I,
and they have shown us acceptance, courage,
gratitude, reverence, faith, hope, and love.

We have taken Communion to the residents
of the nursing home,
my friend and I,
and they have shown us
the Body of Christ.

(Ruth Kulas)

F Read Saint Paul's description of the church as a body (1 Corinthians 12:12–26). Then read the poem "We Took Communion to the Nursing Home, My Friend and I," on page 85 of this textbook. Finally, write an essay on how the poem and Saint Paul's words echo each other.

Like the phrase people of God, the image of the church as the Body of Christ suggests a community of persons who profess faith in Jesus Christ. Perhaps even more vividly, the image of the Body of Christ conveys the notion of a community whose members combine their individual gifts to work together to make him alive and present in the world. F

The church, then, is the continued embodiment of Jesus Christ here on Earth. The members of his Body are Christ's hands and feet and heart ministering to the world today.

### The Temple of the Holy Spirit

What enables the members of the church to embody Jesus Christ in the world? They cannot, by sheer will or effort, pass on God's love to a world that is aching so badly for that love. It is the Holy Spirit, poured out in God's people at Pentecost and down through the ages, who builds up the Body of Christ and gives it vitality. The Spirit dwells in the church. Thus whatever saving and healing actions the members of the church do, whatever genuine truths they teach, whatever light they shine in a dark world—these all come from the work of the Spirit in them. You may have heard it said, echoing Saint Paul, that your body is a temple of the Holy Spirit, a sanctuary or sacred dwelling place. So too is the church a living temple of God's Spirit.

## Building the Reign of God

The church is a sacrament of Christ. Whenever and wherever its members act as Jesus acted, whenever and wherever they preach about and live out the Reign of God that is so dear to Jesus' heart, they make Jesus' presence in the world visible. Just as Jesus preached the good news of liberation to poor people and sinners, so must the church preach the Good News. Just as Jesus fed the hungry, so must the church feed the hungry. And just as Jesus cared for and healed the sick, so must the church care for and heal the sick.

community of faith

The church is to be both a sign and an instrument of the Reign of God, as promised and delivered by God in Jesus Christ. Through its words and actions, the church, empowered by the Spirit, is to carry on Jesus' work of building the Reign of God.

### The Early Church

The early Christians took very seriously their mandate to imitate Jesus; this can be seen in the following testimony, given by a non-Christian man named Aristides to the Roman emperor Hadrian:

> Christians love one another. They never fail to help widows; they save orphans from those who would hurt them. If a man has something, he gives freely to the man who has nothing. If they see a stranger, Christians take him home and are happy, as though he were a real brother. They don't consider themselves brothers in the usual sense, but brothers instead through the Spirit, in God. And if they hear that one of them is in jail, or persecuted for professing the name of their redeemer, they all give him what he needs. If it is possible, they bail him out. If one of them is poor and there isn't enough food to go around, they fast several days to give him the food he needs. . . . This is really a new kind of person. There is something divine in them. (Balasuriya, *The Eucharist and Human Liberation,* page 26)

### The Church Today

Examples abound of the people of God giving witness to Jesus Christ and building the Reign of God today: Ⓖ

- Christians who work at food shelves and homeless shelters make Jesus tangibly present to those they serve.
- Parish members who volunteer to bring confined or elderly persons to Sunday Mass are a sacrament of Jesus.

- Bishops and theologians who work together to issue statements on topics concerning peace and economic justice make Jesus' teachings about the Kingdom come alive in the present day.
- Employers who treat employees with fairness and provide them with safe working conditions and just wages are acting Christlike.
- Persons who reach out to hurting or troubled friends, even if only to listen or lend a shoulder to cry on, bring the healing power of Jesus to their friends.
- Families who gather together for times of celebration, sharing, and relaxation witness the fullness of life desired by God for all and revealed to us by Jesus.

Of course, many more examples could be given. The point is, however, that almost any situation Christians find themselves in offers them the chance to be a sacrament of Christ—in both his divinity and his humanity—to those around them. Whenever persons love others as they love themselves, act with and promote justice, show mercy and compassion, or celebrate and give thanks for the gifts in their lives, they carry on the work of Jesus. In other words, people reveal to one another a God who is loving, gracious, and merciful, and they show by their example humanity at its best. By doing so they in fact are being "the church." Ⓗ

church in the world

Ⓖ Draw an image or a symbol that represents how you view the role of the church in the world.

Ⓗ Research one of the following people and the movement associated with that person. Write a two-page report on that person's and movement's efforts to build the Reign of God.
- Saint Francis of Assisi and the Franciscans
- Saint Elizabeth Ann Seton and the U.S. Catholic school system
- Cesar Chavez and the United Farm Workers
- Mother Teresa of India and the Missionaries of Charity
- Dorothy Day and the Catholic Worker Movement
- Martin Luther King Jr. and the U.S. Civil Rights Movement

we are one
united whole

## The Church as a Sacrament of Unity

As a sacrament of Christ to the world, the church has the specific task of reminding all the world's people that we have a common center—Jesus Christ—and that we are one united whole. As the Second Vatican Council stated in its *Dogmatic Constitution on the Church*, the church "by her relationship with Christ . . . is a kind of sacrament or sign of intimate union with God, and of the unity of all [humankind]" (number 1).

For the church, part of being a sacrament to the world means being an ongoing reminder that all the world has been saved by Christ. The church, like Jesus Christ, is a sacrament of God's compassion. The church proclaims that the Creator and Source of All Being is a loving God, and it points to the people, events, and places in the world where God's love can be found. ▨

for your children

▨ What would you like the experience of the church to be like for the generation that would include your own children? In what ways would you like it to be the same as what you experienced? In what ways would you like it to be different? Write your reflections in a page.

## For Review

6. Why is Pentecost often called the birthday of the Christian church?

7. Identify three images that help Christians understand who the church is. Discuss why each is a helpful image.

8. When or where is the church a sacrament of Jesus Christ to the world? Give three examples of how that happens in today's world.

# Building the Reign of God: Bringing Water to the Slums

The following story is based on a real-life incident from the country of Uruguay in South America. Like the tiny mustard seed that grows into a large plant, small actions on the part of members of the church can have far-reaching effects.

"The children come to school without washing because there is no water in the shantytown," the teacher explained to Teresa. "After nights spent trying to sleep on beds with no mattresses, no sheets, and with only rags for blankets, the children must get up very early just to get to school. It is a long way to fetch a bucket of water, and there is no time. So the children show up sleepy and without even having the chance to wash their face. No wonder they have a hard time paying attention to their studies."

All weekend Teresa heard the same story as she worked in the shantytown with the volunteer youth service team from her middle-class parish, located in another part of the city: There was no water in the shantytown, and its lack was the cause of much hardship among its residents.

Her own privileged position had made Teresa feel uncomfortable—she had never thought twice about washing her face when she got up in the morning or getting a drink when she came in from the heat. Somehow, she sensed, she was responsible for the fact that there was no water in the slums.

"Surely something could be done," Teresa pondered out loud to her father, an engineer for the city's public works department. "How difficult would it be to provide the shantytown with its own water supply?"

Getting water to the shantytown would not be difficult at all, Teresa's father found out. And it would cost next to nothing. Indeed, one Sunday's worth of collections from her parish covered the amount the city was charging for laying the pipes to carry the water to the slum. However, to the shantytown residents, who had long ago unconsciously resigned themselves to the whole situation, such an expenditure of money would have been impossible.

Two weeks after Teresa spoke with her father, the shantytown had its water. Enough money was left over to even build a small community center that contained eight showers and a central water hydrant.

Soon the life of the whole community and the character of the people were transformed. Now the children could come to school with washed faces; the old men who spent the day trudging around the garbage heaps could wash their weary feet at night; and the men and women, who before were easily irritated and hostile with one another because of being unable to find relief from the hot, midday sun, could refresh themselves with a cup of cool, clean water. Now life was a little easier, a little more bearable. (Based on *New Eyes for Reading*, pages 35–36)

# The Seven Sacraments of the Catholic Church

So far the discussion of the church as a sacrament of Christ to the world has focused mainly on the church's practical actions of serving and teaching others in the concrete, everyday world. But there is another, unique way that the Catholic church brings the saving presence of Christ more and more into the world. That is through the celebration of the seven sacraments of Baptism, Confirmation, the Eucharist, Reconciliation (Penance), Anointing of the Sick, Matrimony, and Holy Orders.

To appreciate each particular sacrament, we will first consider the role of the seven sacraments as a whole within the life of the Catholic church. Let's start by considering the following example:

Suppose four friends decide to get together every Monday morning before the school day starts. They just want to have a time and space to talk before the hectic week begins. For a whole school year, each Monday they gather under the stairwell by the lockers, hearing one another's latest good news or dilemmas, sharing a snack, working through occasional differences, and supporting one another.

We might say that the gathering of these friends does two things:
1. It expresses who they are. The weekly gathering is a ritual that says, "We are friends."
2. It nourishes and builds up their friendship.

The seven sacraments function somewhat like that: They (1) express the faith of the church, who the church is, and (2) renew and strengthen the faith of the church by giving us divine life. And what is the faith of the church? That we are God's beloved people, united in Christ and called to pass on God's love to the world through the power of the Holy Spirit dwelling in us.

## Rooted in Jesus' Actions and in Tradition

As we saw earlier in this chapter, at the Ascension when Jesus charged his disciples to be his witnesses "to the ends of the earth," he did not leave them without some clue as to how to go about that task. Along with the promise that he would send his Spirit, Jesus left the disciples with the example of his own life and ministry. The way his disciples would witness Jesus to others would be to preach and act as he did.

As the church grew and developed, Christians recognized seven primary ways in which Jesus Christ himself was a sacrament of God:
- He brought people to new life.
- He forgave people's sins.
- He sacrificed himself out of love.
- He shared the power of his spirit with others.
- He healed people's illnesses.
- He was faithful to the One he called Abba.
- He ministered to people's spiritual needs.

Eventually, all seven kinds of Jesus' actions were ritualized into what are now the official sacraments of the Catholic church.

So where do the seven sacraments come from? They are rooted (1) in the life and ministry of Jesus as shown in the New Testament, and (2) in the Tradition of the Catholic church—the church's wisdom, teaching, and practice handed down through the ages under the guidance of the Holy Spirit. The sacraments are a unique, divinely given way that Christ's saving presence in the world is carried out through the church.

## Divine and Human Dimensions

The seven sacraments are not simply rituals of human making. True, they have many of the characteristics of other communal rituals, like graduations and opening ceremonies of the Olympic Games: Their actions and gestures, supported by words, convey shared meanings. They rely on people's active participation or at least understanding. As celebrations they interrupt life's routines, revealing the extraordinary in the ordinary. They are often connected with life's important moments or passages. They help people express who they are as a community and what they are striving for.

Then what makes the seven sacraments different from rituals of purely human making?

**Power from God.** Jesus Christ himself acts in the sacraments: offering new life, forgiving sins, giving his own body and blood, healing, uniting, consecrating. And through the work of the Holy Spirit,

the transforming grace of Christ's actions is poured into human hearts. The sacraments are divinely **efficacious**—capable of effecting change in us and the world—because of God's power, not our own.

**Response from humans.** Whether the grace given by God actually bears fruit in those who receive the sacraments and in the world around them depends on the human dimension: How well prepared are people for a given sacrament? Is the sacrament celebrated in a meaningful way, or do people simply go through the motions? Are their hearts open and responsive to how God may be working in them, or are they distracted and even

*Student art:* Linocut by Jennifer Khouri, Saint Agnes Academy, Memphis, Tennessee

☐ Brainstorm a list of human-controlled factors that would help someone celebrate Mass in a way that bears good fruit in his or her life. Then brainstorm a list of human factors that would hinder a fruitful celebration of Mass. (They are probably the opposite of the helping factors.) Focus on one hindrance and reflect on how it could be changed into a help.

turned off to God and things of the spirit? These factors are part of what is known as the **disposition** of those who receive the sacraments—their inner attitude and readiness for a particular sacrament. ☐

God's loving power flows through the sacraments to us and to the whole world. God reaches out with love, but human beings are free to respond or not. The power comes from God; the response, from us.

## A Definition

At this point we are ready to summarize the church's understanding of what the sacraments are (in the sense of the seven Catholic sacraments). According to the *Catechism of the Catholic Church*:

> The sacraments are efficacious signs of grace, instituted by Christ and entrusted to the Church, by which divine life is dispensed to us. The visible rites by which the sacraments are celebrated signify and make present the graces proper to each sacrament. They bear fruit in those who receive them with the required dispositions. (Number 1131)

Through the sacraments the ongoing Reign of God is revealed and built up in the world—if we allow ourselves to be wide-open channels of God's grace.

# seven sacraments

## For Review

9. What twofold function do the seven sacraments serve in the Catholic church?

10. How did Jesus' disciples witness Jesus to others?

11. Correlate the seven actions of Jesus Christ listed on page 90 with the seven sacraments of the Catholic church.

12. Where do the seven sacraments come from? In what do they have their roots?

13. What makes the sacraments different from rituals of purely human making?

14. What does it mean to say that the sacraments are divinely efficacious?

15. Why is the disposition of those receiving the sacraments important?

16. Give the *Catechism's* definition of sacraments.

# The Sacraments in History

Over a period of centuries in the history of the church, the church discerned that seven of its rituals—the ones we identify today as the Catholic sacraments—were essential to the faith of the church. That is, they had been passed on by the authentic Tradition of the church as coming from Jesus Christ himself.

Each sacrament has had its own historical development, which will be treated later in each chapter on the sacraments. But before considering the sacraments individually, we will take a look at how the sacraments as a whole emerged in the church. As you will see, the sacraments developed as the church itself did.

The rite of a sacrament (here, Confirmation) both signifies and makes present God's power and grace. The sacrament's fruitfulness in us depends on our inner attitude and readiness to receive God's grace.

# 6

# The Sacraments in History

## changing church, changing sacraments

Christ, the beginning and the end . . .

. . . open to the Spirit . . .

we praise you, as a God of history
    who remains steadfast
    in the struggles, defeats, and triumphs
    of your human family and your church.
Lead us to respect for our past,
    to hope for our future,
    and to creative involvement
    in our present.

                        Amen.

If we are to understand the seven sacraments today, knowing something about the Catholic church's history of formation and reformation is necessary. Upcoming chapters on each of the seven sacraments will discuss their historical development individually. This chapter will look at four major time periods in the church's history and examine how the significant changes that occurred during these periods affected the church's understanding of the sacraments.

The seven sacraments of the Catholic church, as we now experience them, did not suddenly materialize in the life of the early church. Nor was, or is, the sacraments' existence stone-unchanging (and even rocks and mountains change over time!). Rather, the church's understanding and awareness of how God's grace is present to us went through a gradual development, just as family members and their circumstances go through changes—as the following story illustrates:

# forming & reforming

## Sitting out on the deck

of their parents' house, three of Tom and Kate Delaney's six adult children try to break some unusual news to their parents as gently and honestly as possible. The traditional family get-together at Christmas has become unworkable, and the children want a summer gathering at their parents' home instead. Because Tom and Kate will probably be able to hear Sam's "excuse" the easiest, the task of starting things falls to him.

"Ma, we're sorry. I know it means a lot to you and Pa when we come back for Christmas—and it does to us, too—but . . . I don't think we're going to make it this year. Between eight hours in a car with screaming kids and never knowing how bad the weather will be, it's just too much of a hassle. We don't want to get caught spending Christmas in a little Podunk motel halfway between here and home like we did that one year—it's really hard with the kids. We're really sorry.

"We were figuring that it might be a lot easier to have everyone get together in July or August instead of at Christmas. What do you think?"

Sam's younger sister, Audrey, speaks up as soon as Sam finishes, knowing that a

blow like the one Sam just delivered needs to be followed up quick with something positive. "Even Marilyn said she'd come home every year if we hold our family reunions in the summer," Audrey notes. "We've been lucky to see her every other Christmas."

Piping in to confirm what his sister Audrey just said, Loren adds, "Yeah, Ma. Coming home in the summer's a lot easier and a lot more enjoyable for everyone. We don't have to worry about the weather, and we're not all crammed into the house getting on each other's nerves like when it's zero degrees outside. You know how cranky you get, Pa, when that happens. In the summertime, when things get too noisy, you can kick us all outside to the yard or onto the deck, like now. Besides, I like it when we go play ball at the schoolyard like we did last night. Can't do that in the winter in Iowa!"

Figuring her father is starting to see the sense of their suggestion, Audrey slides in an extra bonus. "Just think, Pa— you and Ma not having everyone at home for Christmas means you could come visit Ken and me and the boys in Oklahoma where it's

a lot warmer."

# Change and Opportunities for Renewal: Part of Everyone's History

As hard as it was to face their parents, Sam, Audrey, and Loren recognized that things had changed a lot for their family over the past few years. Now that all of them were married, starting families, and living long distances from where they had grown up, trying to get together at Christmas no longer seemed workable. The commitment to getting together once a year was still strong; it was simply time to change when they did it. Instead of gathering at Christmastime, the Delaney family would reunite during the summer.

In spite of the loss that they would feel with this change in the "ritual" of their family get-togethers, the Delaney children anticipated the opportunity for renewal for their family. Without having to deal with the stresses of traveling over the holidays and during the winter, they would once again be able to look forward to coming home—rather than dreading it as they had begun to do. Family get-togethers would once again be appreciated as special and meaningful.

Change is built into the nature of all creation.

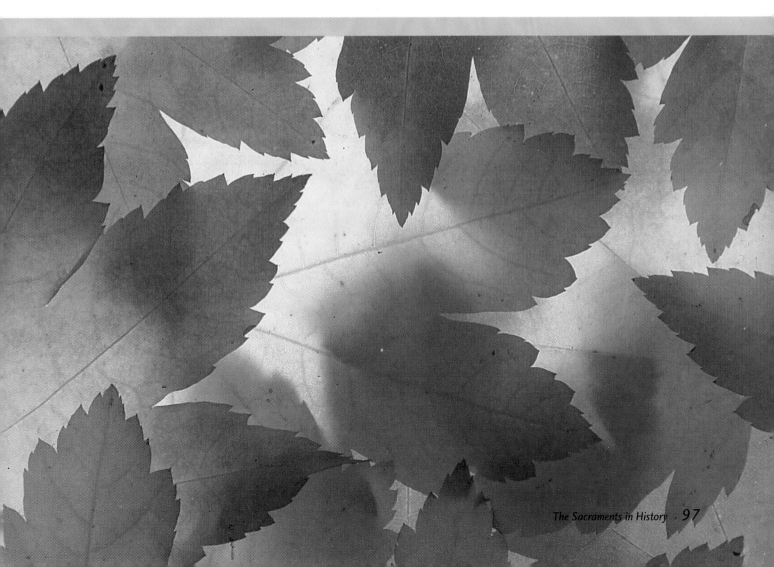

Ⓐ Describe in writing a major change that you or your family experienced. How did this change offer an opportunity for growth or renewal?

## Change: A Fact of Life

As a young person going through a number of changes at this stage in your life, you are probably aware that life is full of changes and opportunities for renewal and growth. As you grew out of childhood and into adolescence, how you acted, how you dressed, and how you related to others most likely changed considerably. In turn all these changes allowed you many opportunities for renewal, such as the following:

- letting go of things that were no longer appropriate for you in your new time or place
- confirming or rediscovering what was most important to you
- deepening your understanding of who you are
- establishing new relationships and enriching old ones

Recognizing change and renewal as part of the "facts of life" provides a helpful basis for understanding history—whether we are looking at our own personal history, the history of our family, school, or country, or even the history of the Catholic church and its sacraments. Ⓐ

## Change, the Church, and the Sacraments

As you read the following broad summary of the history of the church and its sacraments, keep in mind the perspective that change is a fact of life. Although the church is guided by the Holy Spirit and acts as the Body of Christ, it is also a human organization. Like any other human organization, the church grew and changed with the passage of time. Change also came for the church when it found itself in new cultural environments and when it was faced with situations where the old ways of doing things did not work.

Likewise, change and opportunities for renewal were sometimes deliberately sought by the people of God, particularly when the church realized it had lost touch with some of its original roots. In these instances especially, the guidance of the Holy Spirit can be seen. Through the ages the Spirit works with the human dimension of the church, moving hearts and minds to respond to God's call to renewal.

As the church changed throughout its history, there also came changes in how it expressed itself, particularly in its sacraments.

Saint Francis of Assisi, guided by the Holy Spirit, began a renewal of the church in the Middle Ages. This painting by sixteenth-century artist El Greco depicts Francis receiving the stigmata, the marks of the wounds of Christ.

# Phase One: Church and Sacraments Before A.D. 400

## An Early Convert

This section's glimpse at the Christian church and its understanding of the sacraments during its first four hundred years begins with an imaginary personal sketch of a woman named Paulina, who converted to Christianity. The date for the sketch is around the year A.D. 250.

Paulina lived in a Greek-speaking section of Asia Minor north of Palestine. Religion meant little to her. On occasion she attended religious services—usually associated with a festival for one of the many popular gods worshiped in her area—out of a sense of civic duty. She did know of groups for whom religion seemed more meaningful. Often these were sects with mysterious rites.

One such group was the Christians. As an offshoot of Judaism, the Christian religion was known for its strong belief in one God and its high moral standards. Yet Christians also believed the human-divine Jesus had come to usher in a new age. Moreover, they seemed especially concerned about the people who were overlooked by the rest of society: widows, orphans, slaves, foreigners, poor people. Christians' enthusiasm about their religion was even more remarkable considering

their religion had been declared illegal. Christians of the time always lived with the possibility of persecution.

Paulina heard stories about a mysterious Christian rite that some claimed was cannibalism and others said was a drunken orgy. Whatever these Christians were doing on Sunday mornings, however, clearly left an impact. The people that Paulina knew to be Christians were joyful in the face of murderous threats. And they promoted unity and equality in a world where boundaries were solidly built between rich and poor, citizen and noncitizen, free and slave, man and woman.

One day Paulina heard some Christians preaching in the marketplace. They spoke of their former lives and of how their accepting Jesus as Lord had changed them. Paulina chatted with one of the women in the group, who took the time to tell her the story of Jesus and explain his teachings. The woman then invited her to attend one of their gatherings, which she called an agape (pronounced *ah*-guh-pay), or "friendship meal."

Partly out of curiosity, Paulina accepted the invitation and went. She noticed that the small group of people greeted one another warmly, sang psalms with enthusiasm, and listened

The early Christians gathered regularly for a joyful "friendship meal," at which their sharing of bread and wine became a sharing of Christ's body and blood.

**B** If Christianity were illegal in this country today, do you think the church would be stronger or weaker than it is now? Explain your answer in writing.

intently to readings about Jesus that a bishop then applied to their present lives. The woman who had spoken to her earlier then took Paulina aside and explained that the remainder of the celebration was only for baptized members of the community. Through the sharing of bread and wine, the woman explained, Christians believed they shared Jesus' body and blood. She said that by doing this they would enter the mystery of Christ's dying and rising, and it would remind the participants of their commitment to sacrifice themselves in Jesus' name and for his truth.

Paulina was impressed, though still confused. The woman volunteered to be Paulina's sponsor if Paulina wished to begin initiation into the community. The woman used the word *sacrament* for this process of initiation.

Paulina decided to begin. She recognized the risk in becoming a Christian, but the joy, mutual caring, and inner peace that she saw in the community seemed worth the price.

In Paulina's lifetime Christianity was a prohibited organization composed of small, secret communities, and it had been illegal since the reign of Roman Emperor Nero (A.D. 54–68). In spite of its illegal status and the periodic persecutions that came with it, the church managed to survive and spread throughout the Mediterranean area from the foundations laid by the Apostles. Increasingly, converts came from the non-Jewish (Gentile) world. Evidence suggests that early Christian missionaries even made their way as far as India! **B**

# Early Christian Worship

Christians during Paulina's lifetime would have gleaned their models for community life and ritual celebrations from the examples set by the very first Christian communities described in writings such as Saint Paul's epistles and the Acts of the Apostles. These rituals included Baptism, sharing the Lord's Supper, and the laying on of hands.

### Formality Begins to Emerge

By the time Paulina sought to become a Christian, around A.D. 250, the church had already become somewhat formal in its worship and ministry. In the sketch, we read about a gathering called a friendship meal, which has many similarities to today's Mass. There was singing, reading from the Scriptures, the preaching of a "homily" by the bishop (the ordained leader of the community who presided at its liturgical celebrations), and a sharing of bread and wine. The bread and wine, believed by Christians to be the body and blood of Christ, was shared only by the baptized members of the community. All those who were still preparing to become Christians were taken aside during this time. In Paulina's day the church also had a formal initiation process for those who wanted to join.

underground Christianity

### Christian and Pagan Rites Mingle

When new cultural groups converted to Christianity, their traditional religious rites were often mingled with those already in use by Christians. For example, the early church borrowed popular pagan festivals and Christianized them into Christmas and other annual holy days. Likewise, much of the wedding service as we know it originated in common Roman practices. Rings, the mutual kiss, the exchange of promises, and the wedding banquet were all typical elements of weddings in the Mediterranean area before the appearance of Christianity.

The early church's openness to adapting to other cultures is also evident from the fact that the prayers and procedures used at the celebration of the Eucharist differed according to local custom. ©

### Early Church Teachings on Sacraments Emerge

About forty years before Paulina became interested in the church, around the year 210, a Christian writer named Tertullian first used the Latin word *sacramentum* in a sense similar to how Catholic Christians use the word *sacrament* today. At the time, Roman religious rites—such as the initiation ceremony for young Romans entering the army—were called *sacramenta*, the plural of *sacramentum*. In his writings on Baptism, Tertullian borrowed the word to describe this Christian ritual. Eventually, *sacramenta* was used to describe a variety of religious rituals practiced by Christians.

As mentioned earlier, Christians of this historical period looked to the very early church writings (Saint Paul's epistles, the Acts of the Apostles) to find models for their rituals, faith, and practices, including those practices that were being called *sacramenta*. They wanted to know what these rituals and symbols meant. Based on their own experiences and on what they read in the Scriptures, these Christians began to see the connections between the sacraments and the mysteries of Christian faith. And they began to recognize that these rituals and symbols were true encounters with God.

When the church was under Roman persecution, Christians in Rome worshiped secretly in underground cemeteries called catacombs, such as the catacomb of Saint Callistus with its crypts of beloved martyrs—here, the crypt of Saint Cecilia.

© Imagine that you have been asked to create church customs or celebrations that would reflect current North American teenage culture. List three changes in church practice that you would make.

After Christianity became legal in 313, Christians could move their worship "above ground" to practice their faith openly. Before long, they were building magnificent churches like the basilica of Santa Maria Maggiore, constructed in Rome from 432 to 440.

## Christianity Becomes the Official Religion of the Empire

The prospects for the Christian church's continued survival and growth were given a large boost in the fourth century. First, the emperor Constantine lifted the ban on Christian worship in the year 313. Christians could now gather openly and freely without fear of persecution from government authorities. Then, by the end of that century, Christianity was declared not only legal but the *official religion* of the Roman Empire—a far cry from its previous persecuted status.

Christianity's big chance, as we will see, came at about the same time that the Roman Empire was in a serious state of decline—both culturally and politically.

## from underground
### to above ground

### For Review

2. What were some formal elements present in the church's worship and ministry by around A.D. 250?

3. Who lifted the ban on Christian worship in 313, and what effect did lifting the ban have on Christians and Christianity?

# Phase Two: Church and Sacraments During the Dark Ages

The period of Western history from about A.D. 400 to 1000 is often called the Dark Ages. The Dark Ages were brought about by the fall of the Roman Empire in the West.

## The Fall of the Roman Empire in the West

In the year 326, Constantine, the same emperor who had made Christianity legal, angered the citizens of Rome by refusing to participate in a pagan procession. Subsequently, in the year 330, he moved the Roman Empire's headquarters eastward from Rome to the city of Byzantium, or Constantinople, as the city was renamed. When a succeeding emperor died in 395, the Roman Empire was split in two, never again to be reunited.

Over the next century, the Western Empire was constantly being attacked, first by the Huns from central Asia and then by the Vandals, who sailed across the Mediterranean from North Africa. In 476 the last Roman emperor in the West was killed. The collapse of the Western Empire soon followed. In the political and cultural chaos resulting from this collapse, the church and its popes would play an increasing role in governing the West. D

## Saint Augustine: "Administering and Receiving" Sacraments

The general anxiety caused by the decline and fall of the Roman Empire spilled over into the church. By the time Augustine became bishop of the North African city of Hippo in 395, controversy and division plagued the church.

Saint Augustine taught that the sacrament of Baptism confers a new character or a permanent "seal" on the person, marking him or her forever as Christ's. Because a seal was conferred in the sacrament, Augustine spoke of "administering" and "receiving" the sacraments, terms that eventually were tied to the other sacraments as well. Today Baptism, Confirmation, and Holy Orders are said to each confer its own permanent character, and for this reason they can be received only once in a lifetime.

### A Broad View of Sacraments

Although Augustine began to narrow down the church's understanding of what constituted a sacrament, he still thought of sacraments in the broad sense as "signs of a sacred thing." To him, sacraments included not only rituals such as Baptism but also the sign of the cross, the Lord's Prayer, and the oil used for anointing. Augustine believed that almost anything could be a sacrament, or a sign of God, because all of creation was a reflection of God.

### Some Sacraments Seen as More Important

While believing that many things could be sacraments, Augustine also believed that some sacraments were more important to the church than others. He listed these sacraments of greater importance in two categories: "sacraments of the word," such as sermons, prayers, reading of the Scriptures; and "sacraments of action," such as the various

*chaos and change*

D Focus on a time of chaos in the history of your own family, community, or nation. Recall the changes in customs and practices that came about during that time of chaos, and explain in writing how the chaos may have contributed to the changes.

# The Eastern Churches

In A.D. 451 the Council of Chalcedon (the fourth ecumenical, or general, council of the Christian church) declared that the bishop of Rome was the highest authority in the church. At the same time, the patriarch of Constantinople (the head of the church in the East) was named second in authority. Because of the split in the Roman Empire between Rome and Constantinople, relations between the church leaders of the two cities were frequently strained. Eventually, the tensions between western and eastern Christians resulted in a formal split between the churches led by the bishop of Rome and those led by the patriarch of Constantinople.

Today some of these Eastern Christian churches, which have their roots in Asia, northern Africa, and eastern European countries, are officially part of Catholicism and united with the pope. These are called *Eastern Catholic churches,* and they are often referred to as *rites.* For instance, the Byzantine Rite and the Chaldean Rite are Catholic, united with the pope, but they are not in the Latin or Roman Rite of Catholicism, the rite of most of the world's Catholics. The churches called Eastern Orthodox are not officially in union with Rome, although relations between the two are more friendly than they have been in the past.

This course only examines the sacraments as they developed in the Western or Latin Rite Catholic tradition, but be aware of the existence of Eastern Christian churches, both Eastern Catholic and Eastern Orthodox. They too practice the sacraments in their own unique fashions.

symbols and rituals used in Christian worship. It would be more than eight hundred years before the church, guided by the Spirit, limited its use of the word *sacrament* to the seven official rituals celebrated by Catholic Christians today.

## Sacramental Practice in the Dark Ages

After Augustine died, little new thinking about the sacraments took place until about the eleventh century, largely because of the social and cultural upheaval of the Dark Ages.

During the five hundred years or so following the fall of Rome, the church continued to spread across Europe. With that spread and growth, numerous developments in sacramental practices took place as well. Examples include these developments:

- Confirmation became separated from Baptism.
- Public penance was replaced by private confession.
- Lay involvement in the eucharistic liturgy (the Mass) decreased significantly.
- Marriage came to be seen as a sacramental rite.

- Anointing of the Sick became Anointing of the Dying.
- Presbyters (priests) were ordained to preside at liturgical functions as the bishop's representatives.

By the year 1000, social and political stability began to return to Europe, the world of the Roman church. The stability brought with it a revival of activities centered on studying the Christian faith. Once again the climate was ripe for looking at the meaning of sacramental symbols and rituals.

*Below:* The ancient national cathedral in Budapest, Hungary, reflects a vivid sense of the sacred.
✺ *Student art:* Photo by Thomas Eyre, Bishop Shanahan High School, Downingtown, Pennsylvania

## sacramental theology emerges

### For Review

4. What did Augustine teach about the sacrament of Baptism?

5. List three developments in sacramental practices that took place during the Dark Ages.

# Phase Three:
# Church and Sacraments in the High Middle Ages

## A Medieval Christian

The medieval cathedral, such as Notre Dame in Paris, France, was a showplace of beauty and splendor, and a storybook of stone statues and stained-glass windows.

Whereas growth, formation, risk, and turmoil characterized much of the church's first one thousand years of existence, formality and relative stability were the hallmarks of the period between the years 1000 and 1300, a period often referred to as the High Middle Ages.

Let's explore the church's history and its understanding of the sacraments during this period with the help of another imaginary personal sketch, this time of a medieval Christian named Hugh of Lyons.

One thing about Hugh—he knew his place. He was a serf, tied to the land and to his local lord. He was also a Christian; everyone was, except for the pockets of Jews and the infidels across the seas. As a citizen both of his city and of the universal church community known as Christendom, Hugh knew his place.

Hugh had been baptized as an infant and later confirmed by the local bishop. He attended Mass regularly at Lyons Cathedral, which Hugh and his forebears had helped build. The cathedral was a showplace of beauty and splendor and a storybook of stone statues and stained-glass windows. The cathedral contained the tombs of former bishops who had supervised its construction. It also housed numerous relics of saints regarded with respect by the townspeople. Naturally it attracted pilgrims from great distances.

The cathedral itself was a symbol of harmony and symmetry, giving a clear impression of an orderly universe. Within its walls, statues of the twelve Hebrew prophets faced statues of the twelve Apostles. Pictures of the seven deadly vices were balanced by those of the seven virtues. Everything about the cathedral assured Hugh that the world was united under God. And

Harmony & symmetry

everyone worshiped there, from bishop and lord to lowly serf.

Hugh's Christian responsibility, as Hugh perceived it, was to obey his local lord and his bishop. At liturgies and other religious events, he did not have an active role but participated silently and reverently in the worship. Hugh was awed by the richness of the ceremonies.

Hugh's identity was intimately linked with being a Christian. He could not conceive of a life apart from Christianity. The vast array of Christian symbols and rituals, and Christianity's dominance in Hugh's society, supported Hugh in this identity. Although he was a mere serf, he fit into his world. At the same time, his work in building up God's Kingdom on Earth—for instance, his work on the cathedral—was thought to assure him of a lordly place in heaven.

Il Duomo, the cathedral of Milan, Italy

## A Different World

Note the striking contrast between the circumstances experienced by Hugh and those experienced by Paulina, for whom joining the church meant going against the dominant political and cultural forces of her day. For Hugh, to have gone against the dominant culture would have meant not being a Christian. In fact in Hugh's time, the culture of medieval, feudal Europe and that of the Christian church of the West were pretty much the same. Because most political rulers in medieval Europe were Christian, so were their subjects. Not being a Christian meant not being a citizen. In effect the church was the center of life for the ordinary citizens of Europe.

Also different for Hugh were his experiences of the church's rituals, which had become much more formal. By Hugh's time the friendly informality of the Mass that Paulina attended had long been replaced by elaborate ceremonies in enormous cathedrals.

The sacraments in the medieval church had accumulated quite a few "extras" in terms of ornamental details. Part of this accumulation happened because the ceremonies used in the royal courts were often adapted for religious purposes. For example, if, as a medieval person, Hugh had to kiss the ring of an earthly king, he would have felt it only proper to kiss the ring of the Heavenly King's representative, the bishop. Once again, in interacting with its surroundings, the church was naturally influenced by them. E

# The Middle Ages: A Significant Time for Sacramental Theology

Part of an explosion of intellectual interests during the High Middle Ages included a renewed interest in the sacraments by Christian scholars. In many ways the medieval period was a pivotal time, one of the most significant periods of growth and change in the Catholic understanding of sacraments.

### Seven Sacraments Made Official

Up until—and into—the twelfth century, Christian writers shared Augustine's broad view of the sacraments; that is, many symbols and rituals were considered sacraments. One twelfth-century document even listed thirty sacraments! By this time, however, the rituals Catholics now know as the seven sacraments were becoming recognized as different

from other Catholic symbols and rituals. Then in the thirteenth century, the Second Council of Lyons affirmed that there were only seven official sacraments of the church, basically those that Catholics celebrate today. (Later, in the sixteenth century, the Council of Trent would reaffirm this teaching, this time to emphasize the validity of *all seven* sacraments.)

With the word *sacramentum* being restricted in application to the seven rituals of Baptism, Confirmation, the Eucharist, Reconciliation (also called Penance), Anointing of the Dying (now more broadly understood as Anointing of the Sick), Matrimony, and Holy Orders, other changes came as well. Rituals became more standardized, and the theological explanations of them became more uniform.

### Thomas Aquinas and the Sacraments

The medieval church's understanding of the sacraments reached its peak in the work of Saint Thomas Aquinas. One of Aquinas's most significant contributions to the Catholic church's understanding of the sacraments came from his discussion of the sacraments as causes of God's grace. That is, not only were the sacraments signs of sacred reality, as Augustine and others had taught, but the sacraments also served as instruments that actually brought about God's grace.

### An Emphasis on Correct Form Emerges

Over the years a focus on standardizing the sacraments and the proper performance of the sacramental rituals emerged. This became necessary so that people would know when a ritual really was a sacrament in the eyes of the church, and when it was just one person's idea of a sacrament.

People also wondered if the priest's holiness or sinfulness made a difference.

E Would you rather have been a Christian in Paulina's time (the early church) or in Hugh's time? State your reasons in a paragraph.

What if the priest offering Mass was himself a sinner—did the bread and wine indeed become the body and blood of Christ? Were the power and grace of the sacrament truly present regardless? (The answer is yes because the sacrament's power comes from God, not from the minister's personal qualities.)

Minimum requirements were set for a sacrament to be valid and therefore effective—such as the proper materials, symbolic actions, and words to be used.

### Literal Thinking Leads to Magical Thinking

The emphasis on "correct form" in ceremonies was needed to prevent abuses and confusion, but unfortunately this focus tended to encourage literal thinking. As a result many people put their faith in proper performance of the externals rather than in the meaning or experience underlying a ritual.

Inevitably the sacraments were affected by this magical attitude. Merely following the correct forms, it was believed, automatically guaranteed special graces: Saying certain words or doing certain actions was thought to force God to act in a desired way. It was assumed that the sacrament always took in the person regardless of whether the person's heart was receptive to it or whether the person had faith in Jesus Christ as savior.

A fourteenth-century depiction of Saint Thomas Aquinas (top center), enthroned in heaven between holy figures from the Old and New Testaments

What do you think, is the appeal of magic or superstition? Would you consider yourself superstitious? Explain your answer in writing.

In fact the church never officially promoted such a magical approach to the sacraments. It has always taught that a sacrament will have an effect in a person according to the person's disposition to it. But that official teaching did not stop a magical attitude from flourishing among the people.

## On the Brink of a Religious Revolution

There is something to be said for the spirit of wonder and awe underlying an emphasis on objects and actions properly performed. "Magical" attitudes and practices certainly communicate the awesome power of God and of those persons and things viewed as God's intermediaries—priests, sacred objects (such as the relics of saints), and of course, the elements used in the sacraments. However, a superstitious attitude suggests that God's power can be bought, bargained for, or manipulated to suit one's own ends. Superstition fails to distinguish magic from religion; it represents an attempt to control rather than accept God's power. F

Although the superstitious, magical attitude toward the sacraments was never part of the church's official teachings, it was widespread during the Middle Ages. By the late fifteenth and early sixteenth centuries, abuses concerning the sacraments and other church practices were so out of hand that the situation was ripe for a religious revolution. In 1517 a monk named Martin Luther publicly protested these abuses, and a religious revolution indeed took place. The movement that Martin Luther sparked was soon known as the Protestant Reformation.

# toward more formality

## For Review

6. Contrast the circumstances experienced by Paulina in the early church with the circumstances experienced by Hugh in the church of the High Middle Ages.

7. List the seven sacraments that were affirmed as the official sacraments of the Catholic church in the thirteenth century.

8. What significant contribution to the Catholic church's understanding of the sacraments was made by Saint Thomas Aquinas?

9. Why was it important that the sacraments become somewhat standardized, with an emphasis on the correct form? What was an unfortunate result of overemphasizing correct form?

# Phase Four:
# Church and Sacraments
# After the Council of Trent

## Early Attempts at Reform Fail

As suggested by the prevalence of a magical view toward the sacraments and many other pious practices, the stability and optimism of the High Middle Ages had declined during the two centuries preceding the Protestant Reformation.

Martin Luther's call for church reform, a protest that by then was firmly entwined in the politics of Europe, was not the first. Between 1123 and 1517, church leaders officially gathered nine times to deal with clerical and political abuses in the church. By and large, however, these attempts at reforming the church were to no avail.

What came to be called the Protestant Reformation started out as an attempt to reform the Christian church from within. For reasons having as much to do with politics as with religion, the reform movement eventually organized itself into various Protestant denominations that denied the central authority of the pope, the bishop of Rome.

## The Council of Trent: The Catholic Church's Reformation

Although leaders in the Catholic church felt attacked by the reformers, they also recognized that many of the grievances were legitimate. To respond to these grievances, as well as to the doctrinal challenges of the reformers, the Council

of Trent was convened in 1545 and met off and on until 1563.

### Addressing the Major Complaints

One of the major complaints of the reformers was that the church took a casual attitude toward popular superstitions about religious matters. As a result

Martin Luther, as painted by a contemporary of Luther

essential beliefs such as grace and faith in God had become distorted.

To accomplish reform, first, the Council of Trent legislated practical changes aimed at eliminating abuses. Second, it reaffirmed the belief that although the importance of performing good works cannot be denied, grace is an unmerited gift from God that cannot be bargained for.

### Focusing on the Sacraments

The Council of Trent gave much of its attention to the sacraments: over half of its doctrinal teachings dealt with the sacraments. The council participants felt the need to be exact about the church's beliefs and practices pertaining to the sacraments. Otherwise the sacramental rituals and practices would have little consistent foundation, and people might interpret or recognize them differently. Many Protestant groups, for example, recognized only Baptism and the Eucharist as sacraments; other groups recognized no sacraments.

Two main points stressed by the Council of Trent about the sacraments are as follows.

**1. There are seven—and only seven—sacraments.** Council leaders declared that there were "not more nor less than" seven sacraments. (This reaffirmed what the Council of Lyons had taught three hundred years earlier in response to the tendency in that era to identify a multitude of rituals as "sacraments." But Trent's teaching was a response to the Protestant tendency to recognize few sacraments or none at all.) Catholic devotions other than the seven sacraments—like the rosary—were termed *sacramentals.* Sacramentals are religious practices or holy objects used in religious practices that can be spiritually enriching but that are less central to Catholic Christian faith than the seven official sacraments.

The Council of Trent emphasized that the authority to administer the sacraments in Christ's name is given through ordination to the priesthood. *Below:* A newly ordained priest receives from the bishop a paten (plate) and a chalice used at Mass for the consecrated bread and wine.

authority
passed on

# Common Sacramentals After the Council of Trent

In the centuries that followed the Council of Trent, an interesting side effect developed from that council's teachings, in part because of the standardizing of the practices of the seven sacraments. This side effect was the increased use of unofficial sacraments called sacramentals, devotional or pious practices and symbols that helped people get in touch with spiritual realities. Many of these sacramentals are still in use today.

**Prayer books.**  Prayer books containing devotions, prayers, and reflections on some aspect of the Catholic faith (such as the suffering and death of Christ) became a standard part of Catholic piety.

**Devotions to Mary, the Mother of God.**  Devotions and shrines to the Blessed Virgin, which had long been part of Christianity, gained new momentum in the post-Trent period. Ringing the church bells at noon and praying the Angelus became common practices. Praying the rosary, a practice that began in the Middle Ages, picked up considerable popularity after the Council of Trent. Organizations or religious movements devoted to Mary, such as the Legion of Mary, became commonplace.

**Litany prayers.**  Although its origins were in the Middle Ages, the litany became a more widely used form of communal prayer in the centuries after the Council of Trent. A litany consisted of a list of such things as titles of Christ—or of Mary—or names of the saints. These were read aloud by a prayer leader, and after each one, the congregation would respond with a phrase such as, "Pray for us."

**Devotion to the Sacred Heart of Jesus.**  A sacramental image from the sixteenth century that became quite popular during the eighteenth century was the Sacred Heart of Jesus. From that time on, it was not uncommon for Catholics to have pictures or statues of the risen Christ with his heart exposed from under his garment and enlarged with burning love.

**The way of the cross.**  Another sacramental that gained popularity during the post-Trent period was the way of the cross. Even today most Catholic church buildings have fourteen stations of the cross on their walls, depicting the suffering and Crucifixion of Jesus. Making the way of the cross is still a part of many Catholics' observance of Lent.

**Devotion to the Blessed Sacrament.**  An extremely popular and widespread devotional practice following the Council of Trent was the adoration of the Blessed Sacrament. The term *Blessed Sacrament* refers to the consecrated Communion bread that is stored in the tabernacle in the church sanctuary; Catholics believe that the consecrated bread is the body of Jesus Christ. Originally, a forty-hour period of continuous prayer and devotion to the Blessed Sacrament was part of the Holy Thursday observance during Lent. At the time of the Council of Trent, in the sixteenth century, this devotional practice began to be employed outside of Holy Week as well. Eventually, a shorter ritual called the Benediction of the Blessed Sacrament became a common religious practice in Catholic parishes. Today, for many Catholics, this practice is still a much-loved way to revere the Eucharist. Some Catholic institutions have the practice of Perpetual Adoration of the Blessed Sacrament; that is, members of the congregation or community take turns being present with the consecrated host in a twenty-four-hour continuous prayer.

**2. The church approves a scholastic understanding of the sacraments.** The theology of Thomas Aquinas and his successors, which was known as Scholasticism, was deemed the official Catholic interpretation of the sacraments. In particular the council emphasized the sacraments as causes of grace and declared that the sacraments were necessary for salvation. It also affirmed that the sacraments convey grace in and of themselves, not on account of the holiness of the minister or the recipient.

A Mass in the 1950s, before the Second Vatican Council initiated significant reforms in the liturgy

# The Council of Trent: Its Impact on the Church and the Sacraments

The two major emphases of the Council of Trent on how the sacraments would be understood and practiced, as well as the other teachings that came from the council, defined Catholicism for the next four hundred years. Further changes were not made until the Second Vatican Council met (1962–65). In particular the Council of Trent had these two effects:

1. Because the Council of Trent approved only a Scholastic understanding of the sacraments, no new ways of thinking about or different ways of talking about the sacraments were permitted.

2. Soon after the Council of Trent, the official Roman missal for the Mass and an official book on the rites of the other sacraments were published. Both of these publications, which had to be used by all Roman Catholic dioceses throughout the world, imposed greater uniformity in how the sacraments were practiced— including the language used (Latin), the words said, the actions used, and the performance of these actions. Neither book underwent substantial changes until the 1960s.

In short the trend toward standard practices and a unified understanding of the sacraments that began in the Middle Ages became solidified with the Council of Trent.

Much of this uniformity was done to protect the sacraments from the kinds of abuses that came about before the Council of Trent. As a result, however, Catholic Christians were given little room to adapt the symbols and rituals of the sacraments to fit their changing culture or time period. Thus a Mass in South America before the mid-1960s would have been nearly identical to one celebrated in Italy or the United States.

Nearly four hundred years passed before the Catholic church made any significant changes in its official sacramental teachings and practices. This was part of the challenge that Pope John XXIII asked church leaders to address at the Second Vatican Council. Ⓖ

Ⓖ In two columns, one labeled + and one –, list what you think would be the pluses and minuses of standardizing the Mass and other rituals of the Catholic church, so that a Mass in one area of the world would look and sound just like a Mass in another region.

sacraments after Trent

## For Review

10. Briefly explain why the Protestant Reformation came about.

11. What two main points about the sacraments did the Council of Trent stress?

12. Define sacramentals.

13. Describe the trend regarding the sacraments that became solidified with the Council of Trent.

# Phase Five:
# Church and Sacraments in the Twentieth Century

## The Church Rediscovers Its Roots

By the late nineteenth and early twentieth centuries, the Catholic church's defensive stance toward the emerging modern world began to subside. Among the many contributing factors to the church's more open attitudes were several developments happening within the church. Around this time Catholic scholars began to look closely at the teachings of Thomas Aquinas, the worship practices of the early church, and the biblical roots of the Christian faith.

When people began looking into the history of the church in the Middle Ages and earlier, they discovered that church practices and ways of expressing its theology had not always been the same as what they experience. Although this may seem obvious to us living in the 2000s, it was a liberating realization at the time. Eventually, these new developments within the church led Pope John XXIII to call the Second Vatican Council in the 1960s.

## The Second Vatican Council: A Call for Change and Renewal

By calling the Second Vatican Council, or Vatican Council II, Pope John XXIII declared that it was time to examine all aspects of church teachings and practices in an open and forthright manner, using the best information and insights of modern thought. He wanted to "open the windows and let in fresh air."

roots
rediscovered

### Reclaiming the Past

Chief among the concerns at Vatican Council II was helping the church get back in touch with those aspects of its Tradition, especially from the early church, that had been de-emphasized over the centuries. Regaining such elements, the bishops felt, would help the church better respond to the contemporary world.

Given the social and cultural changes that had occurred in the world and within the church itself since the Council of Trent, the church recognized the need to open itself up to other ways of thinking about and practicing the sacraments than those imposed by the sixteenth-century council. Delving into the past and seeing the differences that existed there helped everyone in the church realize that the church's theology and sacramental practices had been changing all the time.

### Keeping the Clear, Letting Go of the Cloudy

In the Second Vatican Council, the church committed itself to renewal based on a fresh look at its origins and its long history. It saw that over the years, many of the changes had helped bring out the true meaning of the sacraments. These changes, the council leaders decided, were worth keeping or reinstating. Other changes had not necessarily been for the better. For instance, over the centuries many unwanted practices and notions had crept into the sacramental life of the church and were clouding the true spirit of the sacraments. These other changes, the council leaders decided, should be set aside.

Pope John XXIII, greeting people from the open window of a train

# A Continuing Challenge

⊞ Interview a Catholic person old enough (fifty or older) to remember the early changes in the sacraments that occurred following the Second Vatican Council. Find out how he or she reacted to the changes at the time. Write up the results of your interview.

With Vatican Council II, the Catholic church entered a new phase in its history and understanding of the sacraments. Once church leaders had studied the historical development of the sacraments, they saw that change and renewal were necessary and even natural. At the same time, they also realized that a great challenge faced the church. This was the challenge of keeping the church's teachings on the sacraments true to the Spirit of Jesus and allowing the church's sacramental practice more effectively to be an instrument of God's grace in the world.

Since the Second Vatican Council, the seven sacraments have undergone changes for the specific purpose of pointing more clearly to the one sacrament who is the center of Christian belief: Jesus. This focus continues today, almost forty years later. The Second Vatican Council also serves as a reminder to the church that the challenge of growth is to remain true to one's spirit while facing the changes that inevitably come along. ⊞

a renewing church

## For Review

14. How did leaders at the Second Vatican Council decide which changes in the rituals of the church should be kept and which should be set aside?

15. What challenge regarding the sacraments did the church face after the Second Vatican Council?

# Mariama—The Church of the Future

During the decades leading up to the year 2000, the number of Catholic churches grew rapidly in the southern half of our world. These relatively young churches with youthful members typically exhibit an enthusiasm for and a delight in the Christian message. Their members—Asian, African, or Latin American—bring unique cultural expressions to their celebrations of the sacraments.

In large part the vitality of these young churches is possible because of the openness reintroduced to the church by Vatican Council II. Here is the story of one modern Christian who is helping to shape the church of the future.

Mariama has been active in her local Christian community ever since her Baptism four years ago. Like many people in her village, Mariama has found in Christianity a cause for hope in an often bleak existence. In particular she finds the Masses held in her simple village church to be moving experiences. She appreciates how the Masses blend the beauty of the Catholic liturgy with elements from her own African and tribal customs. The festive atmosphere that surrounds the Christmas season is a special source of joy and excitement for her and her community. The story of the Christ Child coming into the world to bring peace and good news to poor people is a story she enjoys hearing over and over.

Mariama has five children. She performs regular household chores, along with tending a small stand at the village market. Yet she still finds time to attend meetings and prayer sessions at the local church hall. For Mariama, spending time with other Christian women provides the spiritual support and physical contact that keep her spirits up.

When Mariama was a small child, she saw Christianity as the religion of the white European and American missionaries. Now members of the local Catholic Christian communities and most of their leaders are native Africans. Mariama has seen a growing number of young African women becoming religious sisters working in schools, hospitals, and community centers. Although books and other educational materials are scarce, a real hunger for learning more about the Christian religion exists, especially among the young people in her village. For Mariama and her friends, a discussion about Bible stories often becomes the starting point for similar discussions about family or community events.

Mariama lives a simple life in which basic necessities are barely met—or sometimes not met. Being Christian has helped her question the injustice of her poverty, given her confidence and a community with which to work for change, and provided her with hope for a brighter future.

# The Seven Sacraments

In one of his novels, writer Kurt Vonnegut introduces an alien being who can see forward and backward in time—just as we might look out over a range of mountains, seeing behind us and in front of us. If we could see our own life this way, all at once, it might look very much like a mountain range with peaks and valleys. And at the bottom of each valley, might be a stream or a river or a lake. To get to the next mountain, we have to make a crossing. Some of these crossings would be just simple jumps across narrow streams. Others would be frightening voyages across wide lakes or wild rivers.

The seven sacraments point to the fact that we have many such crossings in our life. For example, we face many new beginnings or rebirths, as symbolized by Baptism. We confront other crucial crossings related to belonging, caring, forgiving, serving, healing, and worshiping. The next seven chapters will deal specifically with each of these crossings. By celebrating all these important crossings, the seven sacraments reflect the whole range of human crossings—from birth to death.

At the same time that the sacraments echo life's crossings, the sacraments' strong connection to the paschal mystery suggests that people can get through life's crossings. At those moments when they feel daunted or trapped by hazardous crossings, Catholics can look to the sacraments to remind them of a mysterious, miraculous truth: Jesus' crossing was a journey through death to new life. And they can count on the sacraments to nourish their spirit through those crossings.

Let's turn our attention now to the seven sacraments celebrated by Catholic Christians.

*Student art:* Photo by Suzanne Marie Hogan, Notre Dame de Sion, Kansas City, Missouri

# 7

# Baptism

## celebrating
## welcome & rebirth

*in the waters of salvation*

… a new way of Life

Giver of Life, be born in me.
I welcome you as you welcome new members
into your church at Baptism.
May my life say welcome to all those
who cross my path.
May my life become new
as I open myself to your Spirit.

**Amen.**

The basis of the whole Christian life is the sacrament of **Baptism.** By Baptism a person's relationship with God is forever changed: Freed from sin and reborn as a son or a daughter of God, the baptized person is given grace and thus shares in the very life of God. Baptism incorporates a person into the Body of Christ, the church. It offers the fullness of the means to salvation—salvation *from* sin and death, and salvation *for* a share in the divine life of the Trinity, the Father, the Son, and the Holy Spirit.

Baptism is the first of the three **sacraments of initiation,** which celebrate a Christian's transformation, entrance, and lifelong growth in the community of Jesus' followers, the church. In the early centuries of Christianity, the other two sacraments of initiation—Confirmation and the Eucharist—were united with Baptism and celebrated in one ritual as part of the process of becoming a Christian. Today adults who join the Catholic church go through a process similar to what the early converts experienced, celebrating all three sacraments together. But for small children and infants entering the church, Baptism is celebrated as a separate sacrament, with Confirmation and the Eucharist following at a later age. The significance of Baptism is best explained by the adult experience of this sacrament, the "original" version. So let's begin our study of Baptism by considering a different but related kind of adult initiation.

# initiation into community

## David can't believe it:

He really is in a new world, at a college halfway across the country from his home. He has dreamed of this day since ninth grade. Now he is at his first day of college orientation in a city he has never been to, in a college he has only read about, in a building he has seen only in pictures. David is trying to appear cool and calm, to pretend it doesn't bother him not to know anyone on campus. He wants to act like he knows exactly what he is doing and where he is going, but he knows his act won't be much of a success. He can't even find his assigned dorm.

Lining up in a gym with four hundred other new students, David waits to pick up his packet of information on the orientation and the college. When he is handed his packet, a guy comes forward, a good-natured grin on his face. "You're David," he says, shaking David's hand. "I'm Tony. I'll be showing you around this week. You got any questions, just ask me. This is my third year here. I know how it feels to be in your shoes—just starting out. It's pretty overwhelming at first, but I think you'll get to like it here. I do. Say, where are you from, anyway?"

David and Tony swap stories about backgrounds and interests as they walk across campus to David's dorm, stopping first to see the student center and the cafeteria.

"The food's not terrific," Tony says. "For lunch I usually go to the snack bar and get a sandwich. That way I know it's fresh. Desserts are good—especially their homemade ice cream." Somehow David no longer feels the need to act cool and experienced. Here is someone who expects him to be curious about everything and will just be a friend while he gets used to things.

Before the first day of the weeklong orientation is over, David is more at ease. Not only does he have Tony to show him the ropes, but he has been teamed up with five other first-year people to talk about what the transition from high school to college means to them. Already David is making friends.

By the end of the week, David feels much more at home, and his enthusiasm has soared. Now he knows lots of people, both newcomers like himself and upper-level students like Tony. He has heard talks from student leaders, teachers, and administrators, and he has registered for classes. The risk he has taken by plunging himself into this new world is beginning to pay off. Already he can sense the great transformation that college life holds in store for him.

Many factors are contributing to David's transformation: the independence of living away from home, the new and exciting relationships, the sense of purpose he feels about his classes and his future, the feeling of belonging to a great college and sharing in the college's own special spirit. . . . David is amazed: He feels like a brand-new person!

Despite all his internal and external changes, David realizes vaguely that his transformation has just begun. But he is ready for more growth. He can't wait to get on with it.

The changes David went through during his college orientation week are just drops compared to the ocean of changes he will go through in the next four years. David cannot possibly anticipate all the highs and lows, the achievements and disappointments, the undreamed-of adventures that are to come. But he has already opened himself to these

experiences.

*Student art:* Photo by Philip Noche, Dominican High School, Whitefish Bay, Wisconsin

## Welcome or Alienation?

In the near future, you may face challenges similar to the challenges faced by David in the previous story. Someday, certainly, you will find yourself at a crossroads, perhaps feeling isolated and in need of friends, support, and reassurance. You may already be familiar with that experience.

Which comes closer to your experience of the world—a world of alienation and cold stares, or a world of friendliness and welcome? You have probably encountered the world as a lonely, impersonal place at times; you have likely found it warm and welcoming at other times. Both portraits of the world are real.

Most of us were born into a welcoming family filled with smiles, support, and sharing. Every human baby needs at least some touching and affection just to survive, so our needs were met in a survival sense. At the same time, however, we were born into a world in which alienation and imperfections exist and are inevitable. A baby's complex physical and psychological needs cannot always be met (or understood!), even by the best-intentioned parents, so every child is bound to feel lonely or abandoned at times. We all eventually discover that the world can be an unfriendly or even hurtful place beyond the security of home or loved ones. And from an early age, most of us have cautionary messages drummed into us: "Stay away from that part of town." "Don't talk to strangers!"

Thus from birth on, we all have experiences that parallel David's experience of walking through a threshold into a new life, experiences where we face either alienation or welcome. Ⓐ

Ⓐ Write about a situation in which you felt uncomfortable and unwelcome. Then write about a situation in which you felt at ease and welcome. Focus on what made the difference for you.

*uncomfortable or at ease*

# What Does Baptism Celebrate?

David's initiation into the world of college has these characteristics:

- He is welcomed into the college community.
- He begins the long-term process of learning and growing in a new, transforming way of life—college life.
- He leaves behind an old identity (high school graduate) for a new one (college student).
- He takes on a new sense of purpose connected with being in college.
- He feels the spirit that energizes the college.

The initiation into the Christian faith highlighted by the sacrament of Baptism has certain parallels with David's journey from alienation to belonging through his college orientation. Christian initiation, and Baptism in particular, celebrates these realities for the Christian:

- being welcomed into the community of Jesus, the church
- beginning a lifelong conversion, turning away from sin to embrace the Christian way of life
- being reborn to a new identity as a son or a daughter of God
- sharing in the mission of Jesus and adopting it as one's own life purpose
- receiving the gift of the Spirit of Jesus that enables the Christian to share in God's life of love

## A Welcome into Jesus' Community

Most of us have experienced feeling both welcome and unwelcome in a group. When you have to linger around the

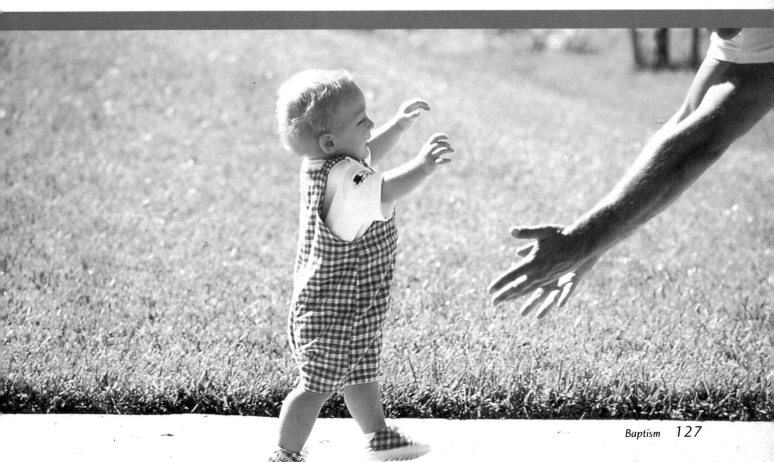

edges of a group, hoping to be noticed and subtly trying to be accepted, you probably do not feel welcome, even if the group members do not reject you outright. People do not have to be cruel to be unwelcoming toward others; they just have to fail to take initiative with others. David, on his first day at college, faced the unknown with fear and insecurity. He began to feel more comfortable when Tony noticed him and made an effort to help him feel like he belonged.

### God Takes the Initiative

Baptism celebrates the good news that God takes the initiative with us human beings. We do not have to do anything to be "noticed" by God. We cannot earn God's favor; it is a gift that God offers to all, inviting us to share in God's own life of love. Whether the one baptized is a newborn baby or an adult who has freely chosen to be baptized, God is the one taking the initiative.

In Baptism the Christian community that gathers for the ritual is the human sign of God's love welcoming the person being baptized into a life of loving relationships.

### A Warm and Welcoming Church

Ideally, local Christian churches would be such warm, welcoming communities that outsiders would sense something remarkably alive about them. People would feel accepted, embraced by the inclusive love of God's open heart. Most people are hungry for that kind of experience, and when they see a spirited community, they feel drawn to it. In fact the parish and school communities where teenagers and adults are coming into the church in great numbers are characteristically vital, caring communities; they are a sign of God's outstretched arms. B

**B** If you were to create an entrance-way banner welcoming people to a local parish church, what would your banner look like? Draw a sketch of your banner and include your written message of welcome.

# A Lifelong Conversion: From Sin to Life

In Christian belief human beings are created good, made in the image of God. They are meant to enjoy a loving life with God and one another forever. But human beings also have the freedom to choose—to love God or to turn their back on God, to care for others or to be concerned only for themselves, to cherish the Earth as a gift or to exploit it destructively. They can choose to sin.

### Original Sin

As the Book of Genesis tells it, the first human beings chose to sin and thereby drove a wedge between themselves and God. According to Catholic teaching, every human being since the beginning of human history (except Mary, the mother of Jesus) has been born into this condition of being alienated from God and tending to choose sin rather than God. This sin at the outset of humankind, and the condition we inherit of tending to choose sin, is called **original sin.** It is a built-in weakness, a penchant for making shortsighted and self-serving choices over wise and generous choices.

Although subject to the effects of the sin of their first parents, human beings are not responsible for or guilty of that first sin. But they are responsible for their own wrongful choices, which are called **personal sins.** We can see the effects of original sin in humankind's history of wars, persecutions, discrimination, and exploitation. These tragedies all come from personal sins for which human beings are responsible.

So original sin—which was human beings' doing, not God's—disrupted the harmonious relationship that was intended to exist between God and humankind.

### Jesus Christ: Salvation from Sin

The Son of God, Jesus Christ, was sent to Earth to restore that relationship, to free human beings from the weight of sin that stood like a boulder between themselves and God. By his life, death, and Resurrection, Jesus overcame sin and gave every human being the chance to live intimately with God.

Thus Catholic teaching is that Baptism—being identified with Christ forever through the waters of new life—takes away original sin, forgives all personal sins and the punishment due to them, and gives grace. Baptism does not take away the effects of original sin, the inclination to choose personal sin, but it offers the abundance of God's grace to overcome that tendency.

Baptism, then, represents a turning away from the old life of sin to embrace the new life in Jesus Christ.

*Student art:* Linocut by Laurel Tomasello, Saint Agnes Academy, Memphis, Tennessee

in the shadows of sin

## The Old Life of Sin

sin
death
fear
slavery
alienation
isolation
hoarding

## The New Life in Christ

grace
life
courage
freedom
welcome
community
sharing

C Reflect on this list of truths that Christians try to live out in the world. Choose the statement that most appeals to you and explain in writing its appeal for you.

### No to Sin, Yes to Grace

In the Rite of Baptism, an adult says no to sin and all his or her sins are forgiven. The adult says yes to God's life of grace, which is more powerful than any sin or any destruction wreaked by sin over centuries. For children too young to comprehend the choice, their parents and sponsors say yes to God's life by renewing their own baptismal promises, with the understanding that they will try to guide the children toward grace and away from sin. This yes implies that the person believes and will try to live out these truths in the world:

- Grace can overcome sin.
- Life can triumph over death.
- Courage can banish fear.
- Freedom to live joyfully in God can overcome slavery to destructive patterns.
- A spirit of welcome can banish alienation.
- Community can replace isolation.
- Sharing can dissolve hoarding. C

The conversion of Baptism marks a profound change in the way people perceive themselves, other people, and the world. But Baptism is not magic. Saying yes to God's life of love will not melt away the legacy of sin's tragic effects. The baptized person will no doubt commit sins during the rest of life. But with God's grace, the person will struggle to overcome her or his worst tendencies and find in God's mercy the strength to go on trying. The conversion to a new way of life, which is symbolized and celebrated in Baptism, will go on for a lifetime.

# Born Again to a New Identity

To appreciate Baptism as an opportunity for rebirth, we need to know something about the life that is left behind and even more about the life that is embraced in this sacrament.

An incident from John's Gospel describes some puzzling remarks that Jesus made about the "rebirth" of Baptism:

> Now there was a Pharisee named Nicodemus, a leader of the Jews. He came to Jesus by night and said to him, "Rabbi, we know that you are a teacher who has come from God; for no one can do these signs that you do apart from the presence of God." Jesus answered him, "Very truly, I tell you, no one can see the kingdom of God without being born from above." Nicodemus said to him, "How can anyone be born after having grown old? Can one enter a second time into the mother's womb and be born?" Jesus answered, "Very truly, I tell you, no one can enter the kingdom of God without being born of water and Spirit. What is born of the flesh is flesh, and what is born of the Spirit is spirit." (3:1–6)

Nicodemus at first did not understand what Jesus meant when he said we must be "born anew," or "born again." Nicodemus heard the phrase literally, not symbolically. So what did Jesus actually mean?

### Born into Risen Life

In speaking of being born anew, Jesus was referring to the inner transformation that comes from people's experience of God's Spirit in their life. Instead of experiencing a new physical birth, people would experience a birth into the Spirit, a rebirth into God's life after passing through a kind of death. Imagine what rebirth into God's life might mean:

- We notice our parents arguing with each other more and more. Their divorce seems almost certain. Can we survive a family breakup? Rebirth into God's life reminds us that Christ journeys with us through all the suffering and dying in our life.
- We struggle with decisions about our priorities in life, about how to balance looking out for ourselves with giving ourselves to others. Remembering that we are born anew into God's life colors the way we look at our life decisions. We try to see things as Jesus would.
- We think back on our childhood experiences and recognize that we carry within us many old wounds from disappointments or mistreatment. The rebirth of Baptism affirms that Christ the healer shares our life. In the end we are never alone.

Baptism, then, plunges a person into the paschal mystery. Through Baptism, Christians are united with Jesus in his life, death, and Resurrection. **D**

### Dying and Rising: An Ongoing Process

Recall again the story of David's entering college. After his first week there, David has a sense of a new identity, but his identity will develop and grow throughout his years in college. Just as David's experience of growth is gradual, the process of rebirth into Christian identity does not happen all at once. Baptism celebrates the mystery of our being continuously reborn, every day of our life. We do not "die and rise with Christ" once but over a lifetime of many "deaths and resurrections," of losses followed by new growth, of failures followed by deeper understandings and victories of the spirit. Our rebirth is ongoing; we are never finished being born again until we

reach our eternal destiny of union with God.

Perhaps you have heard the phrase "born-again Christian" and wondered what it really means. Some people may ask you pointedly, "Have you been born again?" and they may even want to know exactly when in your life you were born again. When these Christians use the phrase "born again," they are referring to a one-time-only, supposedly life-changing event in which a person accepts Jesus as lord and savior. It is obvious that this notion differs significantly from the Catholic understanding of rebirth. Baptism itself celebrates a process of dying and rising to new life within a community, a process that happens over and over again in a person's lifetime.

## Sharing in the Mission of Jesus

In the opening story, college-newcomer David finds a new sense of purpose in his life during his orientation. He may also at times wonder about his purpose beyond college.

### A Life Purpose

Many of us ask ourselves big questions like these:

- What am I going to do with my life?
- What am I here for?
- What's my life all about, anyway?

When we ask ourselves these questions, we are considering our basic purpose in life. **E**

### Jesus' Priority: The Reign of God

With initiation into God's life, the Christian shares in the larger life purpose that Jesus calls his followers to. For instance, Christian initiation challenges Christians to look at war with a different attitude, to show concern for people who are different or distant from themselves,

*a troubling situation*

**D** Imagine how rebirth into God's life might affect a troubling situation in your own life. Describe in a paragraph one possible outcome of that situation.

**E** Choose one of these questions, reflect on it, and write down your reflections.

what's my life about?

and to think critically about the values that are popular in a culture.

In Jesus' set of priorities, life is not simply about taking care of our own needs and wants and those of our family. Jesus' life purpose, and therefore his followers' life purpose, is to usher in the reign of God's justice and peace in the world. The Christian's personal life goals are still important—like getting an education, finding meaningful work, and raising a family. But these goals become just part of the larger life purpose—carrying on Jesus' mission, a task Jesus entrusted to his church. In identifying

with Jesus' life purpose, Christians will no doubt encounter suffering, but they will also experience a deeper, more lasting happiness than the kind that can be attained through success or money.

Conversion and rebirth, as described earlier, do not happen suddenly and completely. Likewise, a person's commitment to Jesus' life purpose does not happen instantaneously with Baptism, even for adult converts. That commitment takes a lifetime of growing into it. Baptism—and indeed, the whole process of initiation—celebrates that the commitment has begun.

*Student art:* Linocut by Amy Foote, Saint Agnes Academy, Memphis, Tennessee

F In writing describe what you like best about your school's or team's spirit. Illustrate your description by recounting at least three concrete incidents in which that spirit was displayed.

# Receiving the Gift of the Spirit of Jesus

Recall that one outcome of David's college orientation was that he shared in a certain spirit of the college. That spirit was apparent in the enthusiasm and the interest of individuals he met that week, but it was bigger than just personal attitudes. It seemed to characterize the college as a whole. Your high school probably has its own school spirit. Sports teams, too, are said to have team spirit.

Becoming part of those groups entails catching the spirit, energy, and vitality that seem to breathe life into the groups.

For the Christian, initiation also involves catching the spirit of the Christian community. But the spirit that enlivens, moves, and guides the community at the deepest level is Jesus' own Spirit, poured out on the disciples at Pentecost, after Jesus' Resurrection, and continuously poured out in history even to the present moment. To become a Christian is to become a "Spirit-ed" person, living in Christ's risen life, because the person shares in the Spirit-life of the Christian community and is thus enlivened, moved, and guided by that Spirit. F

# The Permanent Nature of Baptism

At the beginning of this chapter, it was said that Baptism changes our relationship with God forever. It makes us a son or a daughter of God, and that change is permanent. We cannot get "unbaptized"! Even if we fall away from God for years, we are still God's own beloved. Catholic teaching speaks of the special permanent **character,** or seal, of Baptism. Like the sacraments of Confirmation and Holy Orders, Baptism can be received only once because its effect is permanent.

The Catholic church recognizes the Baptisms that take place in other Christian churches as valid sacraments, if they baptize with water and use the trinitarian formula (see page 137). So if someone baptized in one Christian denomination decided to join the Catholic church, he or she would not be baptized again. Instead, the person would be brought into full membership in the Catholic

Team spirit is catching!
※ *Student art:* Photo by Andrea Jablonski, Saint Vincent de Paul High School, Petaluma, California

church through Confirmation and a formal act of reception.

## Necessary for Salvation

The Catholic church teaches that Baptism is necessary for salvation. What is meant by this?

As we have seen in the story of Nicodemus from the Gospel of John, Jesus himself taught, "No one can enter the kingdom of God without being born of water and Spirit" (3:5). And he commanded his disciples to go out to all nations and baptize everyone (Matthew 28:19). The church teaches that Baptism, through which one becomes a member of Christ's Body, is the fullest means of salvation. For those who have received the Gospel and have the opportunity to be baptized, Baptism is the necessary way to their salvation.

What about all the non-Christians, who make up most of the Earth's population? Does this mean they are not saved? The church teaches that because Christ died for all humankind, all are offered salvation through the paschal mystery, in ways that are known to God. They may not explicitly know or believe in Christ. But those who seek the truth and try to do God's will in accordance with the truth as they understand it can be saved. The assumption is that if they knew of the necessity of Baptism for their salvation, they would desire it, and the desire for Baptism is itself a kind of Baptism.

What about children who die without being baptized? The church entrusts them to God's mercy, in the hope that the God who desires that every human being be saved will not leave innocent children without a means to salvation.

## For Review

1. Describe what happens to a person through Baptism.

2. Name the three sacraments of initiation. In general what do these sacraments celebrate?

3. What five realities for the Christian are celebrated in Baptism?

4. What is meant by original sin? How does Baptism affect original sin?

5. How does the Catholic church's understanding of the phrase "born again" differ from some other Christians' interpretation of that phrase?

6. What does it mean to say that Baptism is necessary for salvation? How can non-Christians be saved?

# The Ritual of Baptism: Symbolic Actions and Words

All the rituals of the sacraments consist of symbols and symbolic actions, along with certain significant words. Together, these express the meaning of the sacrament.

In Baptism, as in all the sacraments, the Christian community—the church—is the primary symbol. In welcoming new members, the Christian community represents God, who takes the initiative in inviting us into divine life. In addition,

four symbols in the Rite of Baptism express different realities of the sacrament. These special symbols are water, oil, a white (or new) garment, and a lighted candle.

Each of these symbols is rich in meaning, and any discussion of their symbolic power is bound to be incomplete. So before reading on, take a few moments to make a list of the meanings that you associate with each of these symbols.

*Student art:* Photo by Samantha Conte, Saint Gertrude High School, Richmond, Virginia

welcoming
new members

# Water: Cleansing and Life-Giving

At the core of the sacrament of Baptism are the action and words of the water rite. This essential rite consists of the minister's pouring water over the person's head or immersing the person in water, while pronouncing the trinitarian formula, **"I baptize you in the name of the Father, and of the Son, and of the Holy Spirit."** Thus the person baptized is freed from all sin and welcomed into the intimate life of the Trinity. Without this action and these words, there is no valid sacrament.

Why is water so central a symbol in Baptism?

### A Natural Symbol

For refreshment or recreation, we often use water. We can drink it, swim in it, ski on it, walk near it, listen to it. Water can restore our energy by cooling us on a hot day and by cleansing us when we are dirty or sweaty. We also get some of our food from fresh and salt waters. And without rainwater, most of what we eat could not grow.

Water is vital for human life: We cannot live without it for more than five days. And although we ourselves did not actually come from water, we do have evolutionary relatives who lived in the sea. It seems, too, that we may not have left the sea far behind; the human body is over 70 percent water.

Of course, water can be destructive as well as creative. Persons who live in places liable to floods know this only too well, as do swimmers and sailors. Being plunged into water can be a deadly experience.

### Scriptural Meanings

Water has special meaning for the Christian community. In the Old Testament, in the very beginning of the Book of Genesis, God breathes on the waters to bring order to Creation. Later, in the story of Noah, the world of sin is destroyed and washed clean through the waters of a flood.

In the Book of Exodus, Moses leads the Israelites out of slavery in Egypt by guiding them miraculously, with God's power, through the great Red Sea and toward freedom and new life in the Promised Land. That sea-crossing was the first step in a long journey for the Israelites. On the way God provided them with life-giving water just when they were feeling hopeless, afraid they would die of thirst wandering in the desert.

In the New Testament, too, water has great significance. Jesus himself is baptized in the water of the Jordan River. Later Jesus would refer to the life he offers people as the "living water." It is no wonder that water is the essential symbol of Christian Baptism.

### Taking the Plunge

In the early years of the Christian church, Baptisms were performed in rivers and streams. The converts would be plunged into the water to symbolize their being cleansed of sin and their dying to an old way of life. Their coming up again would show that they were rising to a new life, a new identity, in Christ. Even when Baptisms moved indoors, new Christians were immersed in a pool of water as a sign of their embracing the mystery of Christ's death and Resurrection. Their plunge into the water also reminded them and the gathered Christian community of how God had rescued the Israelites from slavery, taking the Israelites through the waters of the Red Sea and bringing them out safely to freedom on the other side.

A man is baptized in the Jordan River, the site of Jesus' own baptism.

### A Powerful Communicator

For many centuries Catholics have not seen any dramatic use of water in their baptismal rites. Typically water is poured over the candidate's forehead. In the last few decades, however, many Catholic churches have begun to use the symbol of water in a more powerful fashion in the Rite of Baptism, as it was originally intended. In these churches Baptisms are done either by immersing the whole person in water or by submerging just the person's head. Some Protestant denominations today baptize only by immersion. Consider how much more the symbol of water can communicate about Baptism when it is used this fully. Ⓖ

*teach water*

Ⓖ If you were invited to teach a class of first graders about the symbolism of water, how would you do it? Outline a brief lesson you would give.

# Oil:
# Healing, Strengthening, and Being Chosen

Oil has been used on persons for thousands of years in a variety of ways, many of which find echoes of meaning in the Catholic sacraments.

At the time of the Roman Empire, gladiators and soldiers prepared for battle by covering their bodies with oil for protection against abrasions and infections. Oil was known for its healing qualities. Greek athletes, too, were rubbed with oil as a means of strengthening them. On beaches during the summer months, present-day people guard against the sun's rays using oils from squeeze bottles. Swimmers and other athletes also use protective and healing ointments.

Mixed with perfume, oil was used in ancient times for anointing a person as royalty; anointing was a sign of making the leader sacred for a sacred responsibility. The title Christ actually means "the Anointed One," the Messiah long awaited by the Jews.

In the baptismal rite, anointing with oil on the breast or on both hands occurs before the water ritual of Baptism. This anointing is associated with asking God for strength for the person. The anointing of the new Christian on the crown of the head with chrism (special consecrated oil), which takes place after the water ritual, signifies being chosen and anointed as Christ was chosen, to share in his risen life and to receive the Spirit through him.

## A White Garment: Becoming a New Creation

Treating ourselves to new clothes can help us feel renewed inside. Dressing up on Easter Sunday or for a school prom goes naturally with the freshness of the season and with the excitement of the occasion.

To symbolize the radical newness of a life in Christ, of being "clothed in Christ," the baptized individual receives a white (or new) garment or a white cloth to wear after the water ritual. In appearance as well as in spirit, the person is a "new creation." In the early church, newly baptized people wore this garment the whole week after their Baptism as a constant reminder, to themselves and the community, of their new life and Christian dignity.

(In some cultures today, colors other than white are used because in those cultures white signifies death, not life.)

Some Catholic churches have a pool specifically for Baptism by immersion.

# Baptism in Words and Symbols

**Litany of the Saints**
Holy Mary, Mother of God,
  pray for us. . . .
Saint Peter and Saint Paul,
  pray for us. . . .
All holy men and women,
  pray for us.

**Blessing of the Water**
Through the waters of the Red Sea
you led Israel out of slavery
to be an image of God's holy people,
set free from sin by baptism.

**Renunciation of Sin**
Do you reject sin so as to live in the
freedom of God's children?
  I do.

Do you reject the glamour of evil, and
refuse to be mastered by sin?
  I do.

**Anointing with the Oil of Catechumens**
We anoint you with the oil of salvation
in the name of Christ our Savior;
may he strengthen you with his power,
who lives and reigns for ever and ever.

**Profession of Faith**
Do you believe in God, the Father
almighty, creator of heaven and earth?
  I do.

**Rite of Baptism**
[Name], I baptize you in the name of
    the Father,
and of the Son,
and of the Holy Spirit.

**Anointing After Baptism**
[If there is no sacrament of Confirmation after the Rite of Baptism, an anointing is done.]
[God] now anoints you with the chrism of salvation,
so that, united with his people,
you may remain for ever a member of Christ
who is Priest, Prophet, and King.

**Clothing with the White Garment**
[Name], you have become a new creation,
and have clothed yourself in Christ.

**Presentation of the Lighted Candle**
Walk always as a child of the light
and keep the flame of faith alive in your heart.

# A Lighted Candle: Sharing in the Light of Christ

Imagine yourself in a vast, totally dark room that you have never been in before. You have no idea what awaits you in the room, what you might stumble on, or how you might find your way around the room. You are anxious, even fearful.

Then imagine being handed a candle that is suddenly lit. The light from even this small flame fills the corners of the room. You are relieved and glad to carry the light, and you do not want it to be snuffed out.

The burning of a single candle, especially in darkness, fascinates and captivates us. Light dispels darkness. It guides the lost. It wards off danger and exposes evil. Light is warm, inviting, comforting.

A baptismal candle is lit from the Easter candle, which symbolizes Christ, the light of the world.

Where there is light, there is life. Jesus called himself "the light of the world."

At Baptism the newly baptized person is given a lighted candle to hold. (In the case of an infant or small child, someone from the child's family, such as the father or godfather, lights and holds the candle.) The flame of this candle is received from the large Easter candle, which signifies Christ, the light of the world. In this way the newly baptized person shares in the light of Christ, the hope and warmth of the world, and is encouraged to always walk as a child of the light. ⊞

Who may be baptized? Anyone who has not been baptized before. And who may perform a Baptism? Usually an ordained person—a priest, bishop, or deacon—is the minister of the sacrament. But you may be surprised to hear that in case of necessity (such as when an unbaptized person is in war or in danger of death), any person, even someone who has not been baptized, can baptize another if she or he has the right intention: to do what the church does in baptizing.

*experience with symbols*

⊞ Focus on one of the primary symbols of Baptism—water, oil, a white (or new) garment, or a lighted candle—and complete one of the following two exercises:

1. Write a poem or an essay about an experience you had involving that symbol.
2. Make a collage or draw a picture illustrating the practical importance of that symbol.

## essentials of Baptism

## For Review

7. What are the essential actions and words in the sacrament of Baptism?

8. List three symbolic mentions of water in the Old Testament.

9. What do the two anointings with oil during Baptism signify?

10. What is the significance of the white garment worn in Baptism?

11. Why is a lighted candle given to the newly baptized person?

12. Who may be baptized? Who is the usual minister of the sacrament?

# Baptism's History

## The First Baptisms

At the start of his ministry, Jesus came forward to be baptized in the Jordan River by John the Baptist. Christians have seen in Jesus' own baptism a model of repentance and self-emptying. After his Resurrection Jesus commanded his Apostles to go forth to all nations and baptize all people:

All authority in heaven and on earth has been given to me. Go therefore and make disciples of all nations, baptizing them in the name of the Father and of the Son and of the Holy Spirit, and teaching them to obey everything that I have commanded you. (Matthew 28:18–20)

On the day of Pentecost, the Apostles, who had been huddling in fear since

*Student art:* Photo by Greta Hauge, Oak Knoll School, Summit, New Jersey

living
waters

Jesus' Ascension, were filled with the Holy Spirit. They had been "baptized" by the whole experience of Jesus' life, death, and Resurrection, and now they were filled with the new life of God, ready to share this Pentecost outpouring of the Spirit with others.

So Peter and the other Apostles boldly went out to convert and baptize all who would hear the Good News and believe in Jesus. Following the example of Jesus' own baptism, they baptized with water, which symbolized receiving the Spirit of Jesus as they had received it at Pentecost.

This simple act of Baptism with water later developed into a complex ceremony of initiation, full of the rich symbolism discussed earlier. Let's see how the process evolved.

# In the Early Church

As the fledgling community of Jesus' followers grew and broadened to welcome Gentile (non-Jewish) converts, the church discovered that it needed a more thorough way to prepare persons to become Christians.

### The Catechumenate

From the second century (the 100s) into the fourth and fifth centuries, a process of baptismal preparation called the **catechumenate** developed and flourished, along with the beautiful, powerful rituals of initiation.

As illustrated in the story of Paulina's conversion in chapter 6, becoming a Christian was quite a risky step to take in the earliest centuries of the faith. With Christianity officially illegal, the religion existed "underground"—in secret. Bloody persecutions by the Romans were a constant reminder that becoming a Christian could bring martyrdom. One did not decide lightly to become a Christian.

A person desiring to become a Christian needed to find a Christian who would be a sponsor, who would vouch for her or his character and help the person during the two- to three-year preparation for Baptism. About forty days before the person was to be baptized, the final preparation took place during the period that later evolved into Lent. This preparation consisted of intensive instruction, prayer, fasting, and liturgies involving the group of candidates, or catechumens, with the whole community, led by the bishop. The final step was the Easter Vigil—the only time Baptisms were performed.

### At the Easter Vigil

The Easter Vigil ceremony was preceded by a ritual bathing on Holy Thursday and by two days of fasting. On the Saturday night of the vigil, all the candidates were brought together, men in one room and women in another. Their sponsors—the persons who had guided them toward their new birth—were there. The sponsors were called fathers and mothers by the candidates because sponsors performed a parental role. (Later sponsors would become known as godparents.)

At the start of the ceremony, the candidates faced the West, the place of sunset and darkness. They stretched out their arms and denounced Satan. Suddenly they turned to the East and shouted their attachment to Christ. This physical turnabout by the candidates marked their spiritual turnabout, or conversion. The East was considered the place of light, of the rising sun, and of new life.

Next the candidates went to a room with a pool, often modeled after the Roman public baths. They stripped off their old clothing. Oil was poured over the candidates, who then stepped down into the waist-deep waters. One by one, the bishop submerged the candidates

turn to the east

into the water, usually three times—in the name of the Father, the Son, and the Holy Spirit. After the candidates emerged from the other side of the pool, the bishop anointed them with oil, and they donned new white linen robes, signifying their new life in the risen Jesus. They were embraced in a sign of peace and welcome, and each was handed a lighted candle.

Finally, the candidates were led into the room where the Eucharist was celebrated. By now dawn had come. For the first time, on Easter Sunday, they participated in the total eucharistic celebration.

Before their Baptism the catechumens attended Mass only up to the completion of the sermon. As a matter of fact, the first part of the Mass was called the Mass of the Catechumens because the prayers, readings, and sermon were intended to give instruction to the catechumens. What a joy it must have been for the newly baptized, after three years' preparation, to share the Eucharist with their friends for the first time! It must have been a similar joy for the rest of the community to welcome these long-awaited newcomers to their special Easter meal. 🔲

### Mystagogia

After the Easter Vigil Baptisms and the Easter Eucharist, the new Christians would go through another period of study and intense involvement with the community as they learned more about the mysteries of the faith. This period was known as the **mystagogia.**

Becoming a Christian required abandoning pagan ways and renouncing many comforts, conveniences, and privileges of the time. And before Christianity was made legal in 313 in the Roman Empire, being Christian presented a great risk of martyrdom. Initiation meant sharing one's fate and faith with the Christian community. Considering all that initiation involved, a lengthy process for acceptance into the community certainly made sense.

At the same time, the early Christian leaders realized that Baptism was meant to be a sustained joy, not just a moment of excitement. Developing a joyful, loving community demanded a profound initiation of its newcomers. Today the church has revised the Rite of Baptism, along with the other sacraments of initiation, to recapture the spirit, joy, and meaning of the rites in the early church.

# Evolution into Three Sacraments

The process of initiation just described was appropriate for the adult converts who were joining the faith in the early centuries of Christianity. But later on so many candidates sought initiation into the church that the bishops had difficulty officiating at all the ceremonies. Yet it was considered essential that the bishops conduct the rites.

### A Delayed Anointing

To handle the increased numbers of converts, in the Western church, priests of a given community performed the Baptism with water but delayed the rest of the baptismal ceremony (the anointing with oil by the bishop) until the bishop could get around to the church to "confirm" the initiation at a later time, sometimes even years later. This ritual of anointing and laying on of hands by the bishop became known as Confirmation, and was gradually accepted as a separate sacrament.

imagine

☐ Imagine that you live in third-century Rome and that you were recently baptized at the Easter Vigil along with two other candidates. Write a letter to a friend describing your experience of the ceremony. Include details: Was the ceremony held in a remote location out of fear of persecution? Did the aura of secrecy make it more sacred? Was the water cold? And so on.

Adults baptized in the Catholic church today are confirmed by anointing after their water Baptism.

make a celebration

If relatives of yours asked you to help make their newborn baby's Baptism a true community celebration, what would you suggest to them? Describe in writing at least three recommendations.

### Infant Baptism

By about the year 200, some children of Christian parents were being baptized into the church without going through their own conversion process. By the year 500, when almost everyone in the empire was Christian, infant Baptism was, almost without exception, the way that one became a Christian. Baptizing infants as soon as possible after birth became the norm because it was thought that an unbaptized baby who died would not go to heaven. A Christian family would, naturally, want their child to have access to salvation. So infant Baptism caused a delay between Baptism and the bishop's conferral of Confirmation.

In addition, with the practice of infant Baptism, children did not receive the Eucharist until they were old enough to understand the sacrament. Eventually, in the Western (Roman or Latin Rite) church, the baptized members began to participate in the Eucharist before they were confirmed, and they became confirmed at an even later age. Until recently in Roman Catholicism, these sacraments of initiation remained separate and were celebrated in this sequence: Baptism, the Eucharist, and then Confirmation. Even today debate is going on in the church about how and when in a person's development these sacraments should be celebrated.

### The Eastern Church Practice

In the Eastern churches, the original sequence of initiation was kept. Priests were allowed to baptize, confirm, and offer the Eucharist to the initiates. Today in the Eastern Orthodox churches, and in some of the Eastern Catholic churches, babies and little children receive all three sacraments at one time.

# Since Vatican Council II

After the Second Vatican Council of the 1960s, the church developed two main procedures for Baptism:

1. a ceremony specifically for babies and young children
2. an initiation process for adults (and a parallel process for older children) modeled on the process used in the early church

### For Young Children

Before the special rite for baptizing children was developed, the words of the baptismal ceremony were addressed to the child as if she or he were an adult. Therefore, when infants were baptized—which accounted for the majority of Baptisms during most of Christian history—the adult godparents responded for the children.

**Baptism not consciously chosen.** Today's distinct baptismal rite for young children acknowledges that the awareness and experience of the sacrament differ between adults and small children. For both adults and children, Baptism is a gift from God, not something earned or dependent on the person's own merit. But with adults Baptism is received as a conscious choice. For infants Baptism is not "conscious" (personally felt) or chosen by the children. So during the Baptism of an infant or small child, the parents are addressed rather than the child. No one speaks "for" the child, as the godparents used to do. The parents are recognized as the primary community of the child and as the ones who seek Baptism for their child and want to raise the child in the Christian faith.

As with adult initiation, the new baptismal rite for an infant involves the entire community, not just the child being baptized and the child's close family and godparents. The whole community is reminded of its role in helping the parents raise the child in the faith. All who are present also recall the significance of their own Baptism and their own ongoing initiation into the mystery of Christ. ⏺

Godparents have a special role to play in the life of the child whose parents have chosen them. They are to help the parents and support them as they encourage the unfolding of the child's faith-life. For this reason they need to be baptized and firm believers in Christ.

**"Initiated," one way or another.** In a concrete way, the practice of infant Baptism acknowledges that from our earliest experiences, we are being "initiated" into some way of viewing ourselves and our world. From infancy on we are influenced by the people around us, by our physical environment, and by all our internal and external experiences. Parents can choose to let "initiation" for

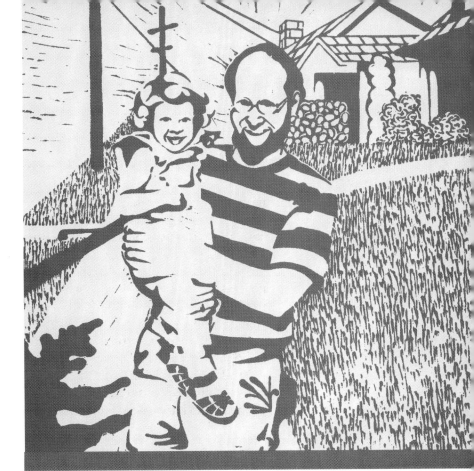

⬛ *Student art:* Linoleum print by Meg Greene, Jesuit High School, Portland, Oregon

their child just happen through exposure to the images, stories, and values communicated by the popular culture and media, like television. Alternatively, parents can put their hopes in the images, stories, and values of the Christian vision as the context for raising their child.

Through Baptism an infant is welcomed into a community that claims as its own the simple beauty of the Christmas story and the dramatic realities of Holy Week. Through Baptism the community celebrates a baby as a child of a loving God, someone whose family ties extend to heaven. Thus infant Baptism signifies the crucial roles that the family, the church community, and the Christian story play in developing within children the Christian view of life. ⓚ

ⓚ Do you agree or disagree with each of the following? Explain your answers in writing.
• When I have children, I won't have them baptized as infants. They can decide for themselves when they grow up.
• If I ran a parish, I would not be willing to baptize children of parents who did not practice their faith.

# Baptized Among a Million Friends

**A**t the 1997 World Youth Day in Paris, France, ten young people were baptized by the pope. The ritual was a living reminder that when we are baptized, we become united with the whole Body of Christ.

Fifteen-year-old Megan Costello held her breath as Pope John Paul II, holding a seashell-like ladle of water, approached her.

She'd been preparing for this moment for two years—ever since joining Saint James Catholic Church in Ogden, Utah. For years before that, she'd been visiting churches of various denominations around her home, looking for one that felt right. The Catholic church had felt like the place she belonged, and now, with nearly a million young people from around the world looking on, she was about to be baptized into it.

She hadn't fainted when the pope greeted her at the beginning of the ceremony, as her friends predicted she might. Instead of being nervous, she had spent much of the ceremony deep in thought.

"I was trying to decide exactly what the whole thing meant to me," she said later. "I still wasn't really sure, so I was going over it in my head."

But there wasn't much time for personal reflection on the mystery of Baptism; before she knew it, the pope was pouring a large measure of cool water over her head, thoroughly drenching her as he said, *"Je te baptise au nom du Pere, et du Fils et du Saint-Ésprit."* And then she breathed again, taking a huge gulp of air as the crowd cheered.

"God acknowledges you as his children and transforms your existence into a story of love with him," the pope said. "Live from now on as children of the light who know they are reconciled by the cross of the Savior."

Then Megan and the nine others who had been baptized with her took their baptismal candles and lit the candles of the assembled cardinals, who in turn passed the flame on to others. Spotlights fixed their beams in a crisscross pattern overhead, making a sort of cathedral of light.

"The light spread out into the audience, so everybody had candles, and it was so pretty," Megan said. "It was a sea of candles. It was beautiful, so moving."

After the catechumens received the sacrament of Confirmation, the ceremony ended in a jubilant riot of waving flags, banners and white sashes as the crowd sang, in one voice, *"Magnificat, magnificat, magnificat anima mea Dominum!"* over and over: "My soul magnifies, magnifies, magnifies the Lord."

Days after returning to her home in Utah, Megan was still full of questions about what the Baptism would mean to her life. But she was certain of one thing: "I felt different after [the Baptism]," she said. "I can't explain what I mean by that, but I felt different. Happy." (Adapted from Daoust, "World Youth Day '97")

### For Adults and Older Children

Since 1972 an official process of initiating adults into the Catholic faith has been in use, and it is modeled after the process the early church used in initiating its new members. The official process today is titled the **Rite of Christian Initiation of Adults.** Popularly called the **RCIA,** it takes into account these realities:

- Becoming a Catholic Christian is a process that takes time.
- Becoming a Catholic Christian means joining a community.

A similar rite is specifically designed for older children—that is, children old enough to learn about and choose the faith.

The RCIA is also a model for receiving into full communion with the Catholic church those persons who have previously been baptized. They could be Catholics who have lost touch with the Catholic church, or they might be Christians who were baptized in another denomination. As mentioned earlier, their Baptisms are considered valid in the Catholic church and thus are not repeated. For those who have not been confirmed in the Catholic church previously, they will receive Confirmation as the sign of full membership.

As a process, the RCIA has a number of stages to help interested persons move along to becoming informed and active members of the Catholic Christian community:

**1. Inquiry.** Before someone enters a formal initiation program, during the phase when she or he and the church are getting to know each other, the person is called an inquirer. When both parties are satisfied that they want to continue with the initiation process, the individual enters the catechumenate stage.

**2. Catechumenate.** A catechumen studies the Catholic faith, accompanied by a sponsor or sponsors, ideally within a community of other catechumens. The catechumens also participate with their sponsors in certain rites that bring them more deeply into the faith and the community. A sponsor should be a committed person who can serve as a mentor in the faith to their catechumen because he or she will be very involved in supporting that person's spiritual journey before and after Baptism.

Ideally the catechumenate period lasts from one to three years. All during this time, the catechumens attend Sunday Mass, but leave the church for their own session after the homily in a formal Rite of Dismissal. This reminds them and the assembly how important full participation in the Eucharist is for Christian life. Toward the end of the catechumenate stage, on the day of election, each candidate is chosen to be among the elect, provided he or she has shown sincerity as a catechumen. Although the community affirms the choosing of the catechumens, it is clear from the Rite of Election that God is doing the choosing. The elect have not "merited" their way into God's favor, like working up through the ranks in scouting. Rather, God has chosen them and they have responded.

joining a
## community

Adults who wish to join the Catholic church participate in a process called the RCIA, which takes a year or more to complete.

**3. Period of enlightenment or illumination.** The season of Lent preceding the Easter Vigil, when the elect will be baptized, is a period of intensive preparation with its own particular rites, consisting of questioning those to be baptized and hearing their profession of faith. As in ancient times, this season gives everyone, the already-baptized members and the elect, the chance to reflect on the mystery of the Resurrection, which they are soon to celebrate at Easter.

Of course, the major event for the candidates and the community is the Easter Vigil. The Easter Vigil service is filled with baptismal imagery so that the new and longer-standing members of the Christian community can reflect on the relationship between the Resurrection of Jesus and the sacraments of initiation. During the service the new members, accompanied by their sponsors, may be baptized and are confirmed. Later in the liturgy, the new members receive the Eucharist for the first time.

**4. Mystagogia.** The process of initiation does not end with Baptism, Confirmation, and the celebration of the Eucharist at Easter. Naturally, new members of a group have special needs. During the time from Easter to Pentecost Sunday, new members and their sponsors reflect together on their experiences of being Christian. The term applied to this period is *mystagogia*, a word related to the word *mystery*. Mystagogia is a time to understand and appreciate more deeply the Christian mysteries.

Throughout the Rite of Christian Initiation of Adults, the church community plays a significant role. Persons are usually drawn to Catholicism because they see some evidence of the life of Christ present within a local Catholic community, or within individuals who have cared about them. During the RCIA process, the catechumens and sponsors gather regularly as a community to share their own life stories and faith stories, and the candidates are affirmed in their journey of faith. The various rites throughout the catechumenate stage are celebrated with the whole gathered community. In fact where the RCIA is experienced as a dynamic process with the involvement of the community, the growing faith of the catechumens presents church community members with a challenge to their own faith. They are often inspired to not be complacent about their faith and to foster the bonds and commitments that build a genuine faith community. Thus the RCIA has the potential to renew local churches in their spirit. Ⓛ

*becoming Catholic*

Ⓛ Interview someone who became Catholic as an adult. Ask why he or she made this decision, what the initiation process was like, and how the person's life has changed since joining the church. Write a brief summary of your interview.

# Baptism's history

## For Review

13. Briefly describe the process called the catechumenate in the early church.

14. Why did the ritual of anointing and laying on of hands, or Confirmation, become separate from the ritual of Baptism?

15. What is the role of godparents?

16. Name and briefly explain the four stages of today's RCIA process.

# Lifelong Initiation, Lifelong Baptism

If you were baptized as an infant, the community of your family and your parents' friends would obviously be significant in your growth as a Christian. But as we have seen, adult Baptism also relies on the community to help new members grow into a Christian life, and it builds up the bonds and commitments in the community.

Baptism is not unique among the sacraments in its emphasis on the crucial role of the community. Each of the seven sacraments is celebrated on behalf of and for the good of the whole community, not just the individuals who are obviously involved.

Each time members of the community witness a Baptism, at the Easter Vigil or at Sunday Mass, they are reminded that their own initiation into the paschal mystery is not yet complete. Initiation will be a lifelong process, a lifelong Baptism in Christ, open to ever-deeper consciousness of the mystery of Jesus and to commitment to his mission.

*Student art:* Ink pen drawing by Katie O'Brien, University of San Diego High School, San Diego, California

8

# Confirmation

## celebrating growth
in the Spirit

...a lifelong journey

Breath of Life may I give witness to your Spirit
                    and light up my corner of the universe
                    by creatively working with others.
            And may I, like your Son,
                    continue to grow
                    in wisdom and age and grace.

                                    **Amen.**

The second of the three sacraments of initiation is **Confirmation,** which celebrates the full outpouring of the Holy Spirit on a baptized person, completing and strengthening the grace given by the Spirit in Baptism. (It is the second sacrament from a theological perspective, but in Catholic practice, Confirmation is not necessarily the second one to be received.) Like Baptism, Confirmation imparts a permanent character or seal in the person, marking him or her as belonging totally to Christ and as united to the church. Thus it may be received only once. Originally celebrated as a part of the early church's initiation ritual, which included Baptism and the Eucharist, Confirmation later developed into a separate sacrament.

Today in Latin Rite Catholicism, Confirmation is celebrated when a Christian is able to be conscious of the Spirit's life in her or him. For people baptized as infants, this means that Confirmation must come at a later age, the age of discretion. (This term is used in Catholicism to describe the age when a person is able to make moral judgments. In practice the age of Confirmation varies across countries and regions, anywhere from age seven to age eighteen.) For older children and adults being baptized, Confirmation is celebrated at the time of initiation, with Baptism and the Eucharist. In either case Confirmation is a sign of growing in the Spirit of Jesus.

Like all the sacraments, Confirmation celebrates a transformation so profound that its meaning can never be captured in any simple description. In Confirmation Christians acknowledge all the wonderful, usually subtle ways that Christ's Spirit is with them—affirming, strengthening, and challenging them. The following story hints at the many ways that the power of the Holy Spirit can be confirmed in a person's life:

# the Spirit's life in us

## Emily wonders

if her life will ever take off—if she will ever have the excitement in her life that seems to come naturally to other girls in her class. She thinks about Mia and Jenna, whose conversation she just overheard. Mia and Jenna went on about the great weekend they were each going to have. Mia and a new guy she is interested in are going to meet at the basketball game that night and then go out later for pizza. Jenna plans to go skiing with a couple of her girlfriends; they will probably meet some guys at the ski lodge and have a great time.

Emily considers her own "plans" for the weekend. Well, there will be the usual farm chores, which have to be done every day. Life on a dairy farm is pretty predictable. Milking twice a day, without fail, is the essential feature.

What else will go on this weekend? Emily thinks about how she might watch some TV shows, baby-sit her little brothers and her sister while her parents go to an auction, and do her homework. The biggest issue of the weekend will be whether to go to Mass Saturday night or Sunday morning. And that will be decided by when the car is available. In a large family like Emily's, there is plenty of demand for a car because the family lives so far from town.

"What a boring life," Emily sighs inside, careful not to let other kids see how down she feels. "My problem is, I'm just a dull person. I never do anything, I never go anywhere. I just exist."

Emily wants to leave school after the last class and get home on the early school bus. Then she can settle down in front of her favorite talk show before chore time.

As Emily rushes for the door, Mrs. Daly, the speech teacher, motions for her to come over. Emily does not want an encounter with such a vigorous, demanding teacher at this point, when she already feels so low. "Oh, no, what did I do now? Maybe she thinks I should change the way I did my speech for class. Like I haven't already put enough time into it!"

But Mrs. Daly is beaming. She doesn't look ready to pounce on her with criticism. "Emily, you did *some* job on that speech today. Marvelous expression—so much feeling you put into it, and in just the right rhythms!"

Emily puts her head down and smiles shyly. "It's easy when you've got Kennedy's words to work with." She had chosen to deliver John F. Kennedy's inaugural address as her major project.

"I've heard students give that speech a hundred times. And believe me, Emily, I never heard it like I heard it from you today."

Emily lifts her head up slightly and catches a glimpse of Mrs. Daly's animated face. "I felt a lot when I was giving it. I guess it showed."

"You bet it did. You know, Emily, you sit there in class so quietly, and I don't often hear from you. Today you amazed me with that speech."

"Yeah, well, I don't usually have much to say. I guess I'm just not very interesting."

"Now that's where you've got it all wrong! You *are* interesting. You're passionate, Emily; you're full of life inside you that's just begging for a chance to come out."

Emily takes in Mrs. Daly's words like a parched field soaking up a gentle rain. Yes, Emily knows she has a lot going on inside her, a lot of vitality; she just never seems to have an outlet for it. So she feels dull. Now here is someone who recognizes what has been in her all along—her tremendous feeling.

"Emily, I would love for you to join the speech team. You've got so much to give."

The early bus is now pulling away from the curb. Emily realizes that it will be 4:30 before she can leave, getting her home just in time for chores. No talk show for her this afternoon. But taking the late bus and missing her talk show doesn't bother Emily like it ordinarily would have.

Looking up into Mrs. Daly's eager eyes, Emily grins. "I'd like that. Yeah, that might be **real neat."**

Emily discovered a gift within her-self—her own deep feeling, her own inner life. Until Mrs. Daly recognized it, this gift had gone largely unnoticed and unrealized. Emily herself was only dimly aware of it as a gift. Channeling that immense inner vitality into a great, passionate speech, and having someone notice her rendering of that speech as special, gave Emily the sense that there was more inside her than met the eye. 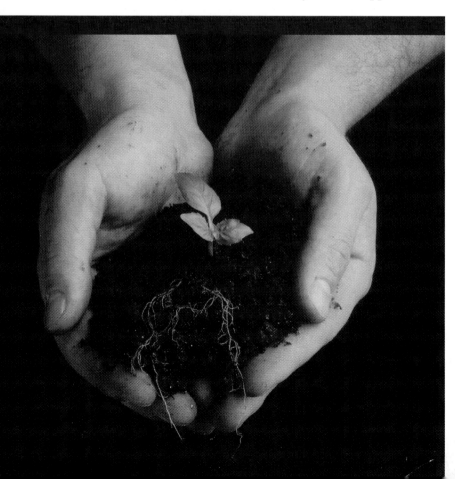[A]

# What Does Confirmation Celebrate?

## Lifelong Growth in the Spirit

aware of a gift

[A] In writing, tell about a gift you have that you were not aware of until another person or an occasion brought it out. Compare your experience with Emily's.

Like Emily in the previous story, all people carry within them great gifts that are not necessarily apparent to themselves or others. Growth in such gifts does not happen all at once. For their part Christians receive the gift of the Spirit in Baptism, but in the sacrament of Confirmation the full outpouring of the Holy Spirit brings baptismal grace to completion. And doesn't something similar happen to us in everyday life? We may be given a gift, like Emily's talent for public speaking, but we are not really ready to share it with the world until it has been "confirmed" in us, as Mrs. Daly did with Emily.

Through the sacrament of Confirmation, the church affirms the view that growth in the Spirit is a continuing, lifelong journey. In recognizing the impact that an individual's faith community can have on his or her journey, the church also affirms the following:

- The Holy Spirit operates in subtle ways throughout people's lives.
- Confirmation itself is one special moment when Christians consciously acknowledge the presence of the Holy Spirit and are given the fullness of the Spirit's grace.
- Caring people are bearers of God's Spirit and "confirmers" of one another's gifts.

### The Breath of God

*Holy Spirit* is the translation of an old Hebrew term that means "wind" or "breath of God." In the Scriptures people experienced the Spirit sometimes as a powerful wind, other times as a gentle breeze or a whisper, and still other times as God breathing life into persons or events. On Pentecost the Apostles felt the Spirit in a dramatic way, as wind and fire. Often in life, however, the Spirit is revealed in subtle ways—more in the breezes than in the strong winds. The Spirit at work in us may become apparent in a simple, gentle moment, like being

# Taking Flight

The following story, based on an African folktale, gives us a way to consider the meaning of Confirmation:

Once upon a time, while she was walking through a forest, a farmer found an eagle tangled in a bush, an eagle too young to fly. She took the young eagle home and put him in the stockyard, where the eagle soon learned to eat chicken feed and to behave as the chickens did.

A month or so later, when the farmer was in the stockyard, she saw the eagle awkwardly pecking at kernels of corn. The farmer thought to herself, "This eagle needed to be here for a while. But now, it is sad to see this king of all birds living in a stockyard with chickens."

"He has never learned to fly," the farmer remarked to her husband. "He behaves as chickens behave. You might say that he is no longer an eagle."

"Still, he has the heart of an eagle and can surely be taught to fly," suggested the farmer's husband.

After talking it over, the two agreed to find out whether this was possible. Gently the farmer took the eagle in her arms and said, "You belong to the sky more than to the Earth. Stretch forth your wings and fly."

The eagle, however, was confused, not knowing who he was. Seeing his friends the chickens, the eagle jumped down to be with them again.

On the following day, the farmer took the eagle up onto the highest cattle hut and urged him again, saying, "You are an eagle. Stretch forth your wings and fly." But the eagle was afraid of his unknown self and jumped down once more to the chicken yard.

On the third day, the farmer rose early, took the eagle out of the stockyard, and climbed with him to a high mountain. There she held the king of birds high above her and encouraged him again, saying, "You are an eagle. You belong to the sky as well as to the Earth. Stretch forth your wings now. Fly!"

The eagle looked around, back toward the stockyard and up to the sky. Still he did not fly. Then the farmer lifted him even higher, straight toward the sun. And it happened that the eagle began to tremble. Slowly, he stretched his wings. At last, with a triumphant cry, he soared away into the heavens.

It may be that the eagle still fondly remembers his friends the chickens. Yet, as far as anyone knows, he has never returned to the chicken yard.

affirmed by a friend or being moved to tears of sympathy. B

### Consciously Accepting the Gift

In the opening narrative about Emily, Emily became aware of her gift of speech when Mrs. Daly commended her for it. In a similar way, if young Christians are to become conscious that Christ's Spirit is truly alive and at work in them, then other people in the community must take the time to recognize and nurture the young persons' growing gifts.

The sacrament of Confirmation provides an opportunity for persons to consciously claim as their own the gift of the Spirit given at Baptism, and now fully poured out by God. Confirmation recognizes that the Spirit is bearing fruit in a person's own emerging talents and personal qualities. Confirmation also "confirms" that the person's initiation into Christ's life at Baptism is now consciously

being embraced. The Spirit can more readily flourish in a heart that willingly accepts the Spirit's gifts. C

### Needing Other People

Notice that in the opening story, Mrs. Daly did not try to make Emily into something she was not. Rather, she recognized Emily's wonderful gift and realized that nurturing it was necessary. Likewise, all of us need such "confirmation" throughout life. When others act in our life as Mrs. Daly acted in Emily's life, they confirm our identity and encourage our growth in the gifts we have been given.

Reflect for a moment on your own life, and ask yourself:

- Which persons have confirmed my identity and encouraged growth of the gifts I have been given?
- Who have been the primary revealers of the Spirit to me?

The people you thought of in answering these questions have been channels for God's grace in your life. In a way they have been your "sponsors"—a term used in the sacraments of initiation to describe people who encourage and nurture the faith of the person being initiated. For example:

- Our parents provide us with food and clothing.
- Our relatives visit our home and take an interest in us.
- Our teachers give their time to help us learn.
- Our friends share their lives with us.
- Many other people whom we meet are friendly to us.

These are some of the sponsors through whom God's grace acts in our life.

In preparation for Confirmation, young people usually choose one person to be their **sponsor,** to accompany them through a particularly significant time of growing in the Spirit. Ideally, the sponsor would be one of the young person's godparents from Baptism, which shows the

B After looking up the various dictionary meanings of the word *spirit,* write about what you think the name Holy Spirit tells us about God. List five ways that you think the Holy Spirit is at work in the world today.

Sponsors are those who have been channels of God's grace for us.
※ *Student art:* Photo by Megan Rulli, Oak Knoll School, Summit, New Jersey

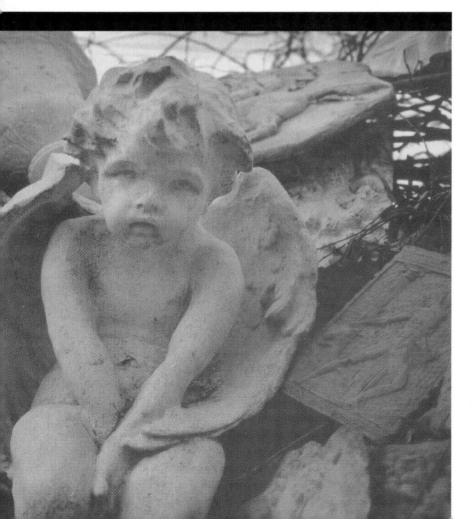

connection between Baptism and Confirmation. At any rate the sponsor should be a baptized person who is fully initiated (having received Confirmation and First Eucharist), active in the Catholic faith, and willing to help the young person grow spiritually. In some parishes, besides the official sponsor chosen by the candidate for Confirmation (who stands with the person at the moment of anointing), another adult, called a **mentor,** is chosen to guide the person spiritually throughout the preparation time. In fact the sponsor is really intended to be that mentor.

### Learning in Community

As chapter 7 discussed, adults and older children who are initiated into the church today through the Rite of Christian Initiation of Adults are confirmed as well as baptized, and they receive the Eucharist at the Easter Vigil. Their celebration of these sacraments follows an extensive period of preparation known as the catechumenate. With other catechumens and their sponsors, they share the story of their own life and learn about how the Good News of Jesus touches them. Over a long process, the catechumens are welcomed more deeply into the life of the community and gradually realize what it means to live in the Spirit of Jesus.

For young persons who were baptized as infants, the period of preparing for Confirmation serves as a stage similar to the catechumenate. Lasting for one or two years, a Confirmation preparation program is meant to give young persons the chance to learn about and grow in the faith they are consciously embracing.

Typically, young people are confirmed as a group in their parish by the bishop of their diocese. Because the bishops are the successors of the Apostles, Confirmation by one's bishop is a vivid sign of full incorporation into the church handed down from the time of Jesus.

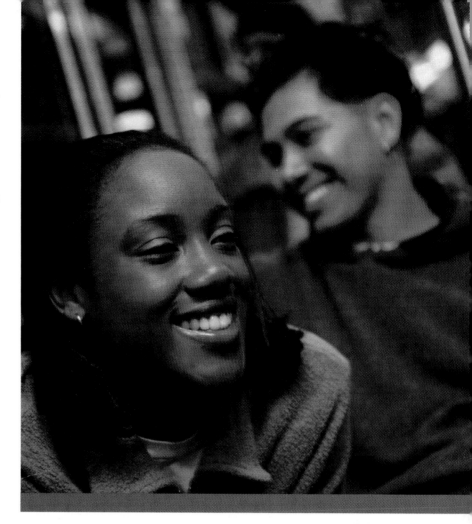

## The Gifts of the Spirit Unfolding

In the opening story, Emily had a special gift that was not being fully expressed; it was lying dormant until it was recognized and nurtured. Likewise, at the time of Confirmation, seven special gifts are called forth and strengthened in those being confirmed. These **gifts of the Holy Spirit** are actually virtues or abilities that were given at Baptism and that gradually unfold in a person as she or he matures. Thus the time of Confirmation, when the young person has already reached a certain level of maturity, is an ideal time to accept these gifts wholeheartedly, be strengthened in them, and try to develop them.

*my life sponsors*

C Are there certain people through whom God's grace acts dynamically in your life—people who encourage and inspire your faith? Think of specific examples of these people's positive influence on you, and write an essay entitled "The Sponsors in My Life."

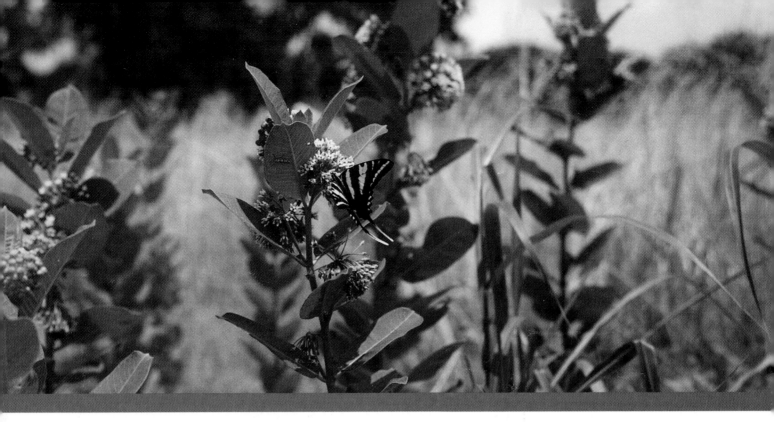

Reverence is an attitude toward God, ourselves, and all creation.
▓ *Student art:* Photo by Sara M. Luczak, North Catholic High School, Pittsburgh, Pennsylvania

*growing in gifts*

D Next to a list of the seven gifts of the Holy Spirit, indicate which two you would most like to grow in. Then for each of the two, reflect in writing on possible opportunities for growth in those gifts—opportunities that might come up in the next week or month that would give you the chance to grow in those gifts.

### The Seven Gifts

In the Rite of Confirmation, the bishop or priest prays that these seven special gifts will grow in the candidates:
- wisdom
- understanding
- right judgment
- courage
- knowledge
- reverence
- wonder and awe in God's presence

By presenting these seven gifts in the form of questions, we can see more clearly the opportunities they offer to grow in Christian maturity.

**Wisdom.** Am I a seeker of wisdom? Do I thoughtfully explore the wisdom of Jesus and of other great teachers of the past? Do I step back to see the whole truth hidden behind the obvious facts at hand? Do I attempt to look at life from many different perspectives besides my own?

**Understanding.** Do I try to understand what I have learned? Do I look closely at underlying causes and not just at results? Am I understanding toward others—especially those who rub me the wrong way? Can I admit my faults?

**Right judgment.** Am I developing my conscience? Do I consult the teachings of the church in trying to make judgments? Do I seek guidance from informed and conscientious people?

**Courage.** Can I freely act on my decisions, remaining faithful to my conscience? Do I act rightly and justly even when risking ridicule or going against the crowd? D

**Knowledge.** Am I challenged but not overwhelmed by the vast amount of information that I can still learn? Am I trying to keep informed about life and its workings? Do I follow the debates on important current issues so that I can make intelligent decisions?

**Reverence.** Do I treat myself and the people and things of the world with reverence? Do I recognize fellow human beings and other creatures of the Earth as my brothers and sisters? Is compassion for others an important measuring stick for my choices?

**Wonder and awe in God's presence.** Do I take time to pray and worship so that I can more deeply appreciate God's presence in my life? Do I reject boredom as a condition of life and instead seek to live with the joy and enthusiasm of a child of God?

Naturally, the development of these gifts cannot happen instantly at the time of Confirmation. These gifts are the fruits of maturing in God's life. Let's examine the notion of what it means to mature.

### Maturity: A Journey, Not a Destination

How do you see yourself ten years from now? Will you be settled down? Will you be working in your lifelong profession? Will you be married? Will you have children? maybe a dog? a house with a TV set and a great sound system? Will you have "arrived"? Will you be an "adult"? Will you be settled and secure until the next stage—retirement? E

Many people have an image of maturity that might be called the destination model, as the previous questions imply. According to that model, we travel through adolescence until one day we arrive at our destination—maturity as an adult. After that our life remains much the same.

Another image of maturity might be called the journey model. This alternative image understands life as a continuing process of growth, filled from start to finish with peaks and valleys, rough roads and straight paths, dyings and risings. It is thus filled with paschal-like events. There is never any set destination we reach that allows us to claim fulfillment in maturity, as in, "Now I've got it made; I've reached maturity; I'm an adult. All I have to do is continue along this same path for the next thirty years, and I will have lived my life."

Much in our culture endorses a destination model of maturity. Adolescence is portrayed merely as the trip that one must take to arrive at a destination—maturity as an adult. Yet the journey model, which is really more consistent with the Christian vision of how we grow, suggests that maturing is a process that takes a lifetime.

in ten years

E Imagine yourself ten years from now. What do you think you will be doing? Name four things you can imagine yourself being involved in or committed to.

taking the journey

choosing service

F If you were in preparation for Confirmation this year and were expected to do some service activity, what service would you choose? Explain your choice in writing.

In taking on the ministry of Jesus, we share our time and talents with others.
※ *Student art:* Photo by Nina Eaglin, Shawe Memorial High School, Madison, Indiana

The story of Emily, recounted earlier in this chapter, offers an unwitting but almost perfect parallel to the journey model of maturity and to the sacrament of Confirmation. Emily had a gift at work in her, but she was only dimly aware of it until Mrs. Daly gave her recognition for it. When Mrs. Daly "confirmed" Emily's gift for speech, she did not say that Emily had reached her highest point or that Emily had no more room for growth and improvement. Rather, Mrs. Daly recognized and encouraged Emily for her gift and her desire to develop that gift. In a similar way, Confirmation does not confer maturity, just as getting married or entering a profession does not confer maturity. Instead, Confirmation recognizes and encourages a person's developing maturity.

In the Christian vision, the process of growing, changing, and maturing goes on in us as long as we are alive.

## Taking On the Ministry of Jesus

To be confirmed in Catholic Christian faith is to consciously accept the gift of Jesus' Spirit given in Baptism—with everything that gift implies. The phrase "with everything that gift implies" is crucial. For implied in the gift of Jesus' Spirit is the call to become more like Jesus, to share completely in the mission of Jesus, to take on as one's own Jesus' ministry of healing, reconciling, and conveying God's love to all persons.

As seen in chapter 7 on Baptism, sharing in the mission of Jesus is an important dimension of being initiated as a Christian. But for an infant or small child being baptized, sharing in Jesus' ministry is a remote reality; it cannot be realized until much later. Young people often experience sharing in Jesus' ministry in a conscious way around the time of their Confirmation. F

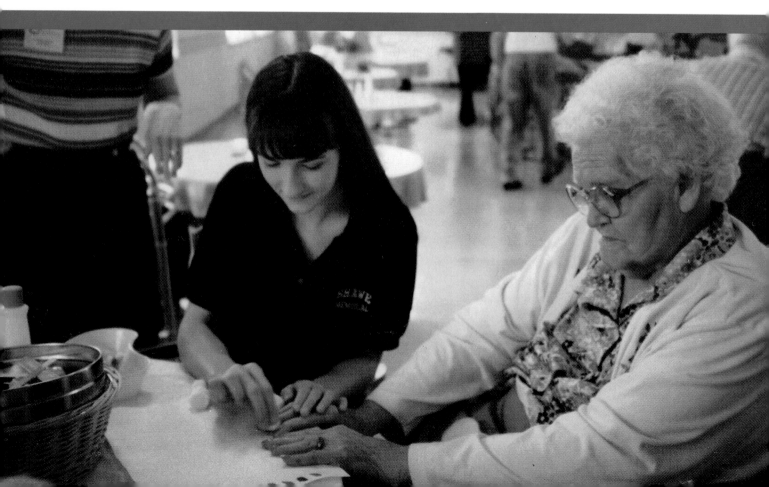

Most programs that prepare young people for Confirmation emphasize that the candidates be involved in service of some kind. The value of such service gets lost if it is viewed as an obligation to be gotten over, as in, "You did your twenty hours; now you can be confirmed." Instead, service experiences are emphasized for two primary reasons: first, to give candidates a taste of living Jesus' life of ministry, and second, to enable them to try out their own gifts for service as a way to discern how they might serve in the future.

Many teenagers give themselves generously to a certain kind of service in preparing for Confirmation. Those who do are often rewarded with personal growth that they never imagined. They discover (and are often surprised by) the skills they have. They discover self-worth. And they discover that in sharing their time and talents with other people, life becomes fuller and richer. Jesus' call to join in his ministry comes with this promise: "I came that they may have life, and have it abundantly" (John 10:10).

## Who May Be Confirmed?

By now it is clear that Confirmation should not be conferred automatically on every Catholic who reaches the age specified for the sacrament in his or her diocese. In Roman Catholicism, Confirmation requires full intention and willingness. Besides being baptized and being of the age of discretion, a person must be the following:
- willing to profess the Catholic faith
- in a state of grace, that is, forgiven of any grave sins through Baptism or the sacrament of Reconciliation (Penance)
- intending to receive the sacrament
- willing to take on the role of a disciple of Christ

The decision to be confirmed is not one to be taken lightly, for it involves both faith and commitment.

## For Review

1. What is the sacrament of Confirmation?

2. When does Confirmation typically take place for people baptized as infants in the Roman Catholic church? When does it take place for those baptized as older children or adults?

3. What is the purpose of a Confirmation preparation program?

4. Why is the bishop's role in Confirmation significant?

5. Name the seven gifts of the Holy Spirit.

6. Explain the two models of maturity discussed in this chapter. Which one is more consistent with the Christian vision?

7. How does the opening story about Emily provide a parallel to the sacrament of Confirmation?

8. Why do most Confirmation preparation programs emphasize service experiences?

9. What is required of baptized persons who have reached the age of discretion, in order for them to be

# The Ritual of Confirmation: Symbolic Actions and Words

ⓖ Recall a personal experience in which hands—yours or someone else's—communicated strength, power, healing, or support. If the hands could have talked, what would they have said? Write an imaginary monologue given by the hands.

*talking hands*

Ideally, candidates for Confirmation go through a process similar to what catechumens go through for Baptism. And like the baptismal process, certain rituals are celebrated with the whole community during the process of Confirmation. The culmination point, the Rite of Confirmation itself, usually takes place in the context of celebrating the Eucharist.

The symbolic actions used at Confirmation are not unique to that sacrament. They are used in other church sacraments, no doubt because they are powerful communicators of meaning. The two rituals central to Confirmation are the laying on of hands and the anointing with chrism.

Amidst the many beautiful prayers of the ritual, certain words and actions are essential to the validity of the sacrament. The words, spoken by the bishop or the priest while laying on a hand and anointing the person, are **"Be sealed with the Gift of the Holy Spirit."**

## The Laying On of Hands: A Powerful Connector

Hands are a symbol of power. Specifically, the laying on of hands refers to an ancient practice of conferring power onto a person by placing both hands on that person's head. In Genesis old Isaac lays his hands on his son Jacob to give him authority over the tribe. Kings and knights traditionally received their official power through a laying on of hands. The practice was also common in the early church to symbolize passing on the power of the Holy Spirit, which the Apostles had received at Pentecost.

### Blessing, Creating, Comforting, Supporting

Hands are a particularly apt symbol for the Holy Spirit working in people. We bless with our hands. The priest at Mass gives the sign of the cross with his hand over the assembly. Friends pat each other on the back to offer encouragement or congratulations. Artists often depict the hand of God creating the world or giving life.

Similarly, we work with our hands, create things with our hands, and "give each other a hand." Hands greet, comfort, and console. Hands touch other people and can help heal simply by their touch. Hands can support and lift up others. They can help to guide. They can be used to reach out and make connections with people. ⓖ

### Spirit Touching Spirit

In the Rite of Confirmation, the bishop initially "lays hands on" all the candidates together by extending his hands over the whole group. Meanwhile, he prays for the Spirit to help and guide the candidates with the seven gifts of the Holy Spirit. A few moments later, when the candidates individually come up to the bishop to be anointed with chrism (the special consecrated oil also used in Baptism), he places a hand on each person's head, which is symbolically the place of wisdom. The feeling of a hand on the head also gives a person the feeling of being strengthened by another's touch. A bond is made; the spirit of one touches the spirit of the other.

gentle & strong power

## Anointing with Chrism: A Commissioning to Service

Have you ever watched public officials take oaths of office? They raise their hand and vow to carry out the duties and responsibilities of their offices. In ancient times anointing with oil served that function. Kings and priests were anointed to symbolize their commission to those roles. Jesus himself is called Christ, which means "the Anointed One." In the Rite of Confirmation, Christians are anointed by the bishop with chrism and thus are commissioned to be Christ for others. This action also recalls their anointing with chrism at Baptism. ⊞

### A Consecration

The anointing at Confirmation is an act of consecrating the person, to share more completely in the mission of Jesus Christ and the church. In the Roman Catholic church, the bishop usually does the anointing, as well as the laying on of hands, to link the person symbolically to the universal church, the church of the Apostles. Where adults or older children are being initiated in a ceremony that includes the sacraments of Baptism, Confirmation, and the Eucharist, a priest, not a bishop, is usually the one presiding.

### A Sign of the Cross

To be anointed the candidates come forward one by one. As each one approaches the bishop, that candidate's sponsor places her or his right hand on

*oil today*

⊞ List all the modern uses of oil and oil-based products that you can think of. Does oil seem like an effective symbol in Confirmation today? Write your opinion in a paragraph.

BE SEALED WITH the Gift of the HOLY Spirit

## Confirmation in Words and Symbols

**Renewal of Baptismal Promises**
Do you reject Satan and all his works
and all his empty promises?
  I do.
Do you believe in God the Father
almighty, creator of heaven and earth?
  I do.

**The Laying On of Hands**
All-powerful God, Father of our Lord
    Jesus Christ,
by water and the Holy Spirit

you freed your sons and daughters from
  sin
and gave them new life.
Send your Holy Spirit upon them
to be their Helper and Guide.
Give them the spirit of wisdom and
    understanding,
the spirit of right judgment and
    courage,
the spirit of knowledge and reverence.

Fill them with the spirit of wonder and
   awe in your presence.
We ask this through Christ our Lord.
   Amen.

### The Anointing with Chrism
[Name], be sealed with the Gift of the
   Holy Spirit.
   Amen.
Peace be with you.
   And also with you.

### General Intercessions
For these sons and daughters of God,
confirmed by the gift of the Spirit,
that they give witness to Christ
by lives built on faith and love:
let us pray to the Lord.
   Lord, hear our prayer.

### Blessing
The Holy Spirit
came down upon the disciples
and set their hearts on fire with love:
may he bless you,
keep you one in faith and love,
and bring you to the joy of God's
   kingdom.
   Amen.

*false values*

◻ If you were to affirm your original baptismal promises today, what particular false values would you think of in rejecting all of Satan's "empty promises"? Jot down these false values on paper, ranking them from most harmful to least harmful.

the candidate's shoulder and gives the bishop the candidate's name. In the essential words and actions of the sacrament, the bishop dips his right thumb in the chrism, puts his hand on the person's head, and makes the sign of the cross on the forehead, saying, "Be sealed with the Gift of the Holy Spirit." The bishop then gives the person the sign of peace.

When it is not celebrated with Baptism, Confirmation includes other actions that echo the baptismal rituals. These actions, the renunciation of sin and the profession of faith, are the same promises made at Baptism and so are a renewal of them. They remind the candidates and the whole community of the essential connection between being baptized and being confirmed. These promises were a part of the candidates' baptismal ceremony long ago, when they were actually pledged by their parents and godparents. ◻

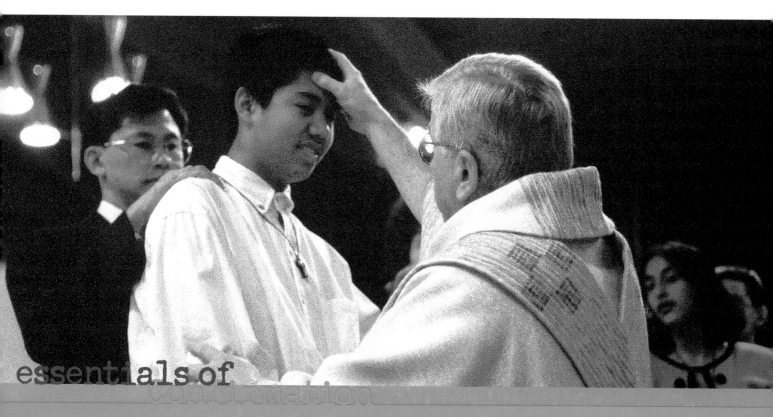

# essentials of confirmation

## For Review

10. What are the essential symbolic actions and words of the sacrament of Confirmation?

11. To what ancient practice does the laying on of hands refer? How does the bishop first perform this action in the Rite of Confirmation?

12. What is the significance of anointing with chrism in the Rite of Confirmation? How is the anointing carried out in the rite?

# Confirmation's History

As discussed in chapter 7 on Baptism, Confirmation cannot be considered apart from Baptism. In the early church, Confirmation was not a separate sacrament. Instead, as the act of anointing with chrism, it was part of the initiation rite for catechumens at the Easter Vigil, which also included Baptism and the celebration of the Eucharist.

## A Separate Ritual

In the Western church, the anointing with chrism by the bishop after the water ritual of Baptism eventually had to take place long after the water ritual. Membership growth had led to more Baptisms being performed (by priests) in widespread communities than there were bishops available to perform the anointing with chrism at Baptism. Delaying the anointing by the bishop allowed priests to continue performing the water ritual and allowed bishops to get around to their communities to "confirm" all the Baptisms that priests had performed over the past months or years. In this manner Confirmation in the Western church took on its own distinct ritual status by the third century. However, this separate anointing became a "regular" practice only after the fifth century, especially with the popularity of infant Baptism.

In the Eastern Catholic and Orthodox churches, Confirmation was never separated from Baptism. Throughout their history, the Eastern churches have baptized, confirmed, and given the Eucharist to infant newcomers in one ceremony, presided over by a priest.

## "Soldiers of Christ"?

In the fifth century, when many people were neglecting the separate anointing of Confirmation, a certain abbot preached that Confirmation was related to preparedness for spiritual combat, to preparing people for their life's battles with the devil. This idea that the sacrament would make an individual a "soldier of Christ" and a "witness for Christ" caught on in the wider church. For the next fifteen centuries, this perspective would influence people's understanding of Confirmation. ⬜

The sign of peace, an embrace that the bishop traditionally gave the person in the anointing ceremony, was administered more and more quickly, until it became a touch. As strange as it may seem, in the Middle Ages, it was misinterpreted as a slap on the cheek, symbolizing the blows and sufferings we must endure for Christ. Gradually, the slap on the cheek came to be standard practice, symbolic of becoming a soldier of Christ. Only in the past few decades has this symbol been dropped from the practice of Confirmation and the sign of peace restored.

## Coming of Age Versus Lifelong Growth in the Spirit

In recent decades a great deal of discussion has taken place in the Catholic church about the meaning of Confirmation. For a time the sacrament was

⬜ List the pros and cons of using the "soldiers of Christ" image to describe what Christians should be. Briefly state and explain your own opinion on the use of the term.

_soldiers of Christ_

thought to represent a kind of coming of age, a reaching of spiritual maturity. This explanation had some appeal, especially because young people were being confirmed more frequently around the time of adolescence. However, along with this notion came the mistaken idea that Confirmation would complete and finish one's learning and formation as a Christian. Nothing could be further from the intent of this sacrament.

The current understanding is that Confirmation does not represent an arrival point, a destination, or a "graduation" from childhood to adulthood. Instead, it celebrates and deepens the ongoing initiation into a new life with Jesus, which began at Baptism. Thus Confirmation readies a person for all the conscious growing and ministering that is ahead in life. It is part of the beginning, not the end, of a person's faith journey.

## A Current Debate

Connected with the Catholic church's discussion about the meaning of Confirmation is a debate about the order in which the sacraments of initiation should be celebrated in a person's life, as well as the age that is most appropriate for Confirmation.

Some theologians argue that the "original sequence" should be restored—that is, Baptism, Confirmation, and the Eucharist should be celebrated in that order. Others claim that with the present practice of infant Baptism, it makes sense to delay Confirmation until the young person is old enough to be truly conscious of the Spirit at work in her or him, that is, later than the age at which First Eucharist is received.

Roman Catholic canon law states that the sacrament should be conferred at the age of discretion—but there are a variety of opinions on when discretion is possible in the life of a young person. The practice in recent decades in the United States has been to confirm young persons anywhere between the ages of seven and eighteen. However, debate and clarification continue in the church about the sequence and administering of these sacraments; the situation is still in flux. [K]

[K] The appropriate age for Confirmation has been debated widely; people in the church variously propose anywhere from infancy to young adulthood. What do you think is the best age for Confirmation? Explain your position in writing.

# Confirmation's history

## For Review

13. Why did Confirmation become a separate sacrament in the Western church?

14. Describe two positions in the Catholic debate about the order in which the sacraments of initiation should be celebrated.

# Toward Full Initiation

The Rites of Baptism and Confirmation are well-defined, identifiable moments that happen only once in a Christian's life. However, these two sacraments of initiation celebrate a reality that is not limited to a certain date or age: the ongoing birth of the Christian into new life. The third sacrament of initiation, the Eucharist, is different in that it is celebrated not once but often in a Christian's life.

Receiving the Eucharist for the first time is a great personal event, and it plunges the Christian more deeply into the paschal mystery, Christ's dying and rising. The Eucharist can then become a frequent event for the Christian, a source of strength and nourishment that can sustain him or her for a lifetime. Let us now turn to this sacrament, which represents the fullness of Christian initiation.

*Student art:* Photo by Clare Major, Saint Joseph's Academy, Baton Rouge, Louisiana

# 9

# The Eucharist

## celebrating Christ's saving presence in our midst

Bread of Life, we meet you while gathered around a table—
laughing, singing, listening,
sharing bread and wine
and our lives in companionship.
Heaven, we know, is like this.
For this we give you our thanks,
our Eucharist.

Amen.

The first two sacraments of initiation—Baptism and Confirmation—celebrate the realities of belonging to Christ, being identified with him, and being gifted by his Spirit in the community of his followers, the church. Like all the sacraments, Baptism and Confirmation are signs that Christ is truly present in the world today, through the church.

But in the sacrament of the **Eucharist**, Catholics have the ultimate sign of Christ's presence in their midst: the sharing of bread and wine, consecrated as Jesus' own body and blood and offered by Jesus out of love for the whole world. Receiving the Eucharist for the first time represents the fullness of Christian initiation by most closely uniting the person with the mystery of Jesus. After that first reception, frequently celebrating the Eucharist becomes a way for Catholics to deepen their lifelong initiation into Christ's life, death, and Resurrection.

All the other sacraments and dimensions of Christian living can be viewed as flowing from or leading up to the Eucharist; this sacrament is central. In the words of Vatican Council II, the Eucharist is "the source and summit of the Christian life" *(Dogmatic Constitution on the Church,* number 11).

Let's look at two stories that shed some light on the meaning of the Eucharist.

## out of love for the world

Having completed the Creation, God looked it over and saw that it was good. Of all the creating, bringing forth man and woman had given God the most delight, for they were made in the image of freedom and love. And so it was that God wanted them, most of all, to remember that their Creator would always be with them.

So God called together representatives of all of Creation besides human beings. Delegations from rock and from fire, from sky and from earth—all were present. Flowers and trees also sent their representatives. And every kind of animal—wild and tame, crawling and swimming, walking and flying—was notified of its right to attend the assembly.

God ushered all the representatives into a huge hall and told them about wanting to give people a sign of love—a sign of God's own continued presence among them. The question God placed before them was, "Whom should I send?"

A loud roar at once shook the assembly hall as all the representatives shouted: "Send me! Send me!" So God sent to humans many messengers—gushing waters and mighty winds, bright sun and protective clouds, the stars and moon of the sky, and the living things of Earth. All these were powerful reminders indeed, and as long as people looked at them—really looked at them—people remembered God.

Yet eventually, some people forgot how to look, and others got too busy, so they no longer saw the reminders. And as brightly as the great sun shone, and as high or low as the cool clouds soared, and as swiftly as the gushing waters flowed, these things no longer reminded people of God's love for them. Everyone ended up confused.

God felt sad and lonely, wanting very much to remind people, but who else could be sent?

Then, in the quiet of one evening, bread came to God and said, "Your people are crying out in hunger, O God. They cry out that you have forgotten them, for they have no food. Send me as a sign that you love them and are with them. They will not be able to forget me, for they will be in need of me every day. Nor will they be alone when they eat me, for I beg to be shared. So I will bring them together. And when they come together to share in me, your bread, then they will remember that you love them and are with them. I am the sign for which you have searched so long."

Of course, thought God, I can send bread! So bread went among God's people. The people shared the gift of bread, and they shared in their God's love. And that is why from that day until this, when people come together to share bread, they know that God loves them and is with them. (Adapted from Juknialis, "Send Me")

* * *

Long ago a family lived in a clearing in the woods. The family was well fed and happy because of the father's prowess as a hunter. But there came a time when game was scarce and the family began to go hungry. When it looked as if they would all starve to death, the woman said to her husband, "This is what you must do. You must kill me and then drag my body in a circle around the clearing." The man refused for several days, though she continued to urge him to do as she had said, until starvation was upon them. Then in desperation he consented to his wife's demand. That night corn grew up wherever the woman's blood had soaked the soil. By morning this new food had grown to maturity and was ready to eat. Ever since, people have eaten corn and remembered Corn Mother's

# gift to them.

(Tinker, "Native Americans")

you are bread

**A** Imagine that you are "bread," called on to report to God after your two thousand years of use in eucharistic celebrations. Write up a one-page report.

In the story, God sent humans many messengers—gushing waters, bright sun, and protective clouds, the living things of Earth. But one simple messenger got through to humans with the message of God's love.

# What Does the Eucharist Celebrate?

## Remembering Love Shared, Life Poured Out

The first of the two previous stories has a simple message familiar to Christians: Bread has been sent to us, to nourish us, as a daily reminder of God's love. In the Gospels we read that at the Last Supper with his disciples, the night before he was put to death,

> [Jesus] took a loaf of bread, and when he had given thanks, he broke it and gave it to them, saying, "This is my body, which is given for you. Do this in remembrance of me." (Luke 22:19)

The Native American story about Corn Mother also contains a theme familiar to Christians: Love poured out as the giving of one's life brings forth new life.

The Gospel account of the Last Supper recalls this truth:

> And [Jesus] did the same with the cup after supper, saying, "This cup that is poured out for you is the new covenant in my blood." (Luke 22:20)

## A Ritual Meal

Jesus placed the meaning of his life and death in the context of an ancient, deeply human action—the sharing of a meal. The Gospels indicate that it was probably not just any meal, but a special Jewish ritual meal called the **Passover seder.** Held yearly in the Israelites' homes since the time of Moses, the Passover seder remembers and celebrates God's saving action of freeing their people from slavery in Egypt. It is essentially a meal of thanksgiving. B

*celebration memories*

B Think back on a particular meal that was also a celebration for you. What rituals were involved? Write about the experience.

*The Last Supper,* a twentieth-century depiction from Brazil

### A Transformed Meaning

At the Last Supper, Jesus transformed the meaning of that ritual Passover meal by identifying the bread and wine, which were customarily blessed and shared at the seder, with his own body and blood, which he was about to give to all humankind on the cross. From that time on, when Christians gather in Jesus' memory for their holy meal, the bread and the wine at this table become, through God's power, Jesus' body, broken and shared for all as nourishment, and Jesus' blood, poured out to give people new life.

The name given to this sacrament, *Eucharist,* is derived from a Greek word that means "thanksgiving." So when Christians celebrate the Eucharist, they are thanking and praising God, in the context of a sacred meal, for all the good God has done for them, through Jesus. Ⓒ

### God's Banquet

It is not surprising that Jesus would have chosen a special meal as the setting for giving himself to his friends. In the stories he told that are recounted in the Gospels, Jesus often used the symbol of a banquet to describe sharing in the Kingdom of God. In one story he refers to a wedding feast. In another he describes a great banquet that the invited guests are too busy to attend; upon learning that the invited guests are not coming, the lord of the house shares the meal with street people instead.

*gifts for you*

Ⓒ The word *Eucharist* is derived from a word that means "thanksgiving." We give thanks by appreciating and enjoying gifts. Name five gifts you have received from God. Write a paragraph explaining what you do to enjoy one of them.

⧄ On the surface, the expression "life-giving sacrifice" sounds self-contradictory—gaining something by giving something up. Using three examples, illustrate how this expression is not self-contradictory but is actually true.

On several occasions Jesus shocked his companions by eating dinner with tax collectors, prostitutes, and other outcasts of his day. God's love takes in everyone, especially those thought to be of little value by society, and a meal was one significant setting for Jesus to use in communicating what God's love is like.

It was quite appropriate, then, for Jesus to offer himself to his followers and say, "Do this in memory of me," while sharing food and drink with them. For Jesus the Last Supper was a banquet whose meaning would be made clearer by his death and Resurrection shortly thereafter. In other words by giving of himself, both symbolically through bread and wine and in deed through his death, Jesus brought about a truly human community worth celebrating in the Eucharist.

The Eucharist thus symbolizes how life and human relationships ought to be: All persons are reconciled. All are invited to gather around the table, forgive one another and make peace, encourage one another, sing songs, and share their life with one another—even going so far as to lay down their life for one another.

## Sacrifice: Giving Life to Bring Life

The Last Supper that Jesus shared with his friends cannot be separated from his death on the cross the next day and his being raised from the dead on Easter. At the Eucharist today, Christians remember and thank God for those saving actions of Jesus' life, death, and Resurrection. The sacrament thus recalls Jesus' sacrifice, his pouring out of life in love for all humankind, to bring life to all persons. ⧄

The Eucharist celebrates more than past deeds, however. It is a memorial meal, but it also brings about a *present* reality—that Jesus gives of himself to us in the here and now, bringing new life to us in the process. Although Jesus' death is over once and for all, his self-gift to us goes on today. It is Jesus Christ himself, through the priest, who offers each eucharistic sacrifice.

By being united to Jesus in the Eucharist, we join our own life struggles and "deaths" (small and large) to his. Our dreams, disappointments, joys, and hurts become one with those of Jesus' own life and death.

Those who gather at the Eucharist are called not only to remember and be grateful for Jesus' sacrifice; they are invited to bring their everyday life to the table of the Lord and unite that life with Jesus' sacrifice. Thus their own life is transformed with new meaning; they are "risen" with Jesus. The paschal mystery is not simply a historical event but becomes a present reality in their own life, and the Eucharist celebrates this truth.

The Eucharist, too, looks forward to the future beyond time when all God's people will be united in love through Jesus in the "heavenly banquet" of God's Kingdom.

our struggles become holy

# The Real Presence

Central to Catholics' understanding of the Eucharist is their belief in the real presence of the risen Christ among them, not just in memory but in the present moment, nourishing them and enabling them to give their own energy and life to others, to be "bread for the world."

### Having "Presence"

What is meant by the real presence of Christ? Let's first consider what we mean when we say that someone has "presence." It is a hard quality to define, but we usually recognize presence when we experience it. A story taken from the Jewish Hasidic tradition may help:

Every evening the disciples of Rabbi Baal Shem Tov (the Hasidic founder) gathered to learn. After the evening prayers, the master would go to his room "where the candles would be lit and 'the mysterious Book of Creation' lay open on the table." Those who sought advice were then allowed in as a group to hear the teacher. "One evening as the students left the room, one apologized to the others for monopolizing so much of the Baal Shem's attention. Throughout the entire audience, the master had spoken to him personally. His friend told him not to talk such nonsense. They had all entered the room together and, from the very beginning, the master had spoken only to him. A third, hearing this, laughed and said that they both were mistaken, for their teacher had carried on an intimate conversation with him alone for the entire evening. A fourth and a fifth made the same claim—that the Baal Shem had spoken to them personally, to the exclusion of everyone else. Only then did they realize what had happened, and all fell silent." (Kushner, quoted in *Context*)

To say that someone has presence is to say that the person is fully there, with all his or her resources gathered to attend to others, to self, and to whatever the situation requires.

Think of the difference between driving a car "absently" versus driving a car "presently." When we drive absently, we do not pay attention to the road, the traffic, or the pedestrians. Our mind is a million miles away; in a sense we are just driving on automatic pilot. Driving presently, however, means that we are fully alert to conditions on the road; we are engaged and attentive, ready to respond to whatever situation arises.

To be fully present to another person is to be completely there for her or him, like the Baal Shem Tov, who was so present that each of his disciples felt personally cared for and responded to.

### How Is Jesus Christ Present in the Eucharist?

Catholic belief is that Jesus Christ is present in the Eucharist in four ways:

1. in the person of the minister of the Eucharist, the presiding priest, through whom Jesus offers himself
2. in the word of God, the Scriptures being proclaimed and preached
3. in the people gathered to celebrate by praying and singing
4. especially in the eucharistic species, the bread and wine that are consecrated as Jesus' body and blood

The consecration of the bread and wine is the most sacred moment in the liturgy. Through the power of the Holy Spirit and Christ's words at the Last Supper spoken by the priest ("This is my body. . . . This is the cup of my blood"), the bread and wine are truly changed. These simple signs become Jesus' body and blood in a way that surpasses human understanding. In Catholic theology this change is called **transubstantiation.** The word means that the bread and wine are not only

truly present

symbols of Jesus' presence; through the consecration, they have *become* Christ present.

For Catholics, receiving the consecrated bread and wine in Communion should be a time of the deepest reverence and joy.

### Are We Present Too?

Christ's presence in the Eucharist is not experienced fully by participants unless they are "truly present" also. Here is an example of how you might be present in a different kind of group event:

Imagine that your school's basketball team is playing in the championship game of the state tournament. You are there in the audience, cheering and stomping, your entire being alive to what is happening in that game, to every basket made or missed, to every time the ball changes hands. You are tuned in to the emotional lifts and falls in your team, in your friends among the crowd, and in yourself. You are all one, present to one another and to the drama of the event.

That kind of peak experience of being present does not happen often in groups. Similarly, most celebrations of the Eucharist are not marked by such intense awareness on the part of the participants, and we cannot expect them to be. But imagine what being truly present, tuned in and attentive, to the mystery of the Eucharist would be like. Through the Eucharist Christians proclaim that Christ —Most Intimate Friend, Savior of the World—is actually in their midst. If we could fully experience Christ's presence, then surely any other kind of transforming experience, such as a worldly success, would pale by comparison. E

### Life and Eucharist as One

At one time or another, you may have been involved in a liturgy that so intensely brought together people's lives, concerns, struggles, dreams, and sorrows that the meaning of the Eucharist came alive in a way it never had before. Consider the experience of the young people at one Catholic high school:

present or absent?

E On paper make two columns, one headed "Present" and the other "Absent." In the appropriate column, list the behaviors, attitudes, and thoughts that you have in a situation where you are truly present versus in a situation where you are truly absent.

Everybody knew Jim was the best rock guitar player in his high school. He had steadily improved since grade school. By his junior year, he had his own group that played at school dances and occasionally at local clubs. He had even played with some professional musicians from the area who recognized his talent. In September of his senior year, however, Jim complained of severe back pain. By December he was in a hospital, barely able to move his lower body. By April he was dead. Cancer had eaten away at Jim's spinal column, ending the life of a promising musician and beloved human being.

What were his friends to do? Practically the entire senior class and many others attended the funeral Mass. Jim was prayed for during school. He was given special mention in the yearbook. Still everyone wanted to do more. Then someone found out that the family was struggling to pay off the heavy debt incurred by Jim's long hospitalization. So the students decided to have a benefit dance. A musical celebration and gathering of friends seemed like an especially appropriate way to remember Jim, and two bands gladly volunteered their time.

Held at the local parish hall, the benefit dance was jammed. To a stranger the dance probably would not have seemed different from any other high school dance—vibrant music and much excitement. Given a closer look, however, it would have been obvious that this was not an ordinary dance. The police were present as usual, but they weren't needed and merely strolled around the parking lot, enjoying the music. Inside, the mood seemed to be a mixture of cheer and sadness. More people than usual smiled at one another. Lots of little groups were

At the Eucharist our lives become one with Christ's life and death, and so also with his Resurrection.

a special spirit

hope and fear, love and longing, joy and trust amid hardship and sorrow. The lyrics that most people were only faintly aware of in church now sank in and hit home. Some people had tears in their eyes.

At Communion, friends of Jim came forward to offer the consecrated bread and wine to their fellow students. Looking into the faces of those giving and receiving Communion, an observer might have said what the pagans used to say about the early Christians: "See how they love one another!" For those participating in the Mass that night, life and Eucharist had become one.

The people privileged to be part of that celebration had experienced the real presence of Christ, fully alive in their midst, in one another and in the sharing of the bread and wine. It was almost as if Jim, like Jesus, had been there with them too, giving them a gift to treasure even in his death. Many of those people would later carry that memory of a transforming Eucharist to the other, more ordinary celebrations of the Mass they were accustomed to. The Eucharist could never quite be just a routine to them again, but a ritual full of meaning—at some times experienced more deeply than at other times.

## The Challenge of the Eucharist: Be the Body of Christ

The incident about Jim, his death, and his classmates' caring response to his family points to the crucial challenge that the Eucharist poses to us. We are challenged in every eucharistic celebration not only to *receive* the body of Christ, under the forms of bread and

dancing together. A special spirit was present—a spirit of friendliness, of togetherness. The promise of a great guitar player had become the reality of a closer, warmer community.

At the end of the evening, around midnight, someone suggested to the campus minister that they close the event with a Mass for anyone who wanted to stay. Almost everyone stayed, even those who didn't usually get into that sort of thing. It just felt right to be there.

Jim's best friend from his band played piano, and the parish hall rang with heartfelt singing that expressed wine, but to *be* the Body of Christ in our everyday life. This transformation is possible only because of the grace of being nourished and strengthened by Jesus in the sacrament of the Eucharist. ⊡

### Becoming What You Receive

The students at Jim's high school discovered the link between the Eucharist and the rest of life when they experienced themselves that night as a welcoming, inclusive community whose members shared one another's concerns. They ached at losing Jim, but they also realized that even in their loss—or perhaps because of it—a new spirit was being born among them as a community. At a level that most of them were only beginning to comprehend, they were uniting their experience with Jesus' death and Resurrection. They were becoming the risen Body of Christ that they were also receiving.

### A Mirror of Everyday Life

The members of the early church recognized that the Eucharist was meant to mirror the way they lived. This is how the Acts of the Apostles describes the Eucharist fitting into the lives of the first Christians:

> All who believed were together and had all things in common; they would sell their possessions and goods and distribute the proceeds to all, as any had need. Day by day, as they spent much time together in the temple, they broke bread at home and ate their food with glad and generous hearts, praising God and having the goodwill of all the people. And day by day the Lord added to their number those who were being saved. (2:44–47)

### Looking at Reality

The Eucharist challenges us to be a welcoming community that offers peace,

⊡ The experience of community is essential to celebrating the Eucharist. Identify a community to which you belong. What shared values and purposes sustain it? How important is this community to you? Write about what you bring to this community and what you get from it.

▦ *Student art:* Photo by Thomas Eyre, Bishop Shanahan High School, Downingtown, Pennsylvania

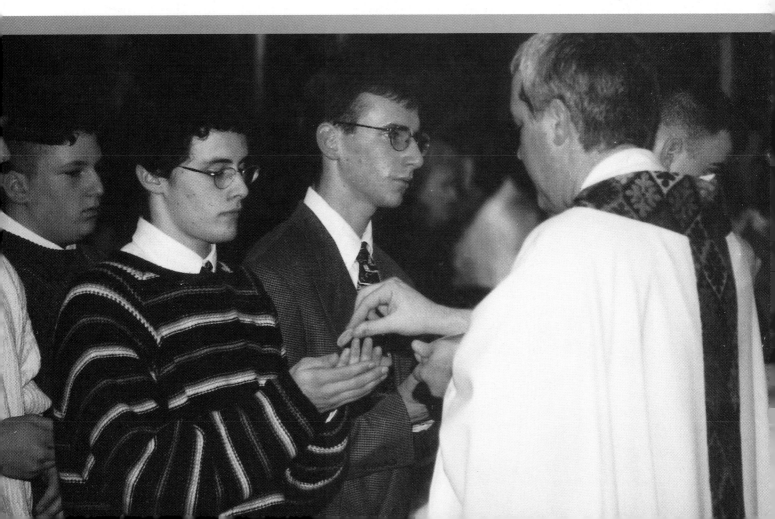

*a challenge*

Ⓖ Which one of the descriptions about the difficulty of living out the Eucharist seems most challenging to you? Write your reflections in a paragraph.

Ⓗ Hunger can take many forms besides physical hunger. Write a one-page essay about a particular hunger that you see in your community.

reconciliation, and sharing to all persons, not just to those we want to associate with as friends. But think about the reality of our church, school, family, and neighborhood communities.

- We can proclaim in the Eucharist that we are open to everyone. But strangers or outsiders may still feel unwelcome in our communities. It is easier to talk about the ideals of unity and inclusiveness than to live them.
- Part of the ritual of the Mass is to offer one another a sign of peace. It is relatively easy to reach over and shake hands with the person next to us in the pew and say, "Peace be with you." It is much harder, however, to reach out to people in our life with whom we have a conflict and to create genuine peace with them.
- We can eat of the same bread and drink wine from the same cup in the Eucharist, and thereby believe that we

share the body and blood of Christ. Yet we may not be "breaking the bread of our life" outside of Mass—sharing what we have, nurturing one another, and sacrificing for one another. To be meaningful, the act of sharing Jesus Christ in the consecrated bread and wine has to be lived out in the rest of life. Ⓖ

The more that Christians share a sense of community, the more they want to celebrate the Eucharist together. If even a small number of people share something of their life during the week, then for them, participating in the Eucharist on Sunday will be much more meaningful. A handsome church building, good music, and trained readers will always enhance genuine liturgies, but the most important element in really celebrating the Eucharist is a sense of belonging, sharing, and community.

### Bread for a Hungry World

The challenge of the Eucharist extends beyond the limits of our own communities and into the wider world, where Christians can respond to many forms of hunger and thus become "bread for the world":

- Millions in our own society and around the world, especially children, go hungry every day. The reasons for this are complex, but chief among them is a gravely unjust worldwide economic system that continues to widen the gap between rich people and poor people, rich nations and poor nations.
- In addition to enduring obvious and glaring deprivation from physical hunger and poverty, some people also experience hunger for hope, for freedom to make decisions that affect their own destiny, for companionship and a sense of community, and for the opportunity to be creative with their life.

*Student art:* Acrylic painting by Christine Della Cioppa, Melbourne Central Catholic High School, Melbourne, Florida

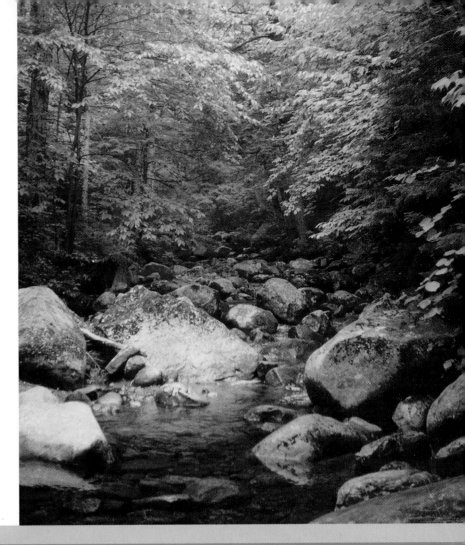

- The whole of creation is threatened by unwise human practices that are destroying many of the Earth's resources and delicate ecosystems. The Earth is hungry to be treated with justice and to have its health restored. When Jesus walked the Earth, the world was hungry for love, justice, peace, and freedom. Jesus gave himself as nourishment to fill that hunger. Today the world is still hungry. Christians now live on a planet that is desperate for hope in the future. The Eucharist, celebrated with conviction, challenges participants. It remains a hopeful sign that Jesus Christ is still nourishing the world through Christians who give themselves to fill the hunger of the world. ⊞

All of creation is hungry for justice.
※ *Student art:* Photo by Kristin Nienkirchen, Immaculate Heart Academy, Washington Township, New Jersey

## For Review

1. What is the sacrament of the Eucharist? What did Vatican Council II say about the centrality of the Eucharist?

2. Why is the word *Eucharist* an appropriate name for this sacrament?

3. Why was a sacred meal or banquet significant as a setting for the Eucharist in Jesus' day?

4. In terms of Jesus' sacrifice, what are Christians who gather at the Eucharist invited to do?

5. How is the Eucharist a celebration of the past, the present, and the future?

6. In what four ways is Jesus Christ present in the Eucharist?

7. What does transubstantiation mean?

8. What is the crucial challenge that the Eucharist poses to Christians?

9. Give three examples from the textbook to show how the reality of our communities may contradict the meaning of the Eucharist.

## "They'll Feed You"

The following account illustrates how one child saw the connection between the Eucharist and hunger in the human family:

Margaret, seven years old, had recently made her First Communion. Her mother, her brother Joe, 14, and she were traveling from Norfolk, Virginia, to New York state to visit relatives. They traveled by bus overnight and arrived in Manhattan very early in the morning.

When they got to Port Authority, New York's huge bus station, they saw many homeless people sleeping there, washing in the bathrooms, getting ready for the day. Joe and Margaret had never seen homeless people before, and their mom had to explain who they were and why they were there.

Since it was so early, and their bus to upstate New York didn't leave until later, they went into the city to sightsee. At that hour, the only thing open was St. Patrick's Cathedral. At altars all around St. Patrick's, they saw priests celebrating Mass. They also saw people sleeping in the pews. "More people without homes," Joe said softly.

Margaret, still excited over being able to receive Communion, began to ask her mother if she could go to Communion now. "Not *now*," said her mother. "We don't have time for Mass. We're sightseeing."

"Please," begged Margaret, until her mother relented. She told Margaret, however, that if she was going to go to Communion, she had to sit quietly for a while and pray first.

So Margaret chose to sit and prepare for Eucharist while her mother and brother continued to tour St. Patrick's. As they came back down the aisle, the two saw that seven-year-old Margaret was speaking to one of the men who had been sleeping in the pew in front of her.

As her mother hurried back, she caught the conversation that her daughter was having with the scruffy man: "I know you must be hungry. They have some bread and wine at those altars. I'm sure if you ask them, they'll feed you."

Margaret, at seven, may not have been able to explain about how we are all the Body of Christ, but she knew in her heart that we have to act like brothers and sisters, no matter who we are. She saw clearly that food for hungry people was part of what Jesus meant by "Take and eat." (Northup, "Why Is the World Hungry?")

# The Ritual of the Eucharist: Symbolic Actions and Words

On the night before he died, Jesus blessed and shared bread and wine with his disciples, identifying these as his own body and blood. Referring to his actions, he said to the disciples, "Do this in remembrance of me" (Luke 22:19). Thus, Catholics have always seen the Eucharist as their central sacrament, a holy ritual filled with great meaning, to be done in memory of Jesus, and with Jesus, until the end of time.

## The Eucharist as the Whole Celebration

Catholics use the term *Eucharist* in a variety of ways, all of which are correct but have slightly different meanings:

- The whole celebration of the **Mass** is referred to as the Eucharist. (The word *Mass* comes from the Latin word *missa*, one of the parting words of the priest

The Eucharist can be adapted to the customs of different cultures, but its essentials are the same wherever it is celebrated around the world—here, in India.

a universal
celebration

a continuing presence

▣ One purpose of a Benediction service is simply to gaze at the Eucharist and realize how wonderful it is that Christ is present. Name some ways that you could keep alive the memory of someone dear to you who is physically gone but present with you nonetheless.

in Latin: *Ite, missa est,* meaning "Go, you are sent forth" or "Go, you are 'missioned.'" It is crucial to the Mass that the assembly is sent forth with a mission—to share Christ with the world.)

- The second part of the Mass, the part that follows the liturgy of the word, is called the liturgy of the Eucharist. This includes the consecration of the bread and wine and the Communion rite.
- **Communion**—consuming the body and blood of Christ under the forms of bread and wine, or only of bread—is the way that an individual receives the sacrament of the Eucharist.
- Catholics believe that the **Blessed Sacrament,** the consecrated bread not consumed during the Mass but reserved in the tabernacle, is Jesus Christ—really present, to be honored and adored. The Blessed Sacrament itself is called the Eucharist. ▣

In this discussion of the Eucharist's symbolic actions and words, we will use the term *Eucharist* to mean the whole Mass. The Eucharist comprises two main parts:

1. the **liturgy of the word**—that is, the proclaiming of the word of God in the Scriptures
2. the **liturgy of the Eucharist**—that is, the outpouring of thanks to God that includes the consecration and sharing of the bread and wine in which Christ is present

These two main parts are surrounded by the **gathering rite** at the beginning of Mass and the **dismissal rite** at the end.

## The Essential Actions

Essential to every eucharistic celebration are the following four actions, which take place during the liturgy of the word and the liturgy of the Eucharist.

I. **Word.** The proclamation of the word of God in the Scriptures
II. **Thanksgiving.** The offering of thanks to God for all the blessings of creation and God's saving acts in history, above all for the gift of Jesus Christ, his Son
III. **Consecration.** The action of Christ, through the priest's saying the words, to change the bread and wine into Christ's body and blood, by the power of the Holy Spirit
IV. **Communion.** The participation in the sacred meal by receiving Jesus Christ in the consecrated bread and wine

Only a validly ordained priest can preside at the Eucharist, pronouncing the words of consecration. But the whole assembly joins with him as the Body of Christ, offering the Mass.

You may be familiar with a ritual called a **Communion service.** Your school may have such services, and parishes that have limited access to priests often use them when they are not able to celebrate the Mass itself. In some ways a Communion service resembles a Mass, because it too has a liturgy of the word and a rite of Communion (using bread consecrated at a Mass at an earlier time). Some of the prayers may be the same as those prayed at the Eucharist, including the Lord's Prayer and the sign of peace. But this kind of service is not a Mass, because it lacks a presiding priest who leads the people in offering the Eucharistic Prayer, including the essential action of the consecration. Those who receive Communion at such a service truly receive the body of Christ, but they have not participated in the whole action of the Eucharist, which differs essentially from a service of the word with Communion.

# The Eucharist in Outline

The movement of the Eucharist from beginning to end of a Sunday Mass typically follows this outline:

## 1. Gathering Rite
- Gathering song and processional
- Penitential rite ("Lord, have mercy . . ." or "I confess to Almighty God")
- Glory to God (always omitted during Advent and Lent)
- Opening prayer

## 2. Liturgy of the Word
- First reading, from the Old Testament or, in some seasons, the Acts of the Apostles or the Book of Revelation
- Responsorial psalm, with antiphon between verses
- Second reading, usually from the letters of Paul or another apostolic writer
- Alleluia and verse to welcome the Gospel
- Gospel reading
- Homily
- The Nicene Creed or the renewal of baptismal promises
- General intercessions, or the prayer of the faithful, that is, petitions for the needs of the church and the world

## 3. Liturgy of the Eucharist
- Preparation of the gifts of bread and wine
- Prayer over the gifts
- Preface and Holy, Holy, Holy
- Eucharistic Prayer, the prayer of the whole Body of Christ voiced by the presiding priest
  - Remembrance and thanksgiving for creation and God's deeds
  - Invoking of the Holy Spirit (the *epiclesis*) to transform the gifts into the body and blood of Jesus
  - Institution narrative ("On the night he was betrayed . . ."), which includes the consecration
  - Memorial acclamation ("Christ has died, Christ is risen . . .")
  - Remembrance of Christ's Passion, death, Resurrection, and Ascension
  - Prayers of intercession, in union with all the saints, for the church and its leaders, for the dead, for the world
  - The Doxology ("Through him, with him, in him . . ."), followed by the Great Amen
- Communion rite
  - The Lord's Prayer
  - The sign of peace
  - The breaking of the bread ("Lamb of God")
  - Communion procession and receiving Communion
  - Prayer after Communion

## 4. Dismissal Rite
- Blessing of the assembly
- Sending forth and commissioning ("Go in peace, to love and serve the Lord.")
- Recessional, often with closing song

encountering God

As befits its status, the **Lectionary,** which is the book of readings used at Mass, is carried and raised high in the liturgical procession, kissed, and generally treated with a great deal of reverence. The readings are understood to be God's revelation, just as Jesus is God's revelation. On Sundays three readings are usually given: one from the Old Testament, one from the letters of Paul or other apostolic writers, and one from the Gospels. Often the people sing a response to the first reading as a way of taking the words to heart. The people sing "Alleluia!" before the Gospel reading and stand during that reading to show their joy at hearing of Jesus, the living Word of God. All these rituals symbolize that the proclamation of the word is special and sacred. The priest's homily after the readings is intended to help the people discover the meaning of the word for their own life. ⬚

Just as the memory of Jesus remains alive for Christians in the breaking of the bread and the sharing of the cup, so too is Jesus Christ alive for Christians, present to them, in their hearing the words and stories of Jesus' life and community.

In response to the proclamation of the word, the congregation proclaims, on Sundays, the Nicene Creed or the renewal of baptismal promises. Then follows the final act of the liturgy of the word, the general intercessions, also called the **prayer of the faithful.** The needs of the whole church and the world, as well as the needs of the local community, are brought in trust to God.

## Proclaiming the Word of God

The ceremony that surrounds the proclamation of the word of God indicates that the reading of the Scriptures is not simply for getting information. It is an opportunity for encountering God.

## The Symbolism of Bread

When the early Christians talked about the Eucharist, they said that they gathered for the "breaking of the bread." As the most basic and essential food of the people in Jesus' culture, bread often represented life and was thus an appropriate symbol for the Eucharist.

## Gift of God and Work of Human Hands

Bread is a basic food for many people and is closely associated with God's and nature's bountifulness. Images of vast wheat fields swaying in the wind or stalks of wheat beside a plate evoke a sense of gratitude for God's gifts to us, especially for our "daily bread." At the same time, bread is the product of human work. It is wheat that has been ground, kneaded, and baked. Bread is both a gift of God and a work of human hands. K

## Blessed, Broken, Given for Others

In the ritual of the Eucharist, bread is transformed. It becomes Christ offered up, broken, and given to his people. The gathered people are reminded that they too are Christ—meant to be bread that is offered up, broken, and given for others.

Consider the example of parents. Fathers and mothers offer up themselves, the "bread of their own lives," to nourish their children. By working to support the children with food, clothing, and shelter, they provide physical nourishment. In addition, they give their love and energy to surround their children with an emotionally and spiritually nourishing home. In a similar way, you have probably had experiences of giving yourself, "breaking the bread of your own life," for the sake of others.

Bread is a powerful symbol; breaking bread is an action that adds to its symbolism, and sharing bread adds another dimension of meaning. However, eating bread most clearly brings out its natural significance. Eating the bread implies gaining life from it. Similarly, receiving the body of Christ in Communion means sharing life in the Body of Christ—the church.

inspiring stories

J The readings at Mass are sacred stories meant to inspire and affirm the faith of the listeners. Ask an older member of your family to tell you a story from the past that she or he found inspiring. Record the story in writing or on tape.

K Compare home-made bread with factory-made bread. Which seems to better symbolize the meaning of the Eucharist and why?

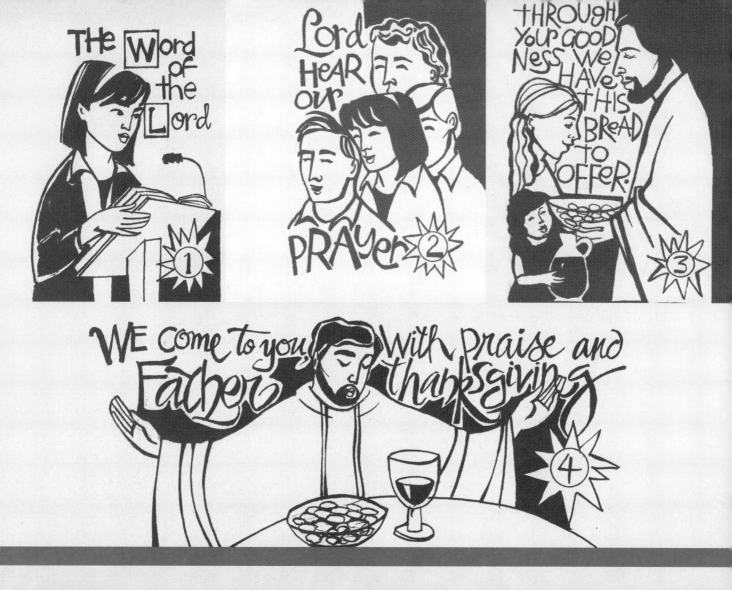

# The Liturgy of the Word

### First Reading
A reading from the book of the prophet Isaiah.

> Rise up in splendor! Your light has come,
>   the glory of the Lord shines upon you.
>                                           (60:1)

The Word of the Lord.
  Thanks be to God.

### Gospel Reading
A reading from the holy Gospel according to Matthew.

> When Jesus was born in Bethlehem of Judea, in the days of King Herod, behold, magi from the east arrived in Jerusalem. (2:1)

The Gospel of the Lord.
  Praise to you, Lord Jesus Christ.

### Prayer of the Faithful
For peace in our families, community, and world, we pray,
  Lord, hear our prayer.

# The Liturgy of the Eucharist

### Presentation of the Gifts
Blessed are you, Lord, God of all creation.
Through your goodness we have this bread to offer,
which earth has given and human hands have made.
It will become for us the bread of life.
  Blessed be God for ever.

**Eucharistic Prayer**

Father, you are holy indeed,
and all creation rightly gives you praise.
All life, all holiness comes from you
through your Son, Jesus Christ our Lord,
by the working of the Holy Spirit. . . .
And so, Father, we bring you these gifts.
We ask you to make them holy by the power of
    your Spirit,
that they may become the body and blood
of your Son, our Lord Jesus Christ. . . .
On the night he was betrayed,
he took bread and gave you thanks and praise.
He broke the bread, gave it to his disciples, and
    said:
**Take this, all of you, and eat it:**
**this is my body which will be given up for you.**
When supper was ended, he took the cup.
Again he gave you thanks and praise,
gave the cup to his disciples, and said:

**Take this, all of you, and drink from it:**
**this is the cup of my blood,**
**the blood of the new and everlasting covenant.**
**It will be shed for you and for all**
**so that sins may be forgiven.**
**Do this in memory of me.**

Let us proclaim the mystery of faith:
    Christ has died, Christ is risen, Christ will come
      again.

**Communion Rite**

Lamb of God, you take away the sins of the world:
    have mercy on us.
Lamb of God, you take away the sins of the world:
    grant us peace.
The body of Christ.
    Amen.
The blood of Christ.
    Amen.

# The Symbolism of Wine

We can survive for about forty days without food but for very few days—perhaps five—without water. Consequently, drink is just as essential to life as food, as basic a "staff of life" as bread. Like bread, wine is both a natural gift of God and the work of human hands. It is the part of nature's bounty that has been harvested and worked on until it becomes a pleasing drink.

### A Sign of Celebration

Wine is not a necessary type of drink, as water is. Wine adds a hint of celebration to the basic symbolism of drink as necessary for survival. As a sign of celebration, wine is an appropriate, awesome symbol for the blood that Christ willingly shed in freeing hu-manity from sin and death. Christians sharing the cup of wine at the Eucharist celebrate the life-giving sacrifice of Christ while committing themselves to pour out their lives for others. And that is a joyful act.

### A Common Cup, Not Individual Cups

Sharing the cup of wine was ritually as significant for the early Christians as drinking the wine itself. They knew that Jesus' blood was shed for all men and women, so they shared joyfully in receiving his life. Thus in the present Catholic eucharistic celebration, each person does not receive an individual cup; rather, everyone drinks from a common cup. Realizing the commitment implied by receiving the Eucharist can bring people to desire the community support symbolized by sharing the cup.

For many centuries before the Second Vatican Council, the Catholic practice was that only the priest who presided at a Mass drank from the cup. This was not the original intent of the Eucharist, however. The cup, as well as the bread, was meant to be shared by all the believers. Now, in many parishes on Sundays, people are invited to partake from the cup after receiving the bread.

the Eucharist's essentials

## For Review

10. What are the two main parts of the Mass?

11. What four actions are essential to every eucharistic celebration? Why is a Communion service essentially different from a Mass?

12. At a typical Sunday Eucharist, from what sources are the three Scripture readings taken?

13. Why is bread an appropriate symbol for the Eucharist?

14. Why is wine an appropriate symbol for the Eucharist?

# The Eucharist's History

## Its Jewish Roots

More than any other sacrament, the Eucharist reveals the Jewish roots of Christianity. That is to say, both major parts of the Mass—the liturgy of the Eucharist and the liturgy of the word—began as Jewish rituals.

### A Jewish Meal: Roots of the Liturgy of the Eucharist

At the Last Supper, Jesus celebrated a Jewish community meal, very likely the Passover seder, with his friends. Meals, especially family meals, are a very important form of worship for Jews. Meals can be steeped in ritual; the Passover meal, which celebrates God's liberation of the Israelites from slavery in Egypt, is a notable example. Often, bread and wine play a central role in the ritual of family meals. And "giving thanks" is generally the theme of a meal. So when Jesus gathered his friends to share bread and wine, he was not doing anything strange or uncommon.

Jesus' actions and words at the Last Supper were unique. First, he identified the bread and wine with himself and with his impending death on the cross, implying that the body and blood he was soon to give up would be the source of liberation for humankind. Second, Jesus commanded the Apostles to continue to share bread and wine in his memory, as his body and blood.

In the early years of the Christian church, on Sunday, the day on which Jesus was resurrected, believers gathered for a meal, which included breaking the bread and sharing the cup in Jesus' memory. In this ritual, believers commemorated the Resurrection and experienced the presence of the risen Jesus with them.

A Jewish family celebrates a Passover seder today.

This shared ritual meal was the origin of the liturgy of the Eucharist as we know it today.

### A Synagogue Service: Roots of the Liturgy of the Word

A Jewish synagogue service traditionally centers around hearing the word of God in the Hebrew Scriptures (what is known as the Old Testament to Christians). The people's prayers, the various songs and chants, and the teaching by the rabbi support that central action. For the Jews the Lord is present in the written word.

The earliest Christians, who were also Jews, naturally attended the synagogue services on Saturday, the Sabbath. But eventually, when the Christians began admitting Gentile converts who were not obligated to keep the Jewish Law, the non-Christian Jews regarded the Christians as a threat to needed Jewish unity. (The Jews had just been crushed by the Romans and fostered an intense nationalistic unity in order to survive.) So the Christians were no longer allowed to attend synagogue services.

The Christians then went their own way, devising their own service of the word, which probably incorporated the letters of Saint Paul, and eventually the Gospel stories, with readings from the Hebrew Scriptures. The early Christians soon combined this service with the eucharistic meal and celebrated it as one service on Sunday: the liturgy of the word and the liturgy of the Eucharist. Thus the basic elements of the Mass as we know it today were established.

## From Supper to Sacrifice

### A "Love Feast"

In the beginning of the church's history, the Eucharist was celebrated as a fellowship meal, or "love feast," called an **agape.** Christians shared the food that each person brought to the Sunday assembly, and they referred to this meal as the Lord's Supper. As the number of members increased, the meal was gradually reduced to a simpler fare of bread and wine, the essential elements of the Eucharist.

For many years after the full meal ceased being common practice, however, Christians still brought food to their services to share with poor people. Today the offertory collection echoes that early spirit of giving at the Eucharist.

*a seder today*

⃞ Interview a Jewish person who is familiar with the Passover seder about how this ritual meal is celebrated today. Write down any similarities you note between the seder and the Eucharist.

⃞ How could church communities share their resources with poor people today? List at least five suggestions.

magnificent ceremonies

### A Ritual Meal of Sacrifice

Over the first three centuries of Christianity, the Eucharist evolved from a fellowship meal to a ritual meal. Some variations in its celebration existed from community to community, but the basic pattern was the same. The eucharistic part of the ritual consisted of an offering (gifts of bread and wine), a thanksgiving prayer over the offered gifts in the earlier Jewish style, a breaking of the bread, and a receiving of the bread and wine by all the participants.

More and more, Christians realized that by participating in this ritual meal, they were entering into the mystery of Christ's sacrifice, death, and Resurrection. They were doing more than sharing a love feast; they were participating in their own redemption.

# From Participants to Silent Spectators

### An Elaborate Ceremony

After Christianity was declared a legal religion in the fourth century, the church's rituals went public. That change set the stage, by the end of the sixth century, for the development of a highly elaborate, almost regal ceremony around what had once been a simple sharing of food and drink. Prayers that had once been offered spontaneously by the presiding bishop were written down and standardized. The place of worship moved from homes, where rituals were carried out secretly during times of persecution, to magnificent church buildings that Christians were proud to build and to celebrate Mass in.

Saint Maurice Cathedral, Angers, France

N The Mass re-enacts a great story, but we can find any story boring if we do not really "hear" it. Rewrite the story of the Last Supper in the first person—as if you were actually there. Make the story as real and as interesting as possible.

The dolphin is a symbol of resurrection and transformation, realities that are made present to us in the Eucharist. *Student art (facing page):* Pastel drawing by Erin Bode, Mercy High School, Omaha, Nebraska

## Less and Less of a Role for the People

The shift in emphasis from the Eucharist as a community meal to the Eucharist as a highly elaborate and dramatic ceremony of sacrifice naturally affected participation in the ritual. Specifically the priest-presider did more and more of the action while the people in attendance participated less and less. By the Middle Ages, priests were "saying" Mass while the people watched in silence. In fact priests often said Mass privately on weekdays, or with only a single server present, for the special intention of some member of the congregation. The community dimension of the Eucharist had all but disappeared.

## Worship from a Distance

At the same time that people's participation in the Eucharist was lessening, the significance of the wine was being de-emphasized, and the bread became more important as a symbol. In fact the awesomeness of the presence of Christ in the bread was so strongly stressed that people hesitated to receive Communion. They contented themselves with viewing the bread elevated at the consecration. People received Communion so infrequently that the church had to require that the faithful receive it at least once a year.

Also, with the emphasis on devotion from a distance, the idea of "gathering around the table" faded. As a result the table became an ornate altar that was set against a decorated wall. The priest, with his back to the people, faced the altar and led the people in the holy sacrifice. Everyone faced the same direction, but the people were unable to see what was going on at the altar. N

## An Unfamiliar Language

At one time in the early church, the language of the Mass in the West had been changed from Greek to Latin be-cause Latin was the language of the people. But in the Middle Ages, Latin continued to be used, even though fewer and fewer of the common people were able to understand it. (The use of Latin in the Mass was standard up until the 1960s.)

## The Presence of God Revealed

As chapter 6 explained, the Council of Trent further solidified the Eucharist as an intricate, standardized sacrament filled with many secondary symbols, prayers, and gestures. In short the original, central rituals had become much-added-onto. The dramatic nature of the eucharistic celebration made attendance at Mass seem more like watching a performance than like sharing a meal. Nevertheless, the awe-inspiring ritual of the Eucharist revealed God's presence through Jesus to millions of faithful Christians of those times, just as the Eucharist continues to reveal God today, but in a simpler, more participatory way.

# A Return to Participation and Table Companionship

To restore the original, communal spirit of the Eucharist, the Second Vatican Council of the 1960s called for vast reforms.

## Changes in the Liturgy

These quite-noticeable changes in the Mass came in the aftermath of Vatican Council II:

- The altar facing the wall became once again a table set in the midst of or close to the congregation, with the priest facing the people.
- The Latin language, used for centuries to celebrate the Mass, was replaced by the common, spoken languages of the

cultures in which the Mass was being celebrated.

- Prayers and responses were spoken by the entire assembly, not just by the altar servers.
- The altar rail that separated the congregation from the sanctuary was removed.
- Kneeling for Communion at the altar rail was replaced by the earlier custom of standing while receiving Communion to express joy and thanksgiving.
- People were invited to take the Communion bread in their hands and to chew the bread, whereas it had once been considered proper to receive Communion only on the tongue.
- Communion wine as well as bread was offered to the whole congregation.
- Singing by the whole congregation was encouraged.

- Prayers of petition addressing the immediate concerns and needs of the people and the wider world were added.
- Laypeople were invited to participate in special roles as lectors (readers), members of the offertory procession, and eucharistic ministers (distributors of Communion). ◙

### Christ Present in the People

The changes brought about by Vatican Council II reaffirmed a simple truth that had become obscured over the centuries: Those who celebrate the Eucharist together are a symbol, with the bread and wine, of Christ's presence. People are to enter actively into the Eucharist, be transformed by it, and live it out. The homily, or sermon, following the readings is intended to bring the word of God

welcome the changes?

◙ Imagine that you were a Catholic in the 1960s and early 1970s when many changes in the Mass, such as the changes listed on this page, came about. Which changes would you have found most striking or noticeable? Would you have welcomed the changes? Why or why not? Write down your reflections.

resurrection
life

# Why Sunday Mass?

The topic of Sunday Mass often brings up the following comments by teenagers:

- "Mass is so boring; it's the same old thing every week."
- "I don't get anything out of going to Mass."
- "I don't need Mass; I worship God in my own way."
- "I don't think Mass should be forced on people."

## Why Mass at All?

All these statements point to a question that has been asked by many young people: "Why should I go to Mass on Sunday?" In several ways the broader question about simply going to Mass—"Why celebrate the Eucharist at all?"—has already been answered in this chapter. Mass is a way to welcome God's presence in our life and a reminder of Jesus' loving sacrifice for us. Catholics also proclaim their faith at Mass, are nourished in that faith, and gain the encouragement of other Christians in living out their faith. In Christians' commitment to celebrate and be the Body of Christ, the Eucharist is not an optional part of being Catholic.

## Why Should I Go to Mass on Sunday?

Behind the question "Why should I go to Mass on Sunday?" lies an issue worth reflecting on—why has the church traditionally placed such great emphasis on Sunday worship and made it an obligation for Catholics to attend Mass on Sunday or on the evening before?

The early Christians celebrated the Eucharist on Sunday because it was the day of the Resurrection. Once Christianity became legitimate, Sunday became the Lord's day, or the day of rest. (And the Lord's day was considered to begin on the Saturday evening before.) An early Christian writer taught that anyone not in the assembly at Sunday Eucharist weakened the church. This suggests that Christians recognized very early on that all the church members together make up the unified Body of Christ. Every Eucharist clearly symbolizes that unified Body. In the earliest reference to the Eucharist in the New Testament, Paul writes, "We who are many are one body, for we all partake of the one bread" (1 Corinthians 10:17). But celebrating the Eucharist on Sunday, when all Catholics are called to participate, most strongly signifies the total, worldwide nature of the Body of Christ.

Receiving the Eucharist at Sunday Mass is unique because it reminds us that the Body of Christ is not only the bread that is eaten but also the entire, worldwide church. Presence at the Sunday Eucharist strengthens the message of support and nourishment for oneself and for others; absence weakens that message. As a symbolically rich day, then, Sunday is a fitting time to celebrate as a community the most pivotal of the seven sacraments.

alive in people's experiences. Presenting the bread and wine at the offertory symbolizes bringing the everyday work and experiences of life to God.

### The Eucharist: At the Heart of the Church's Life

In most Catholic parishes throughout the world, the Eucharist is celebrated in a special way on Sundays, and many parishes have daily Mass as well. Even in places where a priest is not present every week, communities of Catholic Christians gather regularly for a worship service centering on receiving Communion. A number of Catholics attend Mass daily for much of their life, finding in the Eucharist the spiritual nourishment that sustains them. In many Catholic schools, when a major occasion or event like a graduation is celebrated, the Eucharist is typically a central part of the festivities. More than any other sacrament, the Eucharist celebrates Christ's real presence and is thus at the heart of the church's life. P

Through the Eucharist, Jesus continues to be present to us today as he was to the Apostles at the Last Supper: at the table with his friends, in the bread and the wine, and in the sharing of life, sacrificing, and finding of new life by his body and blood. And through the Eucharist, those who receive the body of Christ are strengthened to *be* the body of Christ for others in their life.

*a spirited Sunday*

P Plan a Sunday for you and your friends that would reflect a spirit of worship, recreation, thanksgiving, and enjoyment. Present in writing an outline of your Sunday of worship and rest.

# the Eucharist's history

## For Review

15. What are the Jewish roots of the liturgy of the Eucharist and the liturgy of the word?

16. What effect on people's participation in the Eucharist was caused by the shift in emphasis from its celebration as a community meal to its celebration as a highly elaborate ceremony of sacrifice?

17. Name five changes in the Mass that came about from the reforms of Vatican Council II.

# The Eucharist: Linking Past, Present, and Future

A bronze sculpture of the Last Supper graces the upper room in Jerusalem, the site where it is believed that Jesus and his disciples shared the first Eucharist.

By now it is probably apparent why full initiation into the Catholic faith comes only with the third sacrament of initiation, the Eucharist. The life of the whole church centers on the Eucharist, in which the past, present, and future are brought together in a powerful ritual. To be a full member of the church is to enter into that mystery.

At the Last Supper, Jesus said of his actions, "Do this in remembrance of me." Thus in the Mass the church ritually re-enacts the closing events of his life on Earth. Through the church's symbolic action, Jesus is not relegated to the dead past but instead remains a living presence in the members of his Body, the church. The Eucharist expresses the present condition of the church community, which must receive in order to give the nourishment that will make the world whole again. And the Eucharist anticipates the future Reign of God, the "heavenly banquet" promised by Jesus, while it helps to make that longed-for future a reality even in the present.

In the Mass Catholics unite with all other Christians throughout the world and down through the ages in celebrating Jesus. Because of him Catholics can gather around the table and be one family, at least for a few moments. The Eucharist becomes a constant reminder —all the more powerful because it is a ritual—of the words of the Lord's Prayer: "Thy Kingdom come . . . on Earth as it is in heaven."

# 10

# Reconciliation
## celebrating forgiveness

sin washed away

**Gentle God,** wash me clean, set me free.
Release me from my sins that weigh me down,
liberating God, set me free.
Give me courage to choose wisely,
empowering God, set me free.
Heal me with your forgiveness,
compassionate God, set me free.

Amen.

Two of the Catholic church's seven sacraments recall and bring into our midst the healing ministry of Jesus: the sacraments of Reconciliation and Anointing of the Sick. We will consider Reconciliation in this chapter and Anointing in chapter 11.

The sacrament of **Reconciliation**, also called the sacrament of **Penance**, celebrates the unfailing forgiveness that God extends to us. In his public ministry, Jesus communicated God's forgiveness over and over to those who approached him with sincere faith: "Your sins are forgiven."

Through this sacrament, members of the Catholic church receive God's mercy and forgiveness for their sins and are reconciled with God, with themselves, and with the church—the whole community that is wounded by their sins. The sacrament of Reconciliation also provides a way for us to heal our spirit by telling the story of our own brokenness and failings in confession to a priest, who represents God and the church community.

The following Scandinavian folktale gives us a way to understand the intent behind the sacrament of Reconciliation:

# healing
# our spirit

## Once there was a man

from Iceland, a great poet and storyteller named Ivar. He won fame for his storytelling in the court of Istine, the king of Norway. King Istine thought much of Ivar and bestowed many favors upon him and even upon his brother Thorfin, who also lived in the court.

One day, Ivar's brother decided to return to his native Iceland. Before Thorfin left, however, Ivar asked him to bear a message to Adney, a young woman whom Ivar had loved and who had loved him since childhood. Ivar asked his brother to tell Adney that he would return in the spring to marry her.

When Thorfin arrived in Iceland, he himself fell in love with Adney and she with him. And so they married. Thus when spring came and Ivar arrived in Iceland to marry Adney, he was heartbroken at what he found. Filled with sadness and bitterness, he returned to the court of King Istine in Norway.

Everyone at court noticed a change in Ivar, especially the king. The joy in Ivar's singing was gone. The beautiful truths in his stories were replaced by ugly witticisms. Ivar was a sad man, and his bitterness cast a cold shadow over the entire court.

Wanting to help his friend, the king called Ivar to his throne one night after the evening banquet. Ivar approached the throne, and the king quietly asked the young man what was upsetting him. Ivar merely said, "I am sorry, my lord, but I am not free to disclose what is troubling me."

Guessing that the problem might concern a woman, the king asked, "Is there a woman, Ivar—someone back home, perhaps?" Ivar remained silent. The king knew that he had asked the crucial question. Ivar finally nodded yes.

The king smiled and said: "Ivar, there's no difficulty with that. I am the mightiest king in this part of the world. No one would dare to interfere with my wishes. The next boat that leaves for Iceland will have you on board. You will take a letter from me to this young woman's family, saying that it is my wish that she shall become your bride."

Ivar said, "That is impossible, my lord."

The king looked at him and said, "Do you mean that she is already married?" Ivar nodded.

The king fell silent in thought. Yet after a few moments, he spoke again: "Well, then, Ivar, we must think of something else. The next time I make my rounds of the countryside and visit the villages and towns, I will take you with me. As I take you from place to place, you will meet many beautiful women. Perhaps you will find one of them to satisfy your deepest needs."

Ivar shook his head and said, "No, my lord, for every time I see a beautiful woman, I am reminded of Adney, and my grief is deepened."

The king then said: "Well, then, Ivar, I will give you land and estates—large estates so that you might devote your energies to taking care of the farming and the livestock and all other business matters that will keep you preoccupied and busy for the entire year. With your hands full of work that has to be done, you will soon forget the woman. Then happiness will return to you."

But Ivar said, "No, my lord, I have no wish, no desire, and no ability to do such work."

The king, who cared deeply for Ivar, thought some more and then ventured another idea: "Ivar, I know. I will give you money. I'll give you enough money to travel wherever your heart seeks to go, to the farthest corner of Europe. In your travels, you will see many things and experience many adventures. Then you may forget the woman in Iceland!" Once again Ivar refused, saying he had no desire, no wish, and no ability to travel anywhere.

The king thought and thought and thought. Finally, he offered his last idea: "Ivar, there is one last thing I can think of. I know that this suggestion might seem weak compared to the others. Yet perhaps it may be of some help to you, so I will make it anyway. Ivar, after supper every night, I invite you to stay here with me and to spend as much time as you need to tell me of your feelings for this woman, Adney. You may do that for as long as you need. I will be here."

Reluctantly, Ivar agreed. So every night, when the meal was over and the tables were cleared, Ivar sat next to the throne of King Istine and told him his story. He told his story for days, weeks, and even months. And at the close of each evening, the king never let Ivar leave without some token of his friendship. At the end of each evening, the king gave Ivar a small but meaningful gift.

Finally, after several months, Ivar found that he no longer needed to tell his story. His old joy returned to him, and once again Ivar began to sing and to tell the ancient stories that Scandinavians love so dearly. In the following year, he met a young woman whom he fell in love with and who loved him. Ivar was once again a happy man, but he was now also a wiser person. Thus Ivar soon gained even greater fame as a storyteller whose tales had wise and happy endings.

A Imagine that after one year in Adney and Thorfin's marriage, Adney deeply regrets that she did not marry Ivar. She becomes very sullen, and she constantly treats her husband in a nasty manner. Suppose that she comes to you for help. What would you offer her? Would your approach resemble the king's response to Ivar?

Ivar was lucky to have King Istine as a friend. Istine genuinely cared for Ivar and was willing to help him any way he could. Ivar, however, wanted no bandages to cover up his pain, no matter how fancy the bandage. He felt his pain too deeply to try to hide it. Ivar needed to forgive Thorfin and Adney for the pain they had caused him, even though they had not intended to hurt him by falling in love.

Ivar himself also needed forgiveness for the bitter conduct he had shown to the court. The king finally offered the simplest gift he possessed—himself, his presence in listening to Ivar's story, as long and as often as Ivar needed. That simple gift turned out to be very powerful: Istine gave Ivar the chance to lay his burden down.

# What Does Reconciliation Celebrate?

The forgiveness of God celebrated in the sacrament of Reconciliation, or Penance, happens in many ways in everyday life. Realizing God's forgiveness begins with acknowledging our weaknesses and failings as sin.

## Acknowledging Our Sin

Sometimes we respond to the hurt in our life by passing it on to others, causing even further hurt. We do this through **personal sin,** that is, actions—thoughts, words, or deeds—that alienate us from ourselves, other persons, and God. We may also sin by cooperating in others' sin, even passively by not speaking up against it and thus seeming to approve of it. This is how sin gets perpetuated in the world.

Sin often results from carrying around a legacy of hurt that we refuse to lay down. The burden of that legacy manages to disrupt even our best intentions. Saint Paul understood this dynamic well: "I do not understand my own actions. For I do not do what I want, but I do the very thing I hate" (Romans 7:15).

So out of our own complex history of hurts, we may say words that cut deeply into the hearts of people we love. We may

alienation through sin

make promises and break them. We may see a weakness in another person and never cease to mention it. We may hide the truth about something we did so that people will think well of us. Like Ivar we need to lay down our burden of cutting words, forgotten courtesies, and mistaken actions so that we can be free to love again with a whole heart. This is an acknowledgment of our sin.

An act is a **mortal sin** (mortal means "deadly") if it is a very grave or serious violation of God's Law—such as murder or adultery—done knowingly and freely. Mortal sin completely separates a person from God. A **venial sin** is a less serious offense, a wrong that weakens our relationship with God and others but does not cut it off. Obviously, it is most important that we be freed from our mortal sins through repentance and forgiveness. But venial sins can be destructive in their

own ways, by diminishing the spirit of love in us and hardening our heart over time. Facing up to our venial sins enables us to be open to the fullness of God's grace and love again.

## Telling Our Stories

### Healing Stories: Bringing the Darkness into the Light

We all have our dark side—weaknesses that cause us to do things we would rather not do or things we know we should not do. We have stories that we can barely acknowledge to ourselves, let alone share with other people. So we conceal our hurts and our faults. All of us, then, are in need of healing. The story of Ivar points to the truth that our healing comes from bringing our dark side into the light. Maturity is marked by the

*Student art:* Pen drawing by Jacinto Astiazarán, University of San Diego High School, San Diego, California

storytelling heals

B Recall an instance when storytelling was a healing experience for you. Tell about the incident in writing.

ability to admit that we have a dark side, and by the determination to bring that dark side into the light.

We often seek healing through some kind of storytelling. Isn't the chance to share the story of our own self one of the special things about having a best friend? A best friend is usually someone who knows our whole story—our dark side as well as our bright side—and still accepts us. A best friend is someone with whom we can be ourselves and even make mistakes—without fear of embarrassment or rejection.

## The Gift of a Good Listener

Some persons, like King Istine, are better listeners than others. Often these are people who know their own faults well enough to be able to accept the weak spots in others. They are also able to ask the right questions or are just genuinely interested in people and their problems. Good listeners make it clear through their smiles or warm tones of voice that they accept and care for us. B

During your own childhood, who were your favorite teachers, priests or ministers, relatives, and other adults? Chances

# sharing
our stories

are that they had at least one of two traits: Either they gladly listened to your stories, or they shared their own stories with you. All through our life, we need persons with whom we can share our stories.

### Scenes of Sharing Our Stories

Here are some examples of what the sacrament of Reconciliation celebrates—people sharing the stories of their own weakness, laying down the burdens that have kept them from loving with a whole heart:

- Mike can tell his close friend Jeff things about himself that he cannot admit to anyone else: "You know, after I broke up with Ellie, it hit me that the only reason I'd had the guts to break up was that I thought maybe Cheryl was interested in me again. Which made me feel kind of phony about why I'd been going with Ellie in the first place—I wasn't that crazy about her, but I felt like I had to be going out with *some* girl."

- Megan is in treatment for alcohol addiction, and she is required to go to Alcoholics Anonymous meetings. At her fourth meeting, she admits: "When I first came here, I thought I really wasn't alcoholic, that I wasn't like the rest of you, that I was better. And I was just playing along with this whole AA routine to keep my counselor happy. But I'm starting to see that I have a real problem, like everybody else here. Whenever I'm feeling the least bit anxious or uncomfortable, all I can think of is, 'I gotta have a drink.' I have to admit, I'm not on top of it, and it scares me."

- Joan is alarmed at how enraged she has been getting at her two-year-old son for his almost-constant misbehavior. She confides to her friend Rita: "You know, when I'm spanking him, sometimes I really get carried away—I just feel crazy, like I have to let all this rage and frustration out of me, and I forget about what I'm doing to him. After I calm down, he clings to me and acts so sweet, like he's scared I'm going to get mad and start hitting him again. And then I feel like such a terrible mother."

### Confession as a Ritual of Telling Our Stories

In the sacrament of Reconciliation, the sharing that happens in everyday life, the sharing of one's weakness and woundedness, is ritualized in a process called **confession.** In order to make a good confession, a person must first honestly face the sin that is within him or her. Only then can the person share the story of his or her weakness with a priest, who represents both God and the whole Christian community. In confession the priest listens and offers acceptance, guidance, and forgiveness on their behalf.

The telling of specific sins keeps the process of Reconciliation from becoming too abstract. In the sacrament people do not seek forgiveness "in general" or resolve to change "in general." Rather, they name specific attitudes and behaviors that they find to be trouble spots in their relationships with God and others.

Church teaching states that Catholics must confess at least once a year any mortal sins they have committed, but confession of venial sins is recommended as well. Acknowledging our sins to a priest-confessor and experiencing forgiveness can be profoundly healing and a great help to growth in Christian maturity and love.

# Turning Around

One of the most beloved of Jesus' stories in the Gospels is the parable of the prodigal son (Luke 15:11–32). Recall that in the story the younger son turns his back on his parents, taking his inheritance and going off to spend it in reckless living. But when his money runs out, he is left with feeding pigs as his only means of survival. Finally, he realizes how foolish and shortsighted he has been. He decides to go home and beg forgiveness, hoping to live even as a servant in his parents' house. Ⓒ

## Coming to Our Senses

We know that the father in the story welcomes his son back with open arms, so delighted is he that the young man has returned. He throws a big party for his son, insisting that he be treated specially. The point of the story is to demonstrate God's unconditional, all-embracing forgiveness of those who wander away. But note how the young man opened himself to experiencing forgiveness. In a journey that was both spiritual and physical, he came to his senses, acknowledged his mistakes, made a turnaround, and traveled back to his parents' home in order to make things right with his father. Only after this journey is the young man in his own heart, ready to be received into his father's arms. Ⓓ

Every time we "come to our senses" about an attitude or pattern of behavior we have been engaging in that is hurting our relationship with God, with others, or with self, we begin a conversion of heart. This conversion comes about through the Holy Spirit at work in us, helping us make a change. God's loving

The Homecoming, woodcut print by Marion C. Honors, CSJ

forgiveness is always present, always offered; but to experience God's forgiveness, we must make a turnaround, acknowledging that we have sinned, are sorry for it, and want to change. We must firmly desire not to sin in this way again. It is this conversion that is celebrated in the sacrament of Reconciliation.

To get in touch with where we need both forgiveness and renewal, we can periodically make an examination of conscience, a review of recent personal events using a series of questions about how well we have responded to God's call to love. This kind of self-examination is also a good way to prepare for the sacrament of Reconciliation.

*design a service*

Ⓒ Suppose that you are in charge of designing a reconciliation service for your high school. From the questions on page 215, select and list ten that seem most meaningful to include in a reflection time for an examination of conscience.

Ⓓ Read the story of the prodigal son (Luke 15:11–32). Reflect on the story as it relates to situations you have experienced or known about.

# An Examination of Conscience

Here are some questions that might be used to make an examination of conscience before confession or at any time. They are divided into three areas: relationship with God, relationships with others, and relationship with self.

## Relationship with God
- Have I developed ways to make God's presence active in my life?
- Do I take time for God by participating in Sunday Eucharist and setting aside moments to pray or read the Scriptures?
- Do I bring Jesus' perspective to bear on my decisions about my relationships with others, my use of money and other materials, and my view of myself?
- Do I speak of God and my faith with reverence?

## Relationships with Others
- Do I love and respect my parents and other family members and try to resolve my differences with them peacefully?
- Do I treat other people with respect, not with abuse, prejudice, or manipulation?
- Do I share what I have with those in need and reach out to suffering persons with support?

- Do I reverence all human life, do whatever I can to help life thrive, and avoid actions that harm life?
- Am I truthful, fair, and genuine in my dealings with others?
- Do I work honestly at my job or studies?
- Have I hurt others' reputation by speaking falsely about them or spreading gossip?
- Do I try to become informed on issues affecting society and the whole world?
- Do I treat all of creation with respect and justice?
- Have I honored the sacredness of sexuality by not using another person sexually and by reserving full sexual expression for marriage?
- Am I a faithful friend?
- Do I deal with conflict in a constructive way?
- Do I drive with care and safety?
- Do I waste resources?

## Relationship with Self
- Do I try to develop myself as a person, making full use of my strengths and talents?
- Do I explore my own motivations and attitudes about things to become more honest with myself?
- Do I put myself down?
- Do I try to put destructive attitudes into perspective so they do not control me?
- Do I let fear stand in the way of doing what I think is right?
- Do I take care of my health—eat well, exercise, and get enough rest and relaxation?
- Have I been respectful of my own sexuality and not mistreated who I am as a sexual person?
- Do I seek the help of other, wiser persons when emotions or problems are causing me a lot of distress?
- Do I abuse alcohol, other drugs, or leisure activities such as watching television?

## Restoring Wounded Relationships

Sin always involves a break in a relationship or harm done to a relationship with others, with self, or with God. When we undergo conversion, we come to our senses about how a relationship has been torn apart. This enables us to turn away from the misguided steps we have taken. Then we are freed to seek restoration of the relationship that was broken or strained.

### Living the Paschal Mystery

The process of conversion and the restoration of broken relationships are a part of everyday life. Although we may experience death or woundedness in relationships, by responding to God's grace, we can find new life in them at an even deeper level. This is the paschal mystery lying at the heart of our existence and of the sacraments—the movement from death to resurrection.

Here is a story of such a movement:

Lisa and Michelle, best friends through grade school, began to grow apart in ninth grade. Michelle threw herself into the challenges of schoolwork and into participating in school-sponsored activities. Lisa got swept up in the excitement of spending time with a new group of classmates from across town. This group seemed so different from the classmates Lisa had known since the first grade. It was a "faster" crowd, more daring than Lisa was used to. She found the change exciting and fun.

Michelle and Lisa gradually saw less and less of each other, and they found they no longer had much to talk about together. Michelle ran for class president and won; Lisa started going out with a junior boy who was popular in her new group of friends. Throughout

⒠ Write a critique of this attitude in someone who is approaching the sacrament of Reconciliation: "I'm going to confess about taking that stuff from the department store, to get my guilt out of the way. I know I'll do it again, but then I can just go to confession again and get rid of the guilt."

be critical

### Experiencing Penance as Conversion

Another name for the sacrament of Reconciliation, as mentioned at the beginning of this chapter, is Penance, a word derived from the same roots as *repent,* which means "to be sorry." Penance refers to a conversion of heart, a turnaround. Such a conversion is shown externally in changed behavior, which can indicate the sincerity of the change of heart. That is why as part of the sacrament, the priest advises the person in confession (the penitent) to take some action that will express genuine repentance. Usually this action includes prayer, deeds of kindness, or sacrifices. The action itself is called a penance.

Doing a penance can indicate the sincerity of a person's sorrow for sin. However, what is crucial is that in the person's heart, she or he intends not to do the sin again. In the future the person may actually fall into the same sin again despite the good intention. But without that intention, her or his participation in the sacrament is not genuine. ⒠

ninth grade and into tenth, the girls went their separate ways.

Then came Christmas of their sophomore year. Just before the holidays, Lisa and her mother were called into school to meet with the vice-principal. Apparently, Lisa had been cutting her last class every day and hanging out with her boyfriend at a nearby park. The vice-principal said that Lisa would not be suspended this time, but change needed to occur.

Lisa's mother was furious. "I forbid you to spend time with that crowd ever again."

"But Mom, they're my only friends!" Lisa protested.

"Whatever happened to Michelle?" her mother asked. "Why don't you see her anymore?"

"She's a snob now, Mom," Lisa answered tersely.

Nonetheless, that evening Lisa called Michelle. Michelle already knew about Lisa's trouble, and the conversation was brief and somewhat strained. But after speaking with Lisa, Michelle went to her room and rummaged through her treasures from grade school. There she found a booklet that Lisa had made her for her twelfth birthday. The last page contained a photograph of the two friends smiling and hugging, with the caption "Best Friends Forever!" written underneath it.

Michelle thought about all the times she and Lisa had spent talking together and playing together. To her, they were special moments, and she missed her friend. She decided to pull out the last page of her old birthday booklet and send it to Lisa. Beneath the caption "Best Friends Forever!" Michelle added "Still!" followed by "I miss you" and "Merry Christmas."

Lisa received this gift in the Christmas Eve mail. She cried when she first read the caption and again as she walked over to Michelle's house. When Michelle came to the door, the two girls smiled nervously. But then they began talking about Christmases shared in the past and finally about all the changes that high school had brought for them. By evening they felt their friendship rejuvenated. In fact they found the bond between them stronger than ever, because they knew now that they were more than just fair-weather friends. Lisa discovered that she had a friend she could always turn to, and Michelle found out that Lisa would not let pride stand in the way of making up with her friends.

### Reconciliation as Coming Back Together

The word *reconciliation* literally means "coming back together." Reconciliation among people involves the restoring of relationships that have been broken or wounded. It is the fruit of the process of conversion; it is the new life that comes when we are freed from what has held us back from loving. With conversion we are enabled to embrace others, self, and God with a whole heart. Reconciliations like Lisa and Michelle's are celebrated in the sacrament of Reconciliation.

restoring relationships

Ideally, before celebrating the sacrament, we would go to anyone with whom we needed to patch things up or from whom we needed to ask forgiveness, and we would rebuild that relationship. Then we would be ready to celebrate that restoring of life in the sacrament itself. Or perhaps as a result of the sacrament, we might approach those whom we have hurt to be reconciled. F

### The Ripple Effects of Our Actions

The pain we cause by our wrongdoing goes beyond those whom we have hurt directly. For instance, when we make prejudiced remarks or hold hurtful attitudes about particular individuals because of their race or class or social group, we hurt those individuals. We also add to the climate of negative expectations or cruelty that surrounds all persons in that group. And that creates more barriers for everyone to overcome—more tension, mistrust, and hostility.

Nor is sin against ourselves a totally private issue. Whenever we harm ourselves—whenever we reject God, God's love for us, and our worthiness to be loved—we damage our own ability to love and care for others. We damage our ability to live freely and fully. And because we as human beings live in community, harm to us will also affect others.

Thus sin is not just a matter between "me and God" or "me and one other person." Its scope is much wider than what we immediately see. Just as a pebble tossed into a pond disturbs the entire pool of water, so our actions both for good and for ill have far-reaching effects.

The following story from the tradition of Hasidic Judaism gives a sense of how widespread are the ripple effects of one person's sin and how great is the need for forgiveness:

A wealthy merchant happened to share a compartment on a train with a poorly dressed old man whom he treated rudely and disdainfully. When they arrived at their common destination, the merchant saw in the railroad station a throng of people waiting in ecstatic joy to greet the arrival of one of the holiest and wisest rabbis in all of Europe. To the merchant's chagrin, he then discovered that the old man who had traveled in the compartment with him was himself the great rabbi.

Embarrassed at his own disgraceful behavior and distraught that he had missed a golden opportunity to speak privately with a wise and holy man, the merchant pushed his way through the crowd to the old man. When he reached him, he begged the rabbi's forgiveness and requested his blessing.

The old rabbi looked at him and replied, "I cannot forgive you. To receive forgiveness, you must go out and beg it from every poor, old person in the world." (Adapted from Cavanaugh, *The Sower's Seeds,* page 11)

When we sin we need to ask forgiveness not just from the person or persons we have harmed directly but, in a sense,

# far-reaching
## effects

# Why Tell a Priest?

One author who works with teenagers describes here how she answers a question frequently asked about confession:

I often hear the question, "Why do I have to confess to a priest? Can't God forgive me himself if I tell him I'm sorry?" I argued these points with an experienced pastor several years ago. He explained that Jesus gave us the sacrament because we need it. Although God can and does forgive us whenever we repent, we need to hear his forgiveness for ourselves. It's our humanness that demands visible, audible, tangible signs. We need a time and space when we can put our sin behind us and know that God "remembers not the sins of the past" (see Psalm 79:8). When we commit serious sin, or actually choose to be "outside" the Church, it's all the more vital to present ourselves for "reentry," a welcome back. That's why we as Catholics are required to confess all serious sins to a priest. It is an obligation that is, in reality, an opportunity— an opportunity to start over and an opportunity to grow. (Paiva, "Bless Me, Father")

from the whole community and even the whole world that is worse off because of our sin. But, of course, as in the wealthy merchant's situation, it is impossible to find everyone who has been touched by the ripple effects of our sin and ask their forgiveness. Ⓖ

### Forgiven by God and the Whole Community

The sacrament of Reconciliation provides for our need to be forgiven, not only at the one-to-one level but also at the community level. Reconciliation gives us an opportunity to confess our wrongdoing before someone who represents God and the entire community—a priest—and to hear the words of forgiveness given on their behalf. After experiencing this powerful, community-wide forgiveness, many people discover they have an answer to the questions that previously concerned them: "Why should I confess my sins to a *priest?* Why not just tell the person I hurt or a friend who is a good listener?"

Ⓖ Draw four concentric circles, with the circle in the center representing a stone hitting the water, and the surrounding circles representing the ripples that go out from the stone across the water. On the stone, write something you have done that you know was wrong. In each circle surrounding the stone, write the effects of your actions. Begin with the most direct or closest effects in the nearest circle, and end with the most indirect or remote effects in the farthest.

rebuilding
community

The name given to this sacrament, Reconciliation, highlights its community focus. If sin can be understood as things or actions that break a community apart, then Reconciliation can be understood as the processes or actions that rebuild community. In the sacrament of Reconciliation, community members come together to admit their weakness and celebrate their return to God and one another.

The sacrament of Reconciliation is meant to be not only a way to convey God's forgiveness through the absolution of a priest but also a celebration of the experiences of forgiveness already present in our everyday life. In other words, it is meant to be a peak moment of the daily healing processes that take place around kitchen tables, in cafeterias, during visits to chapel, in classrooms, in workplaces, or on late-night walks.

## For Review

1. What is the sacrament of Reconciliation, or Penance?

2. What was King Istine's gift to Ivar? How did it help Ivar?

3. What is sin? What is the difference between mortal and venial sin?

4. What does penance mean? What is the penance that the priest advises for the penitent in confession meant to indicate?

5. What intention must the penitent have regarding his or her sin?

6. What does reconciliation mean? What does reconciliation among people involve?

7. Give examples of how sin is not just a matter between "me and God" or "me and one other person."

# The Ritual of Reconciliation: Symbolic Actions and Words

Perhaps you have experienced the Rite of Reconciliation at your school or parish in a way that truly felt like a celebration of forgiveness. At a communal service, you may have had the opportunity to look back over your recent past for attitudes and actions that needed to be forgiven. Along with the other people present, you may have acknowledged your sorrow and asked God's help in transforming your life. As part of the ritual, you may have spoken with a priest in confession, who reminded you personally of God's enduring love for you. Leaving the ceremony, maybe you felt refreshed and renewed—walking forward as a more courageous and capable person because you knew that you did not walk alone.

As we will see in the section on the history of this sacrament, Reconciliation evolved from a highly community-focused ritual to a highly individualized, private one. In the aftermath of Vatican Council II, the Rite of Reconciliation was revised to integrate the communal dimension with the emphasis on individual repentance and forgiveness. A scriptural focus was also added to connect the sacrament with its biblical roots.

## Three Forms of the Rite

Three different forms of the Rite of Reconciliation can be celebrated, the third one reserved for emergency situations:
1. a celebration for an individual penitent
2. a communal celebration for several penitents with individual confession and absolution
3. a communal celebration for several penitents with general confession and absolution

Whatever form is used, only a priest or a bishop is the minister of the sacrament and has the authority to give **absolution** for sins—that is, the release of penitents from the guilt of their sins, in the name of Jesus Christ. The priest himself does not forgive sins—God does. But that forgiveness comes through the intervention of the church and its authorized minister of the sacrament.

Forgiveness is given to us in the name of Jesus Christ.
🌸 *Student art:* Pastel drawing by Laura Reestman, Mercy High School, Omaha, Nebraska

H Design a room to be used in the sacrament of Reconciliation for confession. Draw a floor plan and describe in writing the furnishings, decorations, lighting, and so on. Describe your reasons for designing the room as you did.

I As practiced today, the sacrament of Reconciliation emphasizes community and the need for the whole community to seek forgiveness. If our society today were personified—imagined as one person—and that person had the opportunity to go to confession, for what five "sins" should the person most ask forgiveness? Write them down and tell why you think these are society's sins.

## Celebration for an Individual

A person can choose to celebrate the sacrament of Reconciliation with a priest on an individual, one-to-one basis. A parish or school may have times set aside when a priest is available for this purpose. Or an individual might ask for an appointment with a priest, especially when she or he wishes to have ample time for discussion without the pressure of knowing that other people are waiting for their turn.

**Still a community focus.** Even when the sacrament is celebrated for an individual, Reconciliation is still considered a community celebration. Thus the community itself and the priest as its representative are primary symbols in Reconciliation. As a representative of God and the whole church, the priest is a reminder of the loving community that welcomes the person and desires Reconciliation for him or her. The instructions for celebrating the rite explain the importance of the priest's greeting the penitent warmly, conveying the love of God and the community. The guidelines for building parish Reconciliation rooms (where individual confession takes place) state that the room should reflect a spirit of welcome and warmth. In other words, the very physical space where Reconciliation is celebrated individually should mirror the church community as a home where people can experience God's loving forgiveness. H

**Face-to-face or separated.** Spaces set aside for confession usually allow for two possible methods of communicating with the priest—either face-to-face, with the priest and penitent seated in chairs; or separated visually, with a screen between the priest and penitent. This second option is preferred by some persons, especially those more comfortable with the anonymous style of confession that was customary before Vatican Council II.

But a face-to-face, personal confession is more in the spirit of the revised rite.

**A personal exchange.** Whether confession takes place in an anonymous or a face-to-face setting, a genuine, spontaneous exchange is meant to happen between priest and penitent. Individuals celebrating Reconciliation should try to explore not only their actions but also their attitudes and motivations. The priest is to listen in an accepting, nonjudgmental way and offer words of advice and encouragement, along with a suggested penance and the words of absolution. The common but misguided image of confession as a fearful, judgmental event ought to be a thing of the past. Individual confession today, when done as the church intends it, can be a rich, healing, and comforting experience.

### Communal Celebration with Individual Confession and Absolution

The communal celebration of this sacrament was introduced as an option after the Second Vatican Council. This form highlights the communal dimension of Reconciliation in a more obvious way than does individual celebration. The community members gather, sing songs and hear the word of God together, collectively focus on how they need to be reconciled with one another and with God, and join in praising God for forgiving them. Part of the rite is the opportunity for individuals to confess privately to a priest and receive individual counsel and absolution.

### Communal Celebration with General Confession and Absolution

The communal rite with general confession and absolution is reserved only for emergency situations, when there may be neither time nor enough priests to hear confessions individually. So persons would express their confession of sins in a general way as a community and receive absolution together. However, church rules state that once the emergency situation passes, these individuals should confess their serious (mortal) sins to a priest individually.

The ordinary way a person receives the sacrament, even within a communal celebration, is to have individual confession with individual absolution from a priest. But the church provides for emergency situations by allowing general confession and absolution only as an exception. ⬜

## Common Elements of the Three Forms

All three forms of the Rite of Reconciliation have these elements in common:

1. a greeting and blessing by the priest
2. the reading of the word of God (optional or usually abbreviated in the individual form of the rite)
3. the confession of sins by the penitent and offering of counsel by the priest
4. the prayer of contrition of the penitent, expressing sorrow for sins
5. the giving of a penance by the priest and the acceptance of it by the penitent
6. the absolution given by the priest, communicated with the laying on of hands (If the penitent and the priest are face-to-face, the priest can place a hand on the person's head, symbolizing God's reaching out to the individual with healing, reconciling love. If a screen separates them, the priest can simply raise his hand in blessing over the penitent.)
7. a prayer of thanksgiving for God's forgiveness and a blessing by the priest ⬜

At some point before the confession of sins, the penitent makes an examination of conscience. In a communal celebration, this usually takes place after hearing the word of God. In an individual celebration, self-examination takes place before the person enters the Reconciliation room for confession.

*gestures of Reconciliation*

⬜ Describe in writing two ritual gestures, besides the placing of a hand on a person's head in blessing, that could also effectively symbolize reconciliation and forgiveness.

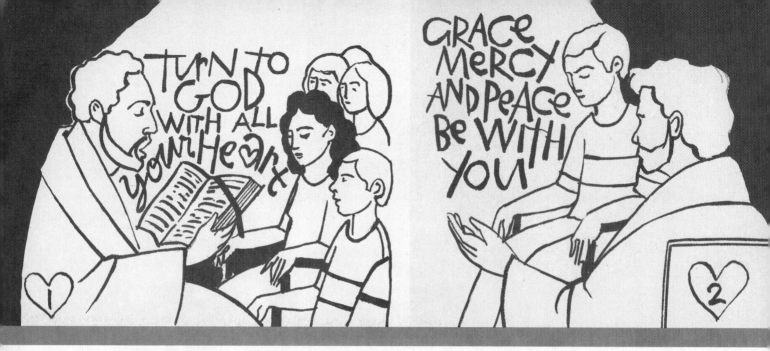

# Reconciliation in Words and Symbols

### Greeting

Grace, mercy, and peace
from God the Father and Jesus Christ his Son
be with you in truth and love.
   Amen.

### The Word of God

Let us listen to the Lord as he speaks to us:

> I will give them a new heart and put a new
> spirit within them; I will remove the stony
> heart from their bodies, and replace it with a
> natural heart, so that they will live according
> to my statutes, and observe and carry out my
> ordinances; thus they shall be my people and
> I will be their God. (Ezekiel 11:19–20)

### Confession of Sins

I confess to almighty God,
and to you, my brothers and sisters,
that I have sinned through my own fault. . . .

### Penitent's Prayer of Contrition

My God,
I am sorry for my sins with all my heart. . . .

### Absolution

God, the Father of mercies,
through the death and resurrection of his Son
has reconciled the world to himself
and sent the Holy Spirit among us
for the forgiveness of sins;
through the ministry of the Church
may God give you pardon and peace,
and I absolve you from your sins
in the name of the Father, and of the Son,
and of the Holy Spirit.
   Amen.

### Praise of God and Dismissal

Give thanks to the Lord, for he is good.
   His mercy endures for ever.
The Lord has freed you from your sins. Go in
   peace.

### The Essentials

Essential to the sacrament are the penitent's contrition, confession of sins, and satisfaction for sin by doing the penance. The words of absolution by the priest are also essential to the sacrament:

> **God, the Father of mercies,**
> **through the death and resurrection of**
> **his Son**
> **has reconciled the world to himself**
> **and sent the Holy Spirit among us**
> **for the forgiveness of sins;**
> **through the ministry of the Church**
> **may God give you pardon and peace,**
> **and I absolve you from your sins**
> **in the name of the Father, and of the**
> **Son,**
> **and of the Holy Spirit.**

### Nonsacramental Services

In recent decades communal reconciliation or penance services that are less formal and that differ from the official rite have become popular. Your school or class may at times hold such services. The reconciliation service may have many of the elements that are part of the official rite. Although individual confession and absolution of sins are not included, this kind of service gives people an opportunity as a community to become aware of what areas of their life need healing, to express sorrow for their sins, to experience a special kind of community spirit, and to be reconciled with God and one another. Such a communal service is a wonderful expression of the spirit of the sacrament of Reconciliation. But it lacks individual confession and absolution and so is not considered a sacrament.

# rituals of forgiveness

## For Review

8. What are the three forms of the Rite of Reconciliation?

9. What is absolution? What is the role of the priest or the bishop in the forgiveness of sins?

10. How does the individual form of the rite incorporate a community focus?

11. What elements do all three forms of the rite have in common?

12. What are the essentials of the sacrament?

# Reconciliation's History

Jesus was a healer. He drew all kinds of people to him—children, women, lepers, outcasts, foreigners, sinners, saints. He healed people's bodies, calmed their minds, and forgave their sins. Belief in Jesus seemed to carry with it a healing of body, mind, and soul all at once.

Throughout its history the church has tried in various ways to be a sacrament of healing forgiveness, in imitation of Jesus the healer. The whole church, laity and clergy, is given the task of healing and reconciling. However, priests' and bishops' particular authority to absolve people from sins is rooted in Jesus' words, spoken to the Apostles after his Resurrection: "If you forgive the sins of any, they are forgiven them; if you retain the sins of any, they are retained" (John 20:23).

## The Early Experience: Community Healing and Forgiveness

For the most part, in the earliest years of the church, the healing process for minor sins took place informally within the community. Members of the community listened to one another's stories in the kind of healing-storytelling process described earlier. This process involved two elements: discernment and thanksgiving. That is, Christians usually tried to determine (discern) just what an individual's problem was—why the person was falling into a certain weakness. Then, as a community, they praised God in thanksgiving for forgiveness.

In the spirit of the early church, the present church teaches that Christians should become reconcilers and healers for one another. The role of reconciling is not solely the priest's; it belongs to all the members of the community.

In the Gospel account of a healing miracle, Jesus first forgives the sins of a paralyzed man. When the scribes grumble that Jesus has no such authority, he shows that he does by curing the man, saying, "Stand up, take your mat and go to your home" (Mark 2:11). When the man walks, all are amazed!

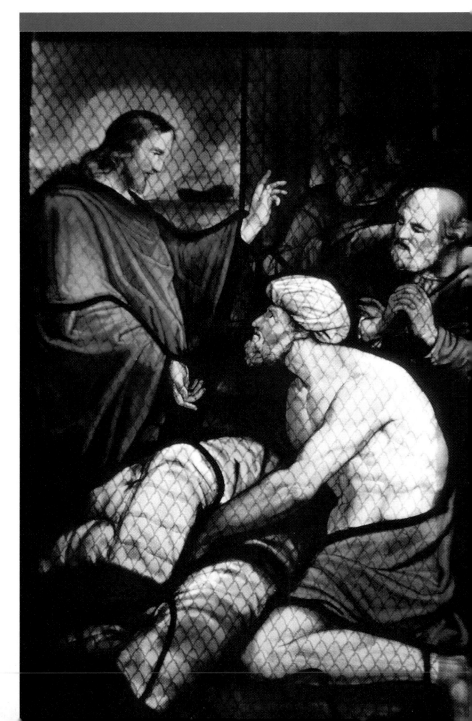

## Reconciliation for Major Sins: Available Only Once

Although celebration of God's forgiveness happened informally and person-to-person in the early church, Baptism was thought to be the primary means of reconciliation between God and a sinner. When converts renounced the life of sin in Baptism, they were considered reconciled with God once and for all. The earliest Christians did not imagine that anyone would actually fall into serious, scandalous sin after the overwhelming liberation of being baptized. In addition, the Eucharist was always there to sustain Christians in their efforts to overcome sin.

### Excommunication as a Break from the Community

Despite the powerful experience of Baptism and the vitality of the early church community, some members occasionally slipped back into their former pagan ways and thus cut themselves off from the community. When members clearly renounced the faith or practice of the church, they were excommunicated—that is, no longer allowed to share the Eucharist with the assembly. They were, in effect, thrown out. This was considered a permanent, irrevocable break with the community.

But the church faced a dilemma: What was the community to do if an excommunicated person sincerely repented and wished to come back and rejoin the church? The answer to this dilemma emerged in the second century with the development of a lengthy process of re-entry into the church.

### A "Second Baptism" for Re-entry

The process for re-entry into the church was modeled after the process of preparing for Baptism. Actually, re-entry was considered something of a second Baptism. As a kind of second chance after Baptism, it was available to a person only once in a lifetime. The excommunicated person joined the Order of Penitents, which was similar to the Order of Catechumens that prepared for Baptism. Penitents could remain in this order for years, until they were judged worthy to re-enter the church. During celebrations of the Eucharist, the penitents sat in the back of the place of worship, left after the homily, and looked forward to the time when they would again share Communion with their friends.

Other members of the community "took on" the sins of the public penitents; they prayed for and with them, and they did penances with them. Lent was a time of intense prayer and fasting to demonstrate a genuine change of heart, not only in the public penitents but in the entire community. The ceremony in which the public penitents returned to

at the
breaking point

Communion took place on Holy Thursday and was presided over by a bishop.

This official, public process of Reconciliation continued for about a thousand years. However, few people took advantage of it, because the process was extremely difficult and long, with severe penances required. Some excommunicated persons preferred to wait until they were on their deathbed to be reconciled; in such an emergency, absolution could be obtained by the dying person without performing penances. Gradually, the serious sins requiring the lengthy process of public Reconciliation were narrowed down to three actions—murder, apostasy (denial of the faith), and adultery.

# Private Confession: Reconciliation with a Personal Touch

As was just stated, most early Christians never went through the official, public process of Penance. Instead, they found forgiveness for their less serious sins by sharing in the Mass, giving alms to the poor, seeking forgiveness from others, and doing other common reconciling actions. Then in the fifth century, a new practice—private confession—began among Irish monks.

### The Irish Monks as Confessors

Dedicated to spiritual perfection, the Irish monks would regularly confess their faults to each other. The monk hearing the confession would pray with the other and prescribe actions to help him overcome the fault. Certain monks came to be renowned for their assistance to the other monks, so they became popular confessors. People outside the monasteries began to take advantage of the help of these monks. Gradually, the practice of private, individual confession spread to the rest of Europe.

### From Public Penance to Private Confession

For a time two major forms of Reconciliation existed in the church. The

Early Irish monks first developed the practice of private confession. They typically lived and prayed in "beehive huts," made of stones with no mortar holding them together. This hut has survived about twelve hundred years on the Dingle Peninsula in Ireland.

back on track

In a paragraph describe how you might support a friend who is trying to get back on track after a period of serious moral problems.

official system of Penance was public, community-centered, available only once, and administered by a bishop. The unofficial system of confession, which grew up alongside the official form, was private, available whenever desired, and administered by a priest. By the ninth century, the public system of Penance was nearly gone. Finally, in the thirteenth century, private confession was decreed the one official form of Penance, and it remained so until the post–Vatican II changes of the 1970s allowed for communal celebrations.

### Confession as Confidential

In various statements over the centuries, the church has upheld the confidentiality of a penitent's confession. That is, a priest is bound by the **seal of confession:** he may not, under any circumstances whatsoever, reveal what has been told him in confession—even in the case of murder. This assures penitents that they can be completely honest before God and the church's representative, without fear that their disclosures will be used by others against them.

# Current Practices: Combining the Individual and the Communal

As was mentioned in the section on the ritual of Reconciliation, the three forms of the Rite of Reconciliation in use today integrate the communal dimension of the early church with the individual focus of later developments. Since Vatican Council II, the changes in the celebration of this sacrament have been remarkable— although perhaps not yet well adjusted to, as evidenced by a drop-off in the use of the sacrament in recent years.

### Why a Drop-Off?

A few decades ago, most Catholics would not have thought of receiving Communion without first going to confession. The lines for confession on Saturday afternoons were long, and priests were kept busy listening attentively in the "confessional box." Now the pendulum seems to have swung in the opposite direction, with the sacrament being celebrated much less often and by many fewer Catholics. Perhaps to some people, even the word *confession* (as the sacrament was formerly called) may carry negative associations with an earlier age, when an emphasis on guilt and judgment was more prominent. Other people may remember how they used to simply reel off their sins to the priest like reading a shopping list. Although they rightly reject such an unthinking approach, they may be unaware of the post–Vatican II changes and mistakenly assume that Reconciliation is supposed to be rote and mechanical.

On the other hand, some Catholics who are aware of the personal tone that is part of the revised rite can feel uncomfortable with that change. They may prefer the more rote, impersonal approach they grew up with. Some people do not wish to talk about themselves and their faults with a priest, reasoning that if they tell God or another person they are sorry, that is enough. They may figure that because they are reconciled to God through the Eucharist, why bother with another sacrament?

### A Needed Symbol of God's Forgiveness

There are other sacraments in which forgiveness takes place—Baptism and the Eucharist, for instance. And as we know, reconciliation does happen in everyday life, apart from the official rite.

Nonetheless, the official sacrament is a specific, tangible way of conveying the forgiving power of God in our life. It offers an opportunity to celebrate forgiveness in a way that is individual as well as communal, private as well as public, focused as well as all-embracing. Many Catholics who regularly take advantage of this sacrament find it a profound experience of Christ's healing forgiveness.

A line of confessionals in a nineteenth-century Irish church

*a history of forgiveness*

## For Review

13. What words of Jesus' are the scriptural foundation of priests' and bishops' authority to absolve people from sins?

14. In the early church, what was thought to be the primary means of reconciliation between God and a sinner?

15. Briefly describe the process in the early church by which an excommunicated person could re-enter the church.

16. When and how did private confession originate?

17. What is meant by the seal of confession?

# Toward Healing the Whole Person

The health of a person's spirit is intimately connected with the health of the whole person. The body and soul are not really separate. Thus many physical illnesses can be traced to spiritual ills—to grudges held onto tightly, for example, or to guilt not relieved. The sacrament of Reconciliation, in providing experiences of healing forgiveness, helps the church to care for the spiritual ills of its members and to carry out the healing ministry of Jesus.

In addition to addressing people's spiritual health, the healing ministry of Jesus also focused on people's physical suffering and sickness. In another sacrament of healing, the sacrament of Anointing of the Sick, the church turns its concern to the needs of those who suffer from physical ills. That sacrament is the focus of chapter 11.

*Student art:* Photo by Kim Hall, Sacred Heart Cathedral Preparatory, San Francisco, California

# Anointing
## of the Sick

### celebrating
### God's healing love

... making life whole

Healing God, strengthen and comfort the sick,
caress those in pain,
and bring peace to the dying.
Restoring God,
make the lives of all of us
healthy, holy, and wholesome.
Amen.

Both the sacrament of Reconciliation and the sacrament of Anointing of the Sick celebrate and carry out the healing ministry of Jesus. Reconciliation deals with the harm caused to a person's relationships by sin. The sacrament of **Anointing of the Sick**, however, offers persons strength, peace, and courage to overcome the hardships of serious illness or the increasing frailty of old age. Its grace is meant to lead primarily to healing of their spirit, and if God wills, to healing of their body. In receiving the sacrament, ill or frail persons can unite their own anguish with the suffering, death, and Resurrection of Jesus, and so join with the Lord in the salvation of the world.

Anointing offers a way for God's love, through the community, to reach us in time of need—as the following story illustrates:

# God's care through community

## Mrs. Beck

has spent the last forty years of her life taking care of her home and family. A devoted Catholic, she attended daily Mass whenever she could and was very active in church and community service projects. To both her neighbors and her family, Mrs. Beck has been a joyful, faith-filled person, always patient and willing to lend a kind word and a helping hand.

Five months ago, however, sickness changed things radically. Just as she once took care of her children, they now take care of her. Previously, she kept busy with many projects. Now she must spend most of her time in bed or in her special chair in the living room. Before her illness Mrs. Beck was seldom concerned about her needs. Presently, her body, so weak and full of discomfort, cries out for attention. And whereas once she would drop in to visit friends occasionally, they now have to come to see her.

Ever since becoming ill, Mrs. Beck has had to wrestle with a whole new image of herself. No longer is she the strong, independent woman whom family and friends once relied on. Many things taken for granted in the past have become matters of great concern for her. Who will help her dress? Should she venture downstairs or wait until she is more rested? Will this be her last Christmas with her family?

Even her prayers have changed. She was used to saying, "Thank you, Lord, for my family and friends, and for all the gifts you have given to me." Now she finds herself praying, "Jesus, into your hands I commend my spirit."

Mrs. Beck is fortunate compared to many seriously sick people; she has a loving family, friends, her faith, and the memories of a lifetime well spent. Yet she still needs all the help she can get. Her doctors do what they can, but the help that she needs in her present illness cannot be found in pills, shots, or bed rest. She needs, more than pills, the touch of loving concern. She needs to hear again the words of Jesus about God's healing and forgiveness and compassion. She needs to hear her family say, "I love you," and her friends say, "We're with you." Loving touches from her children, warm smiles and hellos from her friends, and simple handshakes from parish visitors never meant so much as they do now.

Thus to Mrs. Beck the sacrament of Anointing, offered to her by her pastor, seems to follow naturally from the support she has felt from her family, neighbors, and friends at the parish. The sacrament makes a big difference in how she understands her illness. The anxieties and fears that accompany her discomfort and confinement are eased. Although she is still physically impaired, Mrs. Beck feels healed, somehow more whole. She also feels that she belongs, that she is not alone in her time of suffering. In addition, celebrating the sacrament of Anointing reaffirms her belief in Jesus, who suffered so much himself, and in **his healing touch.**

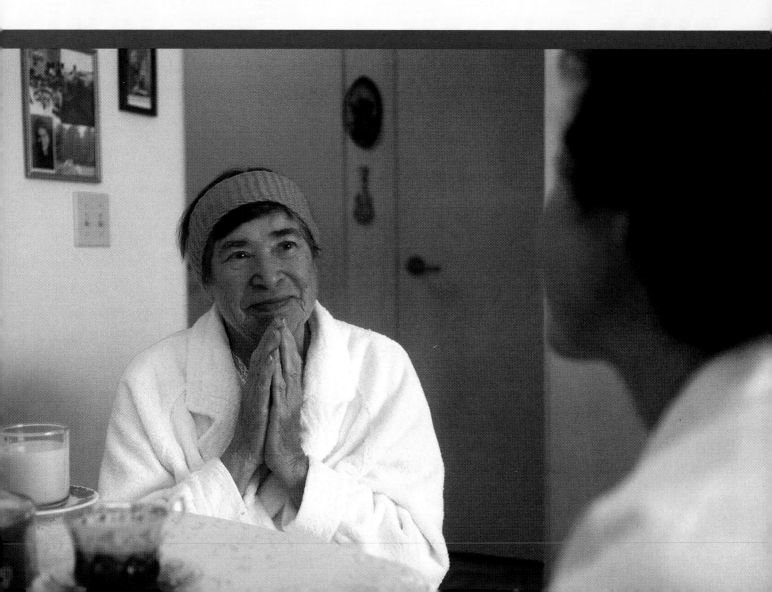

# What Does Anointing Celebrate?

**A** If you were seriously sick, what would you want your friends to do for you? Reflect in writing on how they could support you through the illness.

**B** Remember a time when you were sick enough to stay home at least several days. How did being sick affect your spirit and emotions?

The fears and anxieties felt by Mrs. Beck due to her illness and the drastic changes that illness brought to her life are not uncommon experiences for those suffering from ill health, whether physical or psychological. When people are sick or close to death, they often talk about a great sense of loneliness and isolation, or worry, depression, and helplessness. Some speak of a strong desire to pray, to get more in touch with God. Others, however, report a sense of abandonment

*Student art:* Photo by Cailin Joyce, Sacred Heart High School, Kingston, Massachusetts

*Student art (facing page):* Charcoal drawing by Margaret Ferguson, Sacred Heart High School, Kingston, Massachusetts

by God. To many people, times of illness and suffering seem senseless and devoid of meaning, permeated by an overwhelming emptiness. **A**

The sacrament of Anointing offers a spiritual antidote to the damaging effects of illness. Pain, suffering, and facing one's mortality can greatly undermine a person's sense of well-being, especially one's spirit. Anointing by a priest or a bishop is a statement by the whole Christian community that God's gracious concern does not leave us in times of suffering, illness, and even death. Experiences that try the human spirit need not be seen as hopeless and meaningless. In the midst of suffering, we need to hear most tenderly the healing message of Christian faith:

- God loves and cares for us when we are sick or suffering.
- God heals our spirit and gives us comfort through the love of the Christian community.
- Jesus' suffering and death were not his final fate, and neither are they for us. Jesus' Resurrection gives us hope.

## God's Loving Concern: A Gift to the Whole Person

God's loving concern for sick, suffering, or dying people is the first and foremost truth celebrated in the sacrament of Anointing. In this sacrament the people of God seek not only to remind sick, suffering individuals among them of God's unconditional love and forgiveness, but also to reassure them that God cares about their total well-being.

Knowing that God cares about us when we are hurting can have a powerful healing effect on us. As we read in the opening story of this chapter, Mrs. Beck experienced firsthand the restoring grace that comes by way of Anointing:

- Her fears were relieved and her discomfort eased.
- Her sense of inner wholeness was built up even in the face of her physical decline.
- Her feelings of isolation were dispelled.
- Her faith was renewed and strengthened.
- She was enabled to see her suffering in a new, meaning-filled light.

### Healing the Whole Person

If you or someone close to you has ever been seriously injured or sick, you know that being sick affects all of you—your body, mind, and soul. In other words physical illnesses do not just affect our body. They often have damaging effects on our state of mind and our spiritual well-being. Even something as simple as a headache affects our emotions and our outlook. Likewise, emotional difficulties, such as depression or stress, usually have some sort of negative impact on our physical health. Depression, even in a mild form, often results in a lack of energy. Stress has been linked with ulcers, heart disease, some forms of arthritis, and other kinds of ailments. Ⓑ

An illness that has both physical and emotional causes is considered psychosomatic (from the Greek words *psyche,* meaning "spirit," and *soma,* meaning "body"). Some sickness is clearly psychosomatic. However, most illnesses—and most healthy states—are psychosomatic in the sense that they are more than just physical conditions. Modern medicine acknowledges the relationship between emotional and physical health, and many health-care professionals are giving increasing regard to the emotional and spiritual needs of their patients. Indeed, doctors and other health-care workers who care about more than just physical

when we are hurting

ailments receive high praise for their healing skills from their patients. Ⓒ

The sacrament of Anointing acknowledges and celebrates the wholeness of the human person, paying attention to both physical and spiritual well-being. The sacrament does address the physical, bodily conditions of illness, but the primary emphasis of Anointing is to bring spiritual strength and healing to sick and dying people. Often people do experience physical healing after receiving this sacrament, but that is not its primary purpose. In the words of one Christian teacher,

Ⓒ Interview a person from one of the medical professions. Ask the person what he or she has observed about the spiritual or psychological dimensions of illness and healing. Take notes and report on the interview in class.

The meaning of the sacrament is that God is offering the anointed person the grace to overcome anxiety and despair, to find comfort in an uncomfortable situation, to be healed and whole even if their body is diseased or broken. (Martos, *Doors to the Sacred*, page 339)

**How Do We Know God Really Cares?**

How do Christians know that God cares about people in their experiences of physical, emotional, and psychological pain? Two elements lie beneath the Christian belief in God's compassion. Both come to us from the Gospels, and

Jesus' compassion

both involve actions and undertakings by Jesus:

1. Jesus cast out demons, relieved the suffering of people afflicted with many kinds of physical ailments, and actually restored people to life.
2. Jesus himself experienced suffering, death, and Resurrection.

### Jesus' Healing Actions

The accounts in the following Gospel passages exemplify Jesus' concern for and healing of people:

- In Mark 5:21–43, Jesus brings the daughter of Jairus back to life and cures the woman who has a hemorrhage.
- In Matthew 15:21–28, Jesus cures a Canaanite woman's daughter. Jesus also shows compassion for the Canaanite woman, who in Jesus' day was a marginalized (rejected or outcast) person in society.
- In Matthew 15:29–39, Jesus heals many people—lame, maimed, blind, mute—who have been brought to him by the crowds. Jesus also speaks of his compassion for the crowds and feeds them before sending them away.
- In John 9:1–12, Jesus heals a man born blind. While healing the man, Jesus also refutes the then-common belief expressed by the disciples that the man's physical deformity must have been a direct consequence of personal sin.

From these and many other Gospel accounts, we know that Jesus healed because he felt compassion for hurting people. He wanted to show people first-hand the power and depth of God's compassion. Working through him God's power enabled Jesus to heal people and to work so many wonders. Jesus in action was God in action through him, touching people's lives even at their most painful moments and restoring people to the fullness of life. ▣

# The Healing Power of the Faith Community

When the Christian community brings God's compassion and love to its members who are in pain or near death, as it does through the sacrament of Anointing, the community is acting as an instrument of God's healing grace. Thus the role of the Christian community in carrying on the healing ministry of Jesus is expressed in a variety of ways through the church's **Pastoral Care of the Sick.** This includes visiting the sick (by people in the community, priests, and pastoral ministers), bringing Holy Communion to the sick, and praying for them during Mass and at other times. The sacrament of Anointing of the Sick is a central part of this overall pastoral care the church gives to its weak and ill members.

### The Personal and Social Sides of Sickness

In many ways illness is a deeply personal experience. Although others can empathize with our condition, only we as individual persons feel our pain, discomfort, and anxiety. Illness usually causes us to spend a lot of time asking ourselves why we are sick, what is truly important to us, what our life means, what we have accomplished, and many other soul-searching questions.

Because human beings are profoundly social creatures who live in community, however, illness is never completely personal; it always has a social or communal side to it. Alcoholism, for instance, is a disease that causes much physical and emotional damage in many societies today. The development of alcoholism is often influenced by genetic factors, but alcoholism can also result in part from unhealthy social situations in which people struggle to be accepted, to escape or cope with difficulties, and so on. In

▣ Choose one of the Gospel stories in which Jesus heals someone. Read the story and then re-write it from the point of view of the person being cured. How would that person tell the story?

*Facing page:* Jesus lays his hands on the woman who was bent over for eighteen years, to heal her (see Luke 13:10–17). The depiction is by nineteenth-century artist James Tissot.

# "The Second Coming": A Healing Moment

*Laura Collins attends high school at Merion Mercy Academy in Merion Station, Pennsylvania. She was a fifth grader and a Girl Scout when her troop visited Inglis House (a home for incurably ill people in Philadelphia) at Christmas time, bringing ornaments they had made for the residents. Here are her reflections that grew from a photo taken that day by some unknown person and discovered by Laura a year later:*

We arrived on a chilly December morning, ready to "make a difference." Never would I have imagined the difference that would occur within *me* because of that day. . . .

Our troop made rounds along the floor, chatting with the men and women who lived there, just spreading our youthful cheer and enthusiasm. I can still remember the warm feeling I had while talking to these people.

The final part of our day was to hand out more ornaments to those who chose to watch the Christmas carol show being performed by a Baptist choir from North Philadelphia. Mesmerized by the heavenly voices of this group, I stood in awe as we entered the large common room. The choir was composed of everyone from young children to the elderly. They sang with such joy. All the residents were elated.

All but one. The staff had prewarned our troop of young girls about this man. They told us not to be offended by him. He was confined to a wheelchair and caged by the prison of his deteriorating mind. He never acknowledged his own life, let alone anyone else's presence. If he was capable of smiling, no one there had ever witnessed it. They basically told us that the man was not very well and we should expect him to be painfully distant.

No youthful excitement, handmade Christmas ornament, or innocent smile could reach this man. We all tried, and we all failed. Nonetheless, I left that afternoon with a sense of satisfaction—my first real brushes with my burgeoning spirituality. It was a good experience.

That afternoon would not change my life until an entire year later. It wasn't until I was scrambling around one night in sixth grade, looking for some family pictures for a school project that I would discover my own little miracle.

There, in a box of pictures from years ago, was a photograph from that day at Inglis House.

My fingers graced this picture, "The Second Coming," as I affectionately call it. I was in disbelief. It was of the virtually comatose man, who according to the staff had done nothing but breathe for the last eight years—*smiling*. A real, broad, ear-to-ear smile. Not only that, but he is turned upward, locked in the gaze of the man who led the choir from North Philadelphia. Their hands are clasped in what appears to be a grip of understanding, of brotherhood, of love. Surrounding these two men are three young girls, all smiling and joyful. I can just feel the power of this encounter each time I look at it.

I still don't know who took this picture. I like to think of it as a miracle, because it captured a moment that seemed impossible. . . .

When I look at this picture, I see Christ. I see the Second Coming of Jesus Christ. There he is, in the flesh, breaking the barriers of mental illness and drawing out the inner radiance of a man thought to have lost it long ago. There Christ is, just like in the Bible, reaching out to the rejected, the lonely, the meek, the lost soul, and *loving* him. There Jesus is, surrounded by joyful children, just like in all those Bible stories I had always heard even before I was capable of comprehending them. There is Jesus Christ, alive and working in 1991 in the common room of Inglis House on Belmont Avenue. There the Son of God is, come again, for all to see.

This is why I have had this picture enlarged to put on my bedroom wall among my posters and pictures of political figures, actors, musicians, authors, comedians, family, and friends. . . . This is why I always keep a shrunken copy of this picture in my wallet. This is why you cannot find a space in my room without being able to see this picture.

I have made it the driving force in my life. I have used it to discern many a decision in my life. This is why I call this my most valuable possession. It is why, when I close my eyes, I can recall exactly and as clear as day the deep red of "Jesus'" Nike sweatsuit. And why I can picture the clasped hands, light and dark, intertwined into one. It is why I will never *not* be able to feel the realness of God when I envision this man's ear-to-ear smile.

This picture makes my faith palpable. It is my instrument from God. Whenever I face a tough period, when I feel envy creeping into my mind, or hate into my heart, or falseness into my soul—whenever those evils try to manifest themselves as the driving force behind my life, I sit down, wherever I am, and picture this scene, until I can refocus my motives in life and accept the presence of God in my daily life. . . .

When I interact with people, friends and foes alike, I try to see Christ in the ordinary. In the leaders of a North Philadelphia Baptist choir group. In the popular, the uncool, the homeless, the neglected, the wanted and the unwanted. I try, and admittedly fail often, in my pursuit to see Jesus Christ here and now, on earth, in all people. . . .

I can trust that for all my developing spirituality and the doubts that sometimes plague it, I can always count on God's presence in one moment that will forever be real and miraculously captured in my life—"The Second Coming."

other words, while an individual's illness can affect a community or society, unhealthy conditions or "sicknesses" in society can likewise affect individuals. The effects of illness are interactive at many levels.

### The Personal and Social Sides of Healing

Just as illness has both its personal and social dimensions, so too does healing. Persons who are ill in any way rarely find healing by isolating themselves from others. In fact much scientific research suggests that physical touch and the presence of others are critical to the recovery of sick persons. In the same way, social illnesses like alcoholism call for social solutions and communal efforts. E

The communal aspects of healing can be seen in everyday occurrences. Mrs. Beck, in the chapter's opening story, certainly experienced loving concern and healing from her community. Common, everyday healing actions might include sending cards of sympathy and prayers to people who are sick or to families in mourning; visiting sick friends and bringing them gifts or food; or uniting with family members when a relative has died or is seriously ill. Sometimes people even find themselves offering a consoling touch or words of comfort to a sick person with whom they have never communicated before.

Sharing the burden of an illness is the first step in helping to bring about a cure, whether that "cure" involves actual physical healing or healing the person's spirit. Anointing challenges Catholics to not let their ailing sisters and brothers be cut off from the community, even though illness may prevent these sisters and brothers from full participation in the everyday rhythms and interactions of the community. As Mrs. Beck realized, the support from her family, neighbors, and friends

at her parish greatly aided her own sense of inner healing. She knew she did not bear her suffering alone.

### The Christian Community as "Wounded Healers"

In the Christian tradition, experiences of suffering and healing are linked to service to others. The sacrament of Anointing both celebrates and affirms this reality. To understand the connection between suffering, healing, and service to others, consider the following Chinese tale:

A woman's only son died. In her grief, she went to a holy man and said, "What prayers, what magical incantations do you have to bring my son back to life?"

Instead of sending her away or reasoning with her, he said to her, "Fetch me a mustard seed from a home that has never known sorrow. We will use it to drive the sorrow out of your life." The woman went off at once in search of that magical mustard seed.

She came first to a splendid mansion, knocked at the door, and said, "I am looking for a home that has never known sorrow. Is this such a place? It is very important to me."

They told her, "You've certainly come to the wrong place," and began to describe all the tragic things that recently had befallen them.

The woman said to herself, "Who is better able to help these poor, unfortunate people than I, who have had misfortune of my own?" She stayed to comfort them, then went on in search of a home that had never known sorrow. But wherever she turned, in hovels and in other places, she found one tale after another of sadness and misfortune. She became so involved in ministering to other people's grief that ultimately she forgot about her quest for the magical mustard seed, never

E Within your community what are three priorities, attitudes, or customary behaviors that foster sickness? What are three priorities, attitudes, or customary behaviors in your community that foster wellness? Describe these in writing.

realizing that her compassion had, in fact, driven the sorrow out of her life. (Adapted from Cavanaugh, *The Sower's Seeds,* page 5)

Experiences of sickness and suffering are not in themselves something to be sought after. But they can be healing in a sense if they lead to compassion for others. For instance, the best counselors for drug-dependent people are often formerly addicted persons, who themselves find great healing by helping others. F

The examples of Jesus and his first followers clearly indicate that Christians are not immune from suffering. But rather than let their suffering overwhelm and depress them, Jesus and his followers challenge all who profess Christian faith to transform their suffering into healing for themselves and for those around them. In that sense the Christian community is meant to serve as "wounded healers"—people touched by pain who nonetheless offer healing to one another.

giving while ill

F In a one-page essay, discuss three ways that an ill person can be a help to other members of a community.

*Student art:* Photo by Megan Rulli, Oak Knoll School, Summit, New Jersey

from suffering to healing

# Hope Through the Resurrection

The sacrament of Anointing reminds us of the hope-filled reality of Jesus' own suffering, death, and Resurrection, and allows us to reaffirm our faith in that reality.

### Life, Not Death, Has the Final Word

The Gospels tell us that Jesus himself suffered much mental and physical pain and was finally put to death by the terribly painful method of crucifixion. Significantly, however, the story of Jesus does not end with his Passion and death. As Christians profess in the Nicene Creed, "On the third day, he rose again. . . ." Although Jesus' Resurrection did not eliminate suffering and death from human experience, it did make it clear that they are not the end of life but steps on the way to new life.

This is the powerful, hopeful message of the paschal mystery: The God of Jesus is the God of life. And life, not death, will always have the last word. When an entire community takes part in the sacrament of Anointing, all the members of the community can reaffirm their Resurrection faith. Anointing provides a special opportunity for persons who are sick or dying to reaffirm their faith in the risen Jesus.

### A Sacrament of Hope

Christians are called to struggle against suffering in all its forms, just as Jesus did. They are to pray for healing and do all that they can to bring health and wholeness to themselves and others. Yet Jesus' own suffering and death also challenge believers to recognize that suffering, illness, and death—and life itself—are not totally understandable and controllable realities.

In other words although in the Gospels Jesus is identified as a healer, he and his early followers experienced great suffering and pain. Today the mystery of human suffering continues to baffle us, to disturb us, and to call forth Christian hope.

Despite our best hopes and intentions, however, all our prayers, anointings with oil, invokings of the power of God's Spirit, support, and best medical treatments may leave a person still sick or dying. In such instances Jesus' suffering, death, and Resurrection, as well as the sacrament of Anointing, take on special significance. They stand as testimony to God's loving presence in the midst of human suffering. They give Christians hope that their care and deep concern for the sick person will make her or him feel "whole" in spite of physical suffering. And even though the sick person may die, the sacrament of Anointing enables Catholic Christians to express the hope that their loved one will die healed in the Spirit. Ⓖ

Ⓖ Suppose you were stricken with a serious illness that could cause your death. Write an imaginary journal entry in which you describe your own attempts to struggle against the disease and to cope with the possibility that you might die.

*Student art:* Photo by Lisa Mayor, Bishop O'Dowd High School, Oakland, California

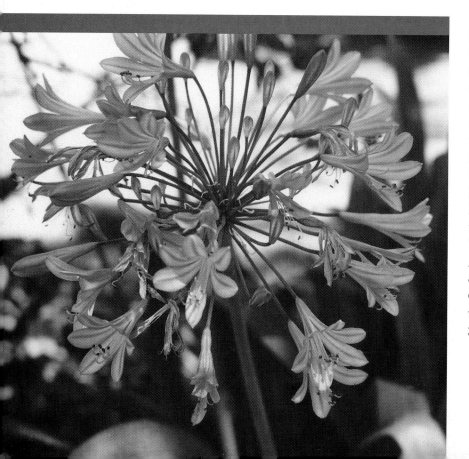

# Healing and the Parable of the Lost Sheep

Jesus' parable of the lost sheep (Luke 15:4–7) vividly portrays the communal dimension of illness and healing. The shepherd has one hundred sheep—that is, a large, complete flock. When one sheep is discovered to be missing, the shepherd leaves the ninety-nine to go off in search of the one that is lost. At first this course of action seems impulsive and impractical— wouldn't it be better to guard the ninety-nine? Jesus explains, however, that no community is truly whole unless all its members are caring for one another. The whole community is affected by the well-being of each member. Likewise, curing one member helps bring about the healing of all.

God's love heals

## For Review

1. What is the sacrament of Anointing of the Sick?

2. What is the foremost truth celebrated in the sacrament of Anointing?

3. What is the primary emphasis of the sacrament of Anointing?

4. Give two examples of Gospel passages that show Jesus healing people. What enabled him to heal people?

5. What are three everyday healing actions that people can do for sick persons or for families in mourning?

6. Describe what it means to say that Christians themselves can be "wounded healers."

7. What is the hopeful message of the paschal mystery with respect to illness and death?

# The Ritual of Anointing: Symbolic Actions and Words

## Different Rites for Different Circumstances

Several slightly different rites are available for celebrating the sacrament of Anointing. The differences allow for the varying circumstances and situations that naturally come up in the community. (There are even directives for baptizing and confirming sick or dying people, if they wish to receive those sacraments and have not done so before.) In all cases

a priest or a bishop administers the sacrament.

**Offered with the wider faith community present.** The sacrament of Anointing can be celebrated with a whole faith community, either as a part of a Mass or in a separate healing service. In the presence of parish members or a school community, a priest gives Anointing to those members whose health is greatly impaired in some way—whether from injury or illness, from emotional or

The healing of the paralyzed man (see Mark 2:1–12), depicted in an African village setting psychological turmoil, or simply from the process of aging.

For instance, every year for Grandparent's Day, one Catholic school in Iowa has a special Mass that includes the sacrament of Anointing. Students, their families, and any members of the parish are invited to participate in the prayers for the sick, and to receive the sacrament themselves if they need it.

**Offered to nonterminally ill persons.** The sacrament of Anointing can also be celebrated by individuals who are seriously, but not terminally, ill—for instance, by people about to undergo major surgery for an illness that is serious but not life threatening. In situations like this, the celebration of the sacrament usually takes place outside the context of a Mass, in the home of the ill person, in a hospital, or in some other institution such as a nursing home. If possible, members of the family or friends gather with their loved one and the priest to participate in the prayers and give their spiritual support.

**Offered to dying persons.** Finally, the sacrament of Anointing is also available to bring a special comfort and peace to those persons who suffer from a terminal illness or are close to death. Again the celebration of the sacrament in these circumstances usually happens apart from a Mass. If death is close at hand, special prayers of commendation, or entrusting the dying person over to Christ, are part of the sacrament. Also included in this situation is a special rite in which the dying person receives his or her last Communion.

Holy Communion offered to a dying person is known as *viaticum*—from the Latin *via*, meaning "way," and *cum*, meaning "with." In other words *viaticum* goes with the dying person as provisions, or nourishment, for a journey on the way to eternity with God. H

### Not Just for Dying Persons

Like Reconciliation and the Eucharist, Anointing may be received by a person more than once. Although the circumstances must be serious to warrant receiving the sacrament, persons can find themselves in such situations more than once in a lifetime.

Over the course of a lifetime, a person might well experience traumatic injury from a car accident, undergo major surgery, grow weak from old age, and inevitably reach her or his deathbed. For someone in each of these situations, receiving the sacrament would certainly be appropriate. Anointing is not just for members of the Catholic community who are dying.

# Common Elements in Anointing

A number of elements are common to all forms of celebrating the sacrament of Anointing:
1. prayers
2. a penitential rite
3. readings from the Scriptures
4. the laying on of hands by the priest
5. anointing with oil on the forehead and hands by the priest
6. Holy Communion

Essential to the sacrament is the anointing by the priest of the person's forehead and hands while praying these words:

> **Through this holy anointing**
> **may the Lord in his love and mercy**
> **help you**
> **with the grace of the Holy Spirit.**
> **Amen.**
> **May the Lord who frees you from sin**
> **save you and raise you up.**
> **Amen.**

*a special farewell*

H If you were giving a farewell dinner for a very close friend who was moving far away, how would you make the meal and the occasion special? Describe what you would do in a paragraph.

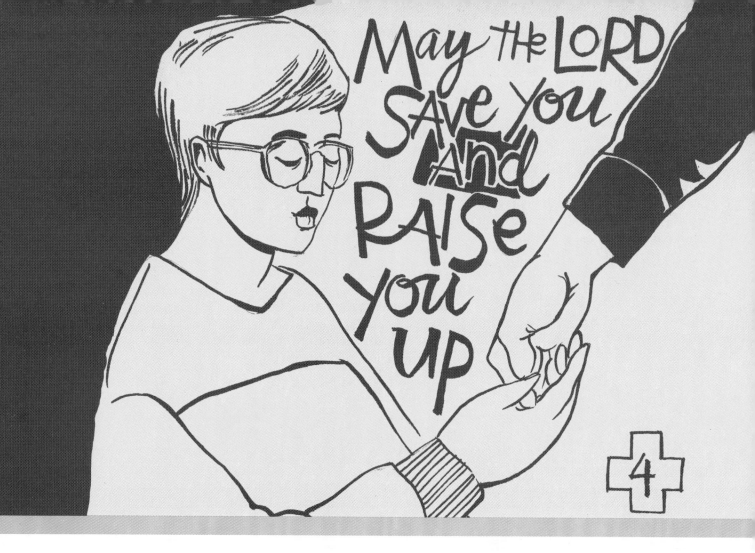

# Anointing in Words and Symbols

**Opening Prayer**

(Anointing within Mass)
God of compassion,
you take every family under your care
and know our physical and spiritual needs.
Transform our weakness by the strength of your grace
and confirm us in your covenant
so that we may grow in faith and love.

**Penitential Rite**

(Anointing outside of Mass)
My brothers and sisters, to prepare ourselves for this
holy anointing, let us call to mind our sins.

**Liturgy of the Word**

(Anointing outside of Mass)
A reading from the holy Gospel of Luke:

> Now there was a man full of leprosy in one of the
> towns where [Jesus] was; and when he saw Jesus, he
> fell prostrate, pleaded with him, and said, "Lord, if
> you wish, you can make me clean." Jesus stretched
> out his hand, touched him, and said, "I do will it. Be
> made clean." And the leprosy left him immediately.
> (5:12–13)

**Liturgy of Anointing**

Laying on of hands
[In silence, the priest lays his hands on the head of
the sick person.]

**Anointing of the forehead**
Through this holy anointing
may the Lord in his love and mercy help you
with the grace of the Holy Spirit.
 Amen.
**Anointing of the hands**
May the Lord who frees you from sin
save you and raise you up.
 Amen.

**Liturgy of Communion**
(Anointing outside of Mass)
All-powerful and ever-living God,
may the body and blood of Christ your Son
be for our brother/sister [name]

a lasting remedy for body and soul.
We ask this through Christ our Lord.
 Amen.

**Blessing**
May the God of all consolation
bless you in every way
and grant you hope all the days of your life.
 Amen.
May God restore you to health
and grant you salvation.
 Amen.
May God fill your heart with peace
and lead you to eternal life.
 Amen.

creating a ritual

⬚ If you were creating a sacrament for sick or dying people, what would you include as symbols, rituals, or activities? What would you want to do for or say to a person you loved who was dying? Explain your recommendations in writing.

## Symbolic Actions in Other Sacraments

The sacrament of Anointing makes use of many of the same symbols and symbolic actions that are used in the other sacraments: anointing with oil (Baptism, Confirmation, and Holy Orders), the laying on of hands (Confirmation, Reconciliation, and Holy Orders), and Holy Communion (the Eucharist). The opportunity for confession of sin in the sacrament of Reconciliation is also offered. In short in the sacrament of Anointing, the Catholic faith community employs many of its resources to help its ailing members.

## Attending to the Whole Person

The sacrament conveys the concern of God and the church for persons in their entirety—their body, mind, and spirit, their individual and social well-being:

- The penitential component of the sacrament seeks to restore the person's harmony with others and with God. During illness we naturally tend to reflect on past experiences and the state of our relationships with God and our friends. Sacramental reconciliation is provided in order to assist healing in those relationships.
- Both the forehead, as a symbol of mental powers, and the hands, as a symbol of physical strength, are anointed with oil.
- The oil has been blessed previously by the local bishop, so it symbolizes the connection to the wider church community.
- Prayers and readings from the Scriptures focus the heart and mind on healing as the action of Jesus.
- The laying on of hands and receiving of Communion emphasize that healing occurs in the context of a caring community. ⬚

# rituals of Anointing

## For Review

8. Describe three different options for celebrating the sacrament of Anointing.

9. Name the six elements common to all forms of the sacrament of Anointing. What actions and words are essential?

10. What do the laying on of hands and receiving of Communion emphasize in Anointing, and in what other sacraments are these rituals found?

# Anointing's History

## Healing in the Early Church

As faithful followers of Christ, the Apostles and the first Christian communities carried on his healing mission. In the Gospel of Mark, we read that the Apostles did so even while Jesus was with them on Earth: "So they went out and proclaimed that all should repent. They cast out many demons, and anointed with oil many who were sick and cured them" (6:12–13).

The Letter of James, written to members of the early Christian church, suggests that prayer, the laying on of hands, and the use of blessed oil were all common healing practices among them:

> Are any among you sick? They should call for the elders of the church and have them pray over them, anointing them with oil in the name of the Lord. The prayer of faith will save the sick, and the Lord will raise them up; and anyone who has committed sins will be forgiven. Therefore confess your sins to one another, so that you may be healed. The prayer of the righteous is powerful and effective. (5:14–16)

During the early period of the sacrament's history, evidence suggests that any Christian could pray for sick people or anoint them with oil or lay hands on them, calling on the Spirit to heal them. The oil, blessed by the bishop, was used as an ointment on the injured part of the body or as a balm that covered the entire body. Sometimes it was even drunk. In many instances ill Christians were anointed with the blessed oil on a regular basis. ⬜

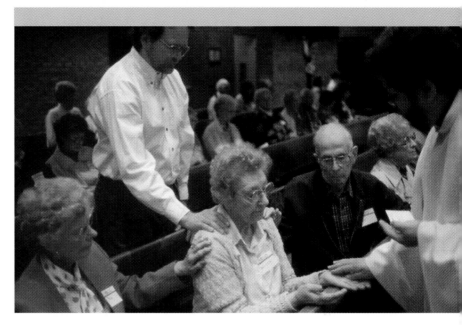

## Anointing Becomes a Preparation for Dying

Gradually, from about the eighth to the twelfth century, significant changes in the sacrament of Anointing occurred. By this time some people had begun treating the blessed oil like a magic potion. This exaggerated regard for the oil, along with a general increase in priests' sacramental duties, accounts in part for the ministry of Anointing becoming reserved for priests.

During this period Anointing also became associated with the sacrament of Penance, which, as chapter 10 noted, was generally administered to excommunicated persons only when they were near death. The sacrament of Anointing therefore came to be seen as a preparation for death rather than as an act of healing. By the twelfth century, the sacrament was officially called Extreme

Family members gather to support their loved one as she is anointed in a church service.

praying for the sick

⬜ Do you agree or disagree with the following statement? Explain your reasons in a paragraph.
• Praying for someone who is ill is a significant act with great value and purpose. I would want to be prayed for if I were ill.

Unction—a term meaning "last anointing"; it was even called "the last rites." For the most part, the association of Anointing with impending death prevailed until changes were made in the sacrament by the Second Vatican Council.

## Original Purpose Is Restored

Today Anointing's original purpose—healing—is once again emphasized. The official designation of Anointing as part of the Catholic church's overall pastoral care and concern for sick and dying people strongly indicates this fact.

Anointing, as it is celebrated today, highlights Jesus' healing presence in the church. Although the priest has the special role of minister of the sacrament, all the members of the faith community are called to participate in the church's healing ministry. Here are just a few suggestions for how you could do that:

- By taking time out during school to pray for a classmate who is in the hospital, you would be participating in the pastoral care of the sick.
- By sending a card or visiting the person in the hospital, you would be participating in a more personal way.
- By praying with the person, or actually laying hands on the person, you would be tangibly adding to your personal participation.
- And by giving volunteer service in a hospital or nursing home, or by becoming a member of one of the healing professions, you would clearly be giving witness to the healing that the church celebrates in its sacrament.

The Rite of Anointing is one moment in a healing process that can take a long time, but it is an intensely grace-filled moment. Ideally, the sacrament symbolizes and culminates all the pastoral care performed by the caring community in praying for sick people, visiting them, helping their families, and taking on other activities in the service of healing.

In the sacrament of Anointing, Catholics are reminded of God's healing power that keeps flowing through Jesus into the Christian community, the church. And they participate in the mysterious truth that—as in Jesus' life—suffering, sickness, and even death can be part of the healing journey toward resurrected life and wholeness. Ⓚ

[K] From your own experience or from history or the news, recall an individual for whom suffering, sickness, or even death was not a defeat but a path toward victory, toward a new, richer life.

# Anointing's history

## For Review

11. In the early church, how did Christians carry out the healing mission of Jesus?

12. What does Extreme Unction mean? Why was this term used for the sacrament of Anointing until recent decades?

13. What purpose of Anointing has been restored and emphasized since Vatican Council II?

# From the Healing Sacraments to the Sacraments of Vocation

Reconciliation and Anointing, as the two sacraments that celebrate God's healing in our life, minister to the physical, emotional, and spiritual well-being of church members. Like the other sacraments, they inevitably focus on a person's relationships in community—on forgiving one another, caring for one another, and surrounding one another with God's love, especially at times of hurt or suffering.

Christians who experience the healing ministry of other Christians, in the sacraments of healing and in everyday life, are thereby strengthened to respond generously to the life call that God offers them. The last two sacraments, of Matrimony and Holy Orders, are concerned with specific life callings, or vocations, to service in the community.

God's care and healing are with us in the sunrises and the sunsets of life.
*Student art:* Photo by Jason W. Chan, La Salle High School, Pasadena, California

# 12

# Matrimony

## celebrating
## the covenant of love

...in good times and in bad

. . . each child a blessing

Compassionate God, when two become one in marriage,
we are reminded that you became one
with us through your Son, Jesus.
God of men and women,
give strength to couples
and to all those who seek
a life of love and generosity.

Amen.

Every Christian has a vocation, or calling, to become holy and to spread the Good News of Jesus Christ. Through Baptism and Confirmation, we are consecrated to share in the common priesthood of all God's people. Catholicism celebrates two particular vocations as well in the sacraments of Matrimony and Holy Orders. Termed the **sacraments at the service of communion,** they consecrate people to special roles of service in the Body of Christ. This chapter focuses on Matrimony (also called Marriage); chapter 13 considers Holy Orders.

The sacrament of **Matrimony** is a sacred bond, or covenant, between a man and a woman that pledges them to be faithful lifelong spouses, loving and caring for each other and lovingly raising and guiding the children they bring into the world. Through the sacrament the couple are given the graces they need to be true to their pledge.

The following abbreviated version of "The Gift of the Magi," a classic short story by 1900-era writer O. Henry, offers a tender portrait of a marriage relationship:

# portrait of
## a marriage

## One dollar and eighty-seven cents.

Despite the cheer of the Christmas season, Della was heartsick. With all her careful saving of pennies, she had only a pittance with which to buy her beloved husband, Jim, a nice present. Times were hard, and after the rent on their apartment was paid, there was barely enough from their twenty-dollar-a-week income to take care of essentials, let alone buy extras like gifts.

Despite their poverty, Della and Jim had two possessions in which they took great pride: Jim's gold watch, which was a family heirloom, and Della's long, beautiful hair. Della's hair, unpinned, fell around her like a cloak and reached below her knees, like a shining waterfall of brown. These two treasures were all the couple had of any material worth.

In the midst of her Christmas Eve sadness, while gazing into a mirror, Della suddenly realized how she could afford to buy Jim a present. There were shops that bought hair for wigs—why not get her hair cut off and sell it? The sum it would bring would be enough to buy a gift worthy of Jim!

An hour later, twenty dollars richer, and sporting a short, new, chorus-girl haircut, Della went shopping gleefully for Jim's present. She found the perfect gift: a simple but elegant platinum chain that Jim could use with his precious watch, to replace the old leather strap he now used with some embarrassment. The chain cost twenty-one dollars; Della paid gladly and hurried home.

By the time Jim came home, Della had curled her short, boyish hair. Jim reacted strangely to seeing her this way, and Della, thinking he might be overly shocked, assured him that she would not miss the hair, that it would grow back, and that it had gone for a good cause— him.

Jim then showed her the present he had gotten for her: a set of beautiful, expensive, tortoiseshell combs, combs that Della had seen in a shop window and yearned over for weeks, knowing she could never own them. And now her beautiful hair, in which the combs could have been worn so perfectly, was gone. Her tears and sad laughter soon passed, and Della quickly presented Jim eagerly with his present—the watch chain.

"Isn't it a dandy, Jim? I hunted all over town to find it. You'll have to look at the time a hundred times a day now. Give me your watch. I want to see how it looks on it."

Instead of obeying, Jim tumbled down on the couch and put his hands under the back of his head and smiled.

"Dell," said he, "let's put our Christmas presents away and keep 'em a while. They're too nice to use just at present. I sold the watch to get the money to buy your combs."

A Do you think that Della and Jim were better off or worse off after their exchange of Christmas gifts?

# What Does Matrimony Celebrate?

As a sacrament, Matrimony is an encounter with God. Specifically, it celebrates a couple's commitment to share the whole of their life together and to reveal God's love to themselves, their children, and others through their marriage relationship. Della and Jim's story warmly portrays the essence of the meaning of marriage. In this chapter we explore four concepts that underscore the rich, sacramental quality of the marriage bond: **mutual self-giving, covenantal faithfulness, the becoming of one's real self,** and **creativity.**

*Student art:* Marker pen by Amy Wibowo, Saint Aloysius, Vicksburg Catholic School, Vicksburg, Mississippi

## Mutual Self-Giving

Wherever there is human love and friendship, God is revealed. The First Letter of John expresses this reality with a beautiful simplicity: "God is love, and those who abide in love abide in God, and God abides in them" (4:16).

Because of the unique aspects of the friendship that is the marriage relationship, Matrimony has always had a special place in the Judeo-Christian vision as a way of revealing God's love in human terms. Of all human relationships, the marriage relationship represents in the most vivid way how God relates to us. In a real sense, a husband and wife reveal God to themselves and those around

revealing God's love

them through their own love for each other.

Of course, no marriage is perfect. However imperfect a particular marriage may be, though, it is sacramental insofar as it is the place where wife and husband, children, family, and family friends meet the living God. Recognizing the sacramental nature of marriage reminds us that in all our attempts to give and to love, God is the principal actor, the one behind it all who is the source of all love.

## A Symbol of God's Gift of Self, Freely Bestowed

From the beginning years of the church, marriage has been regarded as a symbol of God's total gift of self to human beings. For Christians in particular, the mutual giving and love between a husband and wife help us understand Jesus' loving gift of self in his death and Resurrection. Like the sacrifices that Della and Jim made for each other in the opening story, Jesus' sacrifice for humankind transforms, heals, and nurtures human existence.

Relating marriage to Jesus' love for us points to what the sacrament ideally can be. The gift of self in marriage, like Jesus' gift of self, must be freely given or it is not love at all. Freedom in giving ourselves to another person implies that we feel good about ourselves, that we recognize we have much to offer another person and deserve that person's respect in return. Freedom makes possible the move from "I" to "we" that is married love. When we can love someone genuinely for his or her own sake and as a free and confident person ourselves, we reveal God's way of loving.

## A Countercultural Vision

The act of giving oneself freely runs counter to an acquisitive, possessive impulse in society that affects many contemporary attitudes and behaviors,

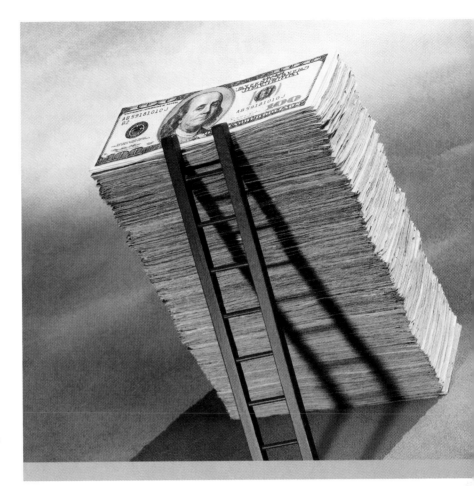

including those toward marriage. One Christian couple, writers Mitch and Kathy Finley, offer this critique of the way marriage is handled in our society:

> The prevailing assumption is that a happy marriage depends upon all kinds of material and economic realities, realities which end up taking first place in the life of the couple. A consumer culture encourages this attitude toward marriage from the moment the engagement is first announced.
>
> The message broadcast to engaged couples is that the future success of their marriage depends on how much money they spend on the engagement ring. Then their future happiness depends on how elaborate the wedding

The pursuit of greater affluence may get in the way of a couple's focus on their relationship.

B Interview two couples who have been married for at least five years. Ask the partners what sacrifices they made for each other in the early years of their marriage, what motivated those sacrifices, and whether those sacrifices still seem like losses. Write up the results of your interview.

C Recall someone who has stood by you faithfully, in good times and in bad. Consider the ways this person supported you and kept faith with you in a hard time. Do you think this person would recall you as someone who has been faithful to her or him? Why or why not?

and reception can be. Next, the more money the couple spend on their honeymoon, the more likely that their marriage will be a good one. And we're off and running: our marriage will be all it can be if only we have a big beautiful house filled with new furniture and appliances—even if we must go deeply into debt for this to be possible. And of course, we really do need a brand new car before we can feel really married. . . .

Of course, once the couple is married, the same set of superficial materialistic values begin to take other forms. . . . The things we buy for our child determines our effectiveness as parents. That's the message.

. . . Husband and wife may continue to say that their marriage is most important for them. . . . [But] in the pursuit of greater affluence, many couples neglect the marital relationship. (*Building Christian Families*, pages 65–67)

A Christian vision of marriage counteracts the trap of consumerism by putting the emphasis for partners on the free gift of self to each other rather than on the relentless quest for the "perfect" household. The sacrament of Matrimony affirms that no amount of possessions will ever bring the hope and joy that two people can feel when they love each other freely and generously. B

### "A Communion of the Whole of Life"

When we think about what marriage involves, we often focus on the sexual intimacy that ideally accompanies marriage. Actually, the mutual physical gift of self that happens in sexual intercourse is meant to express a man and woman's sharing of their most intimate selves at every level of life. They share life while

talking and laughing, struggling over finances, expressing hopes and dreams, raising children, working out conflicts, settling on a common lifestyle, clarifying values, going on family vacations, suffering loss or grief, and learning, changing, and growing together.

Sexual intercourse is intended only for marriage because it embodies the total sharing of a whole committed life together. In the words of a Catholic church document, marriage is "a communion of the whole of life." A loving sexual relationship can joyfully and pleasurably express that communion.

## The Faithfulness of a Covenant

Legally, marriage is a contract, and traditionally it has been thought of in contractual terms. That is, marriage is thought of as holding the man and woman to certain obligations and conferring on them certain rights.

### Covenant: More Than a Contract

In the Judeo-Christian tradition, alongside the notion of marriage as a legal contract grew the idea of marriage as a covenant, modeled on the Covenant between God and the Chosen People (the Jews), or between Christ and the church. **Covenant** is a key biblical concept, perhaps the central concept of the Old Testament. In its secular sense, a covenant is a solemn promise between two parties. In its theological sense, the Covenant is the community of personal partnership between God and humans, established by God's unconditional free love, for the salvation of human beings. In the Covenant God and humans are bound to each other with promises of love and faithfulness.

## Between God and the Chosen People

In the Old Testament, we learn that God established a covenant with Abraham and his descendants, and later renewed it by giving the Israelites the Law on Mount Sinai. The essence of that Covenant was the promise between God and the people that they would be faithful to each other. From the history told in the Old Testament, we know the people often broke the Covenant; they were repeatedly unfaithful to God through idolatry and injustice. But God never abandoned the promise of the Sinai Covenant, remaining faithful to the people in good times and in bad.

Over time the prophets helped the people to understand that God's love for them was like the absolute, undying love of a person who has been hurt by a spouse's infidelity but nonetheless remains faithful and constant. C

*Student art:* Granite and colored pencil by Tracy deEscobar, Coyle-Cassidy High School, Taunton, Massachusetts

### Between Christ and the Church

The early Christians saw the Sinai Covenant as applying to the relationship between Christ and the church. The marriage bond was also interpreted as a covenant, in terms of the love between Christ and the church. Thus Saint Paul urged the Ephesians:

> Husbands, love your wives, just as Christ loved the church and gave himself up for her. . . . In the same way, husbands should love their wives as they do their own bodies. He who loves his wife loves himself. For no one ever hates his own body, but he nourishes and tenderly cares for it, just as Christ does for the church, because we are members of his body. "For this reason a man will leave his father and mother and be joined to his wife, and the two will become one flesh." This is a great mystery, and I am applying it to Christ and the church. Each of you, however, should love his wife as himself, and a wife should respect her husband. (Ephesians 5:25–33)

In speaking of the mystery of marriage, both Jesus and Paul referred to a well-known passage from Genesis: "Therefore a man leaves his father and mother and clings to his wife" (2:24). But to further clarify the unbreakable and sacred nature of the relationship between husband and wife, Jesus added: "So they are no longer two, but one flesh. Therefore what God has joined together, let no one separate" (Mark 10:8–9).

Paul's message that husbands should love their wives as Christ loves the church stood in stark contrast to the assumptions of a culture that saw women as basically inferior and as having few rights. Now, of course, we take it for granted that there should be deep, mutual love and respect between spouses, but this was a radical notion in the first-century Mediterranean world. Today, too, we would not draw quite the same analogy that Paul drew in equating the husband with Christ and the wife with the church. Rather, we would see both the husband and the wife as called to love their partner as Christ loves the church (or, in the terms of the Old Testament, as God loves the Chosen People).

### Covenantal Faithfulness: Images for Today

We receive from our culture many messages about what love, married life, and family life should be like. Movies, TV shows, and romance novels often offer unrealistic portraits of intense and passionate relationships that real-life marriages seldom achieve. Comparing marriage to God's Covenant is not meant to place a heavy burden on couples—presenting a divine ideal not humanly achievable. The challenges of living together and sharing a lifetime are great enough. However, referring to marriage as a covenant places before couples a model of fidelity that can help them build up their relationship and make it more loving.

In the sacrament of Matrimony, Christ is at the center of the union between husband and wife.

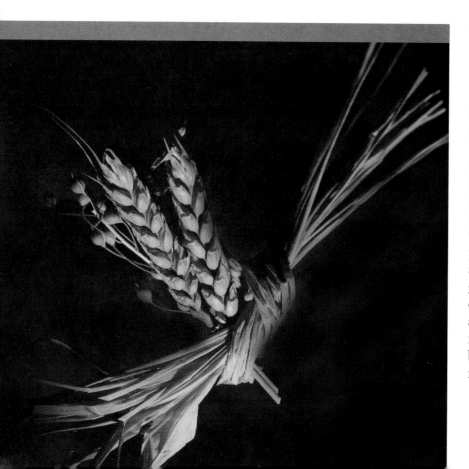

struggle through problems

Faithfulness implies more than just sexual fidelity, which means that the spouses reserve their sexual intimacy exclusively for each other. True marital faithfulness goes beyond only sexual exclusivity to encompass these four characteristics:

**Permanence.** God is faithful to the Covenant forever, and the permanence of God's love for the people is mirrored in the permanence of the marriage bond. "What God has joined together, let no one separate" (Mark 10:9). So in Christian marriage, the husband and wife's faithfulness is not for "this period in our life when we feel committed." Marital fidelity is "until death do us part."

**Constancy.** Fidelity implies the ability to love through all the ups and downs of life, in times of joy and hardship. In the traditional words of the marriage vows, the partners promise to be true to each other "for better, for worse, for richer, for poorer, in sickness and in health, until death do us part." Such faithfulness requires a constant concern for each other's well-being, not only during the romantic times but during the day-in and day-out, year-in and year-out routines that develop in a life spent together. This fidelity is not a couple's simply resigning themselves to being "stuck" with each other, no matter what. Instead, it is their commitment to grow together in supporting and caring for each other.

**Loving confrontation.** Fidelity includes caring enough about the relationship to confront problems honestly and struggle through them together. The ability to confront lovingly assumes that

D Of the four characteristics of fidelity discussed here— permanence, constancy, loving confrontation, and lived values— which one do you think would be the most difficult for you in a marriage? Explain your answer in writing.

E Using the passage from *The Velveteen Rabbit* as a starting point, write a one-page reflection entitled "Romance Versus Love: What's the Difference?"

✦ *Student art:* Photo by Thomas Eyre, Bishop Shanahan High School, Downingtown, Pennsylvania

the spouses believe in each other's inherent goodness and lovableness, even when certain behaviors or personality traits are annoying or even hurtful.

**Lived values.** Fidelity includes actively living out values and priorities. Do the spouses choose to put a priority on their relationship by giving it the time and nurturance that it needs to grow? In this connection a wise saying applies:

> Where you spend your time
> is where you spend your life.
> And where you spend your life
> is where you spend your love. D

## Becoming One's Real Self

Obviously, a marriage covenant implies a lot more than does a marriage contract. A marriage covenant is a commitment freely and gladly given, a sign to the world of the love that sustains life. This special covenantal relationship does not leave untouched those who enter it; it will cause tears and scars. However, insofar as the couple give themselves to each other in the marriage relationship, they are marked with deeper sensitivity and a stronger identity. This process is part of the paschal mystery, which moves

from death and suffering to risen life. As we have seen throughout this course, that mystery is a central reality celebrated in all the church's sacraments.

Over a lifetime together, married partners become persons they never would have become if it were not for their marriage to each other. Blessed by the grace of the sacrament of Matrimony, a couple can believe, even in the hardest times, that God has given them each other as the means to their own salvation, to their own individual, ultimate destiny as a "real" person. E

## Creativity

The mutual self-giving, the faithfulness, and the personal development of partners in marriage all manifest God's love and grace in the world. Yet the loving relationship of the spouses is not the only purpose of marriage. Just as God's love is creative and always brings forth goodness and new life, the couple's love is meant to lead to something wonderful beyond itself.

Certainly, a marriage goes through phases in turning inward versus turning outward. Particularly in the beginning, the couple may be intensely absorbed in each other and in the relationship itself. At times, partners will need to renew that focus on themselves and their own bond.

The point of marriage, however, is not to begin and end with the couple. Love not eventually shared with others becomes stagnant, resulting not in genuine love but in mutual self-absorption. In other words the assured and enthusiastic statement "We care for each other" needs to become "We care for others as well," in order for love to be creative.

There are many ways for couples to be creative and fruitful. The most obvious

# What Is "Real"?

A beloved children's story, *The Velveteen Rabbit*, by Margery Williams, tells of the wondrous, almost miraculous transformation that the love of one person can cause to happen in another. In a conversation between two children's stuffed toys, one of them, the Skin Horse, tells the Rabbit about becoming "Real." As you read the passage, try to connect the conversation with the paschal-like mystery of marriage.

"What is REAL?" asked the Rabbit one day. . . . "Does it mean having things that buzz inside you and a stick-out handle?"

"Real isn't how you are made," said the Skin Horse. "It's a thing that happens to you. When a child loves you for a long, long time, not just to play with, but REALLY loves you, then you become Real."

"Does it hurt?" asked the Rabbit.

"Sometimes," said the Skin Horse, for he was always truthful. "When you are Real, you don't mind being hurt."

"Does it happen all at once, like being wound up," he asked, "or bit by bit?"

"It doesn't happen all at once," said the Skin Horse. "You become. It takes a long time. That's why it doesn't often happen to people who break easily, or have sharp edges, or who have to be carefully kept. Generally, by the time you are Real, most of your hair has been loved off, and your eyes drop out and you get loose in the joints and very shabby. But these things don't matter at all, because once you are Real you can't be ugly, except to people who don't understand." (Pages 16–17)

To become "Real" is to become the person one is meant to be by God. Through God's grace, which sustains a couple's love over a lifetime, husband and wife help each other become "Real."

and natural way is for couples to bring children into the world and raise them.

### Children as a Blessing, Not a Burden

Vital to the sacrament of Matrimony is the couple's willingness to welcome any children that may come from their union. This intention is so central to marriage's meaning that the church does not permit a sacramental marriage between a man and a woman if they as individuals or as a couple are not open to having children, provided they are physically able. If they are incapable of having children, or decide not to adopt children, there are many other ways they can share their love with those around them. Their

# a spirit of welcome

marriage can be just as fruitful as one that brings forth children, but in different ways.

Of greater importance than the number of children brought into the world by a couple is the couple's generosity and spirit of welcoming new life, treating each child as a blessing to the family, not a burden. Babies and children inevitably change a childless marriage or lifestyle, and they can require immense sacrifices from parents. But raising children brings growth, joy, and love as well, and in a loving marriage, the sense of welcome and gratitude for a new life supersedes the awareness of the sacrifices that are sure to come.

Here is an account of how one couple lived the spirit of openness that characterizes families where children truly feel like blessings:

Susan was into her eighth month of pregnancy, but vacation plans had been made the year before. "The children will be disappointed if we don't go on holiday," she told her husband, Joe. "I'll be fine." So off the family went to the seashore, their station wagon bulging with bicycles, beach chairs, and children.

Susan set up her base of operations in the enclosed porch of the beach house, where she could oversee the comings and goings of all family members. No one came or went without checking in with Mom.

Four days into the vacation, Susan began having labor contractions regularly. "It's time to go to the hospital," she told Joe. She gave last-minute instructions to all the children, and then she and Joe sped off to the hospital, which was over two hours away. Halfway into the ride, both driver and passenger had visions of a child being born at a highway rest stop, but with only minutes to spare, they made it to the hospital.

A baby boy was born that night into a boisterous but loving family. Susan still orchestrates family activities, and although family outings are busier, livelier, and more complicated with the addition of a new little one, they are also more loving than ever. ⒡

### Where Faith Is Nurtured

In the family a child first receives the proclamation of the faith—in words and in deeds. Catholic parents are responsible not only to bring their baby to the parish for Baptism, but to live the faith into which their child has been welcomed by the church. The home is where parents teach children simple prayers and basic concepts about God and Jesus, before they ever receive formal religious instruction. Children also learn from their parents the meaning of Christian feasts like Christmas and Easter. When parents participate in the sacramental life of the church, their children have models to follow and a sense of belonging to a faith community. Perhaps most important, by loving them with wisdom and compassion, parents give their children a crucial formative experience of God's love for them.

So important is the family for the faith development of the child that the Second Vatican Council called the family the "domestic church."

### Being Creative for the Reign of God

Creativity and fruitfulness in marriage are not limited to raising children. A husband and wife are called to bring new life into the world, but this new life can take many forms. The spirit of welcome and hospitality with which the couple anticipate children often leads to involvement in the wider community, in making their local or global environment better for all people.

*the place of children*

⒡ React to this statement in writing:
• Intending to have and raise children is central to the meaning of a marriage.

A family can do service projects together as a way of being creative in building the Reign of God.

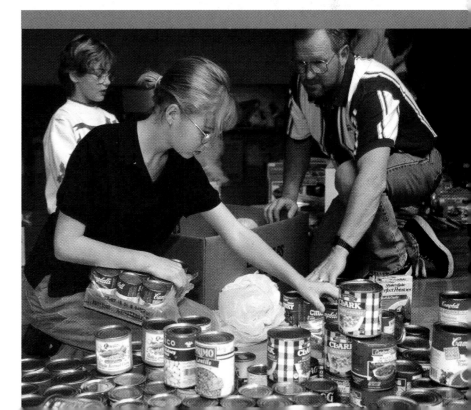

Thus couples seeking ways to be creative as a family might become involved in improving their community's schools, working against racial discrimination in their neighborhood, or helping to improve the recycling system in their city. They may take on a special family-oriented service, like welcoming people who are poor or considered different or strange in their community. In these ways marriage partners share in building the Reign of God as a couple, not merely as individuals. The creative intent of marriage is oriented ultimately toward making God's love, justice, and peace a reality in the world.

Marriage "until death do us part" with the qualities described above may seem impossible to achieve in a culture of temporary commitments where divorce is as common as lifelong marriage. And on their own, a man and woman cannot do what is required to make this kind of marriage a reality. They need the grace of the sacrament of Matrimony, God's moving, active presence with them. God is there for them every moment of their life together, to help them be true to their marriage promises.

# grace every moment

## For Review

1. What is the sacrament of Matrimony?

2. From the beginning years of the church, what has marriage been regarded as a symbol of?

3. In what sense does the Christian vision of marriage counteract the trap of consumerism?

4. What is sexual intercourse meant to express in marriage?

5. What is a covenant?

6. In addition to sexual fidelity, what are four characteristics that are included in marital faithfulness?

7. If one or both members of an engaged couple were not open to having children and wanted to be married in the Catholic church, what would the church's stance be? Why?

8. Explain how parents are expected to be the first proclaimers of the faith to their children.

9. Besides having children, in what ways can married couples be creative for God's Reign?

10. What does the grace of the sacrament of Matrimony do for the spouses?

# The Ritual of Matrimony: Symbolic Actions and Words

## Living Out the Sacrament

The sacrament of Matrimony, as you might guess by now, is not just the ceremony that takes place on the wedding day. Rather, the sacrament is the couple's sharing of the whole of their life together. The wedding ceremony itself is a one-time event that celebrates and affirms the sacrament that encompasses a lifetime. As described earlier, marriage is "a communion of the whole of life."

We have already talked about other sacraments as lifetime endeavors. Baptism, it has been said, is not just a ceremony that happens once and then is ignored. Nor is the Eucharist just a Sunday morning event with no connection to the rest of the week. In an even more obvious way, the sacrament of Matrimony is not simply the wedding ceremony; it is the living out of the meaning of that ritual.

## The Husband and Wife as the Primary Symbols

The husband and wife themselves are the primary symbols in the sacrament of Matrimony. In the Roman rite of Catholicism, they, not the priest or deacon, are the ministers of the sacrament through their mutual consent. In Eastern rites the priest or bishop is the minister of the sacrament (called "Crowning," because the minister, after receiving the consent of the bride and groom, crowns each one as a sign of the marriage bond). All the acts of love that the couple perform in their married life are "rituals" of a sort. When a husband and wife linger over an evening meal and share stories about their day, they are celebrating their marriage. When they support each other in a volunteer project for the community, they experience the sacrament's bearing of fruit. The most powerful love ritual, of course, is sexual intercourse, which symbolizes and brings about physical and

Marrying "in the church" means the couple make their promises to each other with the support and presence of the faith community.

why not?

**G** Suppose that a woman has written to an advice column with this question:
• My boyfriend and I love each other deeply and plan to be together always. We've made our commitment to each other. So why should we get married? Why not just live together?

Answer the question with some wise advice.

spiritual union in marriage. Children born from this union or welcomed by adoption into the couple's relationship are the clearest statement that a marriage is greater than the joining of the couple themselves. So the sacrament is not a one-time-only event but an ongoing shared life.

### The Community as a Symbol

When people decide to marry, they are making a choice that will affect their whole community and will require the support of that community—relatives, friends, and the wider church they belong to. To marry "in the church" means much more than simply having a "church wedding"—that is, a wedding that happens to take place in a church building. Marriage in the church means the couple make their promises to each other with the support and presence of the faith community. The community is there to celebrate the man and woman's love and let them know they will help the couple be faithful to the commitment they are making. The community itself is one of the symbols in a celebration of Matrimony. The priest or deacon at the wedding of a Catholic is a witness of the marriage who receives the mutual consent of the couple in the name of the whole church and gives the blessing of the church. **G**

# The Ritual Itself: Adaptable to Various Needs

### Within or Outside the Mass

Normally and ideally, the marriage ritual for Catholics takes place within the celebration of a Mass. This is particularly appropriate because the Eucharist both symbolizes and brings about oneness in Christ.

In a marriage between a Catholic and a non-Catholic, however, frequently the couple will choose not to have their wedding during Mass. This is generally a matter of courtesy to persons attending who are not Catholic, because Catholic church practice is that only Catholics may receive Communion. To exclude from receiving Communion one member of the couple and potentially half of the congregation at a wedding—which is intended to celebrate the couple's unity—would not be in the spirit of the celebration.

### The Location

Since Vatican Council II, much greater flexibility is possible for the wedding of a Catholic and a non-Catholic than had previously existed. Although the ideal place for the wedding is in the Catholic parish church, permission can be obtained in most dioceses from the bishop or the parish priest to hold the wedding in another Christian church, whose minister might officiate rather than the Catholic priest. Sometimes a bishop may give permission for the wedding to be held in a suitable place other than a church.

### Common Elements of Matrimony Rituals

There are three possible rites for this sacrament in the Catholic church:
• the rite for celebrating Matrimony during Mass
• the rite for celebrating Matrimony outside Mass (which can be used for the marriage of a Catholic and a baptized non-Catholic)
• the rite for celebrating Matrimony between a Catholic and an unbaptized person

Regardless of which rite is used, the ceremony itself combines a focus on the couple with a recognition that marriage

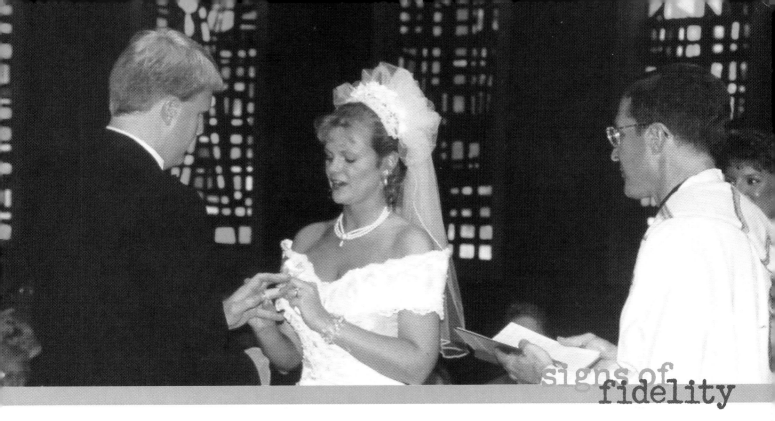

is an event greater and more encompassing than what happens between two individuals alone. Common to the three possible rites are these elements:

1. the liturgy of the word
2. the consent (traditionally known as the vows)
3. the blessing and exchange of rings
4. the nuptial blessing
5. the final blessing

The liturgy of the word, as learned in chapter 9, is the proclaiming of the word of God in the Scriptures. And the final blessing is simply that—a final blessing and prayer for the couple spoken by the minister or priest on behalf of the gathered community. Let's examine the other three elements of the Rite of Matrimony a bit more closely.

**Consent.** The exchange of promises, or consent, during the ceremony gives the couple the opportunity to say yes to each other publicly. Even though the couple have told each other of their love many times before this moment, the promises (vows) gain meaning because they are proclaimed in a formal, public setting with the church as witness. This consent, freely given and sealed by God, is the essential part of the rite. The wording may vary from couple to couple and across cultures, but without free consent, a sacramental marriage does not exist.

**Blessing and exchange of rings.** The words accompanying the blessing and exchange of rings refer to the rings as "signs of love and fidelity." Rings are an ancient symbol of wholeness and unity. Kings and queens wore rings as a sign of their office. Some fantasy tales center on losing or finding rings with magical powers attached to them. On a more practical level, wearing a ring given by another person keeps that person in our thoughts and reminds us of that person's love. In some cultures, however, the exchange of rings does not fit in with the people's customs, so it can be omitted. ⊞

**Nuptial blessing.** The nuptial blessing is a prayer for God's grace, peace, love, and strength to be with the couple through all their life together, and for the gift of children.

circles of unity

⊞ Circles and rings are used symbolically in many cultures and religions and in the art, architecture, celebrations, and writings of those cultures and religions. Create an artwork or write a story or poem that incorporates circles or rings as symbols of wholeness and unity.

# Matrimony in Words and Symbols

### Liturgy of the Word
A reading from the First Letter of John:

Beloved, let us love one another, because love is of God; everyone who loves is begotten by God and knows God. Whoever is without love does not know God, for God is love. (4:7–8)

### Consent
[The couple join hands.]
I, [name], take you, [name], to be my wife [or husband]. I promise to be true to you in good times and in bad, in sickness and in health. I will love you and honor you all the days of my life.

### Blessing and Exchange of Rings
Lord,
bless and consecrate [name] and [name]
in their love for each other.

May these rings be a symbol
of true faith in each other,
and always remind them of their love.  . . .

[Name], take this ring as a sign of my love and fidelity. In the name of the Father, and of the Son, and of the Holy Spirit.

### Nuptial Blessing
Father, to reveal the plan of your love,
you made the union of husband and wife
an image of the covenant between you and your
    people.
In the fulfillment of this sacrament,
the marriage of Christian man and woman
is a sign of the marriage between Christ and the
    Church.

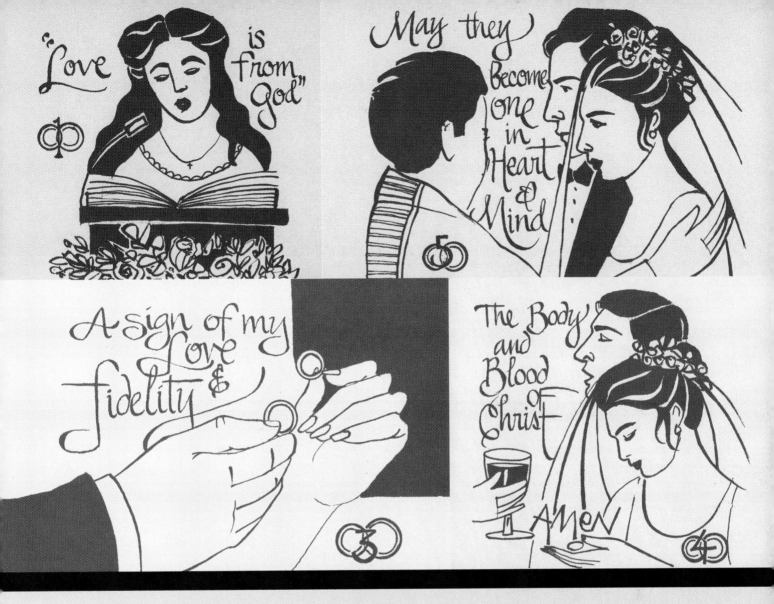

Father, stretch out your hand, and bless [name]
    and [name].
Lord, grant that as they begin to live this sacrament
they may share with each other the gifts of your
    love
and become one in heart and mind
as witnesses to your presence in their marriage.
Help them to create a home together
(and give them children to be formed by the gospel
and to have a place in your family).

**Final Blessing**
May almighty God, with his Word of blessing, unite
your hearts in the never-ending bond of pure love.
. . .

May your children bring you happiness, and may
your generous love for them be returned to you,
many times over. . . .
May you have true friends to stand by you, both in
joy and in sorrow.
May you be ready and willing to help and comfort
all who come to you in need. . . .
May daily problems never cause you undue anxiety,
nor the desire for earthly possessions dominate
your lives. . . .
May the Lord bless you with many happy years
together, so that you may enjoy the rewards of a
good life. . . .

### Personalizing a Wedding

The bride and the groom can personalize their wedding by selecting from the many scriptural readings and various versions of the prayers and blessings those that seem most fitting to their experience and circumstances. The couple can compose petitions for the Prayers of Intercession and select their music with the help of someone versed in liturgical music. There are two standard forms of the consent (vows) to choose from in the United States—the traditional and the revised—but many couples compose their own vows, finding that the writing itself is a clarifying and unifying process. The couple's friends and relatives can be invited to participate in special ways in the rite, as lectors, eucharistic ministers, musicians, and so on.

Some couples have added to their celebration a gift for the world's poor people, symbolized by bringing a basket of food to the altar. Other couples have given a certain percentage of their wedding's total cost to groups or organizations involved in helping poor people. This action is a reminder to themselves and the community that they want to foster, in their marriage, an openness and a reaching out to persons in need.

### Cultural Variations

Different cultures have different symbols and rituals within the marriage ceremony. In the Eastern Catholic church, for example, the crowning of the bride and groom by the priest is a central ritual during a wedding. Many Hispanic weddings include customs such as the offer-

*Different wedding customs symbolize the meaning of the union of a woman and a man. Student art: Photo by Maria E. S. Lopez, Pomona Catholic High School, Pomona, California*

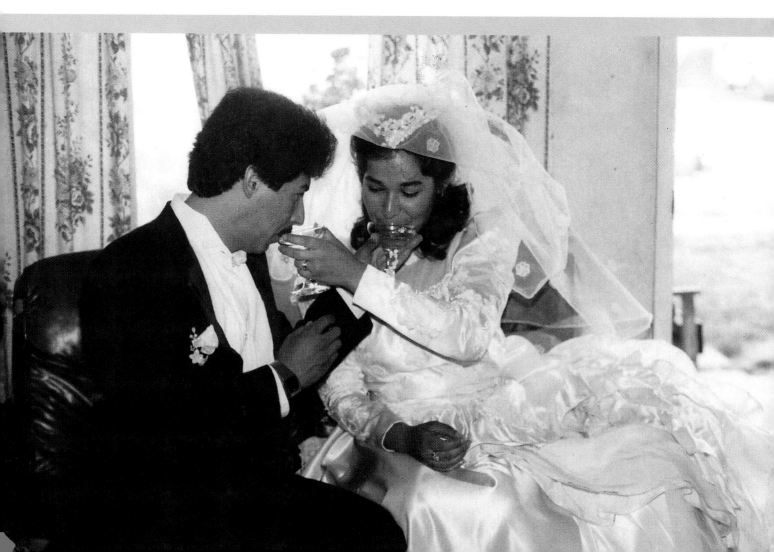

ing of the Lazo, a figure-eight band or "true-lovers' knot" (made, for instance, by putting two rosaries together) as a symbol of the union of the man and woman. Another Hispanic custom is the bride's offering of her bouquet to the Blessed Mother as a way of asking her protection over the marriage.

Parents or other guests might extend good wishes or blessings to the couple at some point in the ceremony. Persons from cultures that have long-standing wedding customs are encouraged to incorporate their customs into the church ceremony, provided the customs do not detract from the meaning of the celebration.

A custom that has gained popularity in North American weddings is the lighting of the unity candle, in which the couple, now joined by their mutual vows, light a single candle from two candles lit earlier by their parents. ▯

### Customs from Pre-Christian Cultures

Interestingly, many wedding customs that people have assumed to be Christian are actually rooted in pre-Christian cultures. For instance, in Greek and Roman cultures just before the time of Christ, marriage consisted of three basic activities still sometimes observed today. First, the father of the bride hands over his daughter to the groom. Second, the bride, in a white gown and a veil and holding flowers, solemnly proceeds to her husband's house, where her husband picks her up and carries her over the threshold. Third, once in the house, the couple eat a special wedding cake.

When considering such customs for inclusion in their wedding, many modern-day couples find it helpful to look at why the customs were originally practiced. Consider one custom we still see today—the father walking his daughter down the aisle and "giving away the bride." This practice originally arose because the father *owned* his daughter. At the time of her wedding, he was simply transferring his "property" over to the husband, who would now own the young woman as his wife. Recognizing the traditional roots of this custom, many contemporary couples prefer other variations for their wedding procession, such as the bride's being accompanied by her mother and father, or the couple's being accompanied by both sets of parents.

▯ Of the various ways you could personalize your wedding or incorporate traditions from your own culture, which two ways would mean the most to you? For each one, explain in writing what you would do and why.

## rituals of Matrimony

### For Review

11. How is the sacrament of Matrimony different from the wedding ceremony?

12. What are the primary symbols of Matrimony?

13. What are the three possible rites for Matrimony in the Catholic church?

14. What is essential to the marriage ritual, without which there is no sacramental marriage?

15. Describe three things couples can do to personalize their own wedding.

# Matrimony's History

## A Gradual Increase of Church Involvement

From its beginning the church recognized the marriages of baptized persons as sacred undertakings with a covenantal meaning. The Christians' rejection of divorce and infidelity contrasted sharply with the practices of the non-Christian Romans of the time, who treated the bond of marriage rather lightly. However, during its early history, the church took no special role in the wedding ceremonies of its members. The early Christians married the same way everyone else did in their various cultures.

Eventually, the church got more involved because many couples presented themselves to their bishop after their wedding to receive the bishop's blessing, although the church did not require this. Also, priests or bishops often attended the weddings of Christians, adding a greater sense of church approval.

Not until the period from the seventh to the eleventh centuries, when the church was the most stable force in society, did it become actively involved in marriage laws and rites. At the time, no other authority existed in Europe that could protect people from abuses of marriage laws, so the church began to fill that role.

By the twelfth century, the typical marriage ceremony took place in front of the church building, was presided over by a priest, and was followed by everyone's going into the church for Mass. Gradually, marriages took place more often in the actual church building and during Mass. By the thirteenth century, marriage was viewed as one of the seven official sacraments of the church.

## A Tradition of Marriage's Permanence

Since its earliest times, the church has maintained that a valid marriage is permanent and cannot be dissolved—a belief based on Jesus' teachings in the Gospels (Mark 10:8–9). In practice, however, a man was sometimes allowed to divorce and remarry if his first wife had been unfaithful to him. However, the reverse did not hold true. Even though a man might be adulterous, his wife was obligated to remain married to him. ⏧

### An Unequivocal Teaching
Saint Ambrose, a fourth-century bishop, reiterated Jesus' teaching that marriage could not be dissolved under any circumstances. A few years later, one of his students, Saint Augustine, taught that divorce and remarriage for either a man or a woman was prohibited. This teaching has essentially been handed down through various official church statements over the centuries. At the time of the Protestant Reformation, Catholicism re-emphasized its clear teaching that the bond of marriage is permanent.

### Annulment Versus Divorce
The Catholic church has always recognized that there are cases in which a marriage blessed by the church was never actually valid as a sacrament. This could be because, at the time of the marriage ceremony, either or both of the partners had not entered the marriage willingly, had been dishonest about their intent, or had been unable to make a permanent commitment. In such a case, after a thorough investigation of the situation,

*pressures on marriage*

⏧ People who marry today often face pressures that did not exist a century ago. Name and discuss in writing three changes in modern culture or in the way society operates that have added pressures to married life today.

Ⓚ Imagine yourself in your late fifties, still married to your spouse after thirty loving years together. Imagine, too, that your spouse, though physically healthy for the time being, has developed Alzheimer's disease in the last couple of years and now does not even recognize you. Would you want to divorce your spouse because you are now strangers? Why or why not? Would this disease be grounds for an annulment granted by the church? Explain your answer in writing.

a local church marriage tribunal may determine that the marriage never existed sacramentally in the first place. A person whose marriage has been annulled is free to marry again according to church law.

An annulment is not the same as a divorce. A divorce dissolves a marriage that once existed, and a divorce is given by civil authorities. An **annulment** given by the church, on the other hand, declares that a valid sacramental marriage never did exist in the first place. The Catholic church maintains that a valid sacramental marriage can never be dissolved or annulled. K

A belief in the permanence of marriage frees a couple to love each other wholeheartedly, without putting conditions and qualifications on their union.

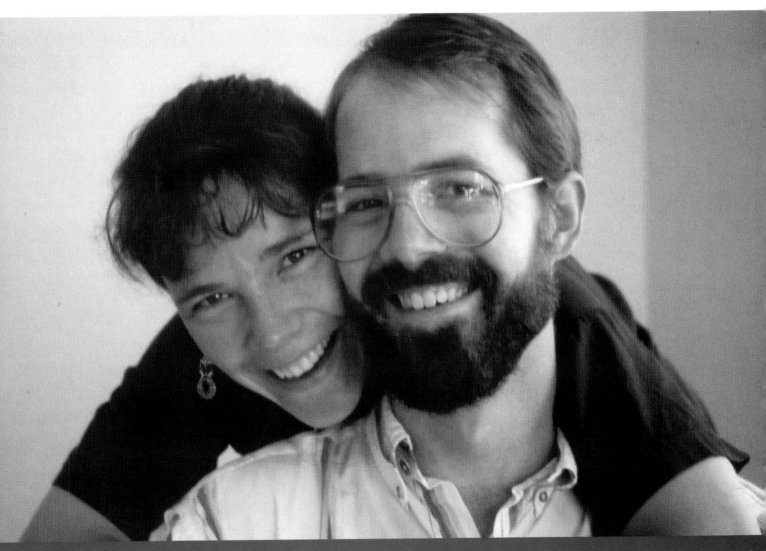

## For Review

16. Why did the church first become actively involved in marriage laws and rites?

17. What is the Catholic church's teaching on whether a valid marriage can be dissolved?

18. What is the difference between an annulment and a divorce?

# A Joyful Hope for the World

Marriage is a natural experience and a powerful symbol. As a sacrament Matrimony depicts God's covenantal relationship with people in the very human "body language" of two persons becoming one flesh. On the human level, such a total gift of self through the whole of a life together is an ideal that can never be completely reached. Nonetheless, with the grace of the sacrament and the support of the church community, couples continue to desire and strive for that ideal. They know, almost instinctively, that the rewards for such a relationship are great. When husbands can, in Saint Paul's words, "love their wives as they do their own bodies" (Ephesians 5:28), and when wives can do likewise, a joyful hope is created that becomes light to the world.

Like the sacrament of Matrimony, the sacrament of Holy Orders celebrates a life path that reveals God's goodness and love to the world and builds up the Body of Christ. We will turn to Holy Orders, the other sacrament at the service of communion, in chapter 13.

*Student art:* Photo by Greta Hauge, Oak Knoll High School, Summit, New Jersey

# 13 Holy Orders

### celebrating ministry in Christ's name

GOSPEL

✠ A reading from the holy gospel according to this world

Jesus knew that his hour had come to depart
and go to the Father.
During the supper he said to his disciples,
"Do not let your hearts be troubled.
Believe in God, believe also in me. dwelling places.
In my Father's house there are you?
If it were not so, would I you?
that I go to prepare a place for you.
And if I go and prepare will take you to myself,
so that where there you may be also.
And you know the way to the place where I am going."

Thomas who do not know where you are going.
"Lord, we know the way?"
said to him.
I am the way, and the truth, and the life.
No one comes to the Father except through me."

The gospel of the Lord.

## 284 SATURDAY

### FIRST READING

A reading from the Acts of the Apostles

[illegible body text]

The word of the Lord.

A period of silence is observed after the reading.

### RESPONSORIAL PSALM

R. All the ends of the earth have seen
the saving power of God.

or: Alleluia. (Two or three times)

O sing to the Lord a new song,
for he has done marvellous things.
His right hand and his holy arm
have won him victory. R.

The Lord has made known his victory,
he has revealed his vindication in the sight of the nations.
He has remembered his steadfast love and faithfulness
to the house of Israel. R.

All the ends of the earth have seen
the victory of our God.
Make a joyful noise to the Lord, all the earth;
break forth into joyous song and sing praises. R.

Jesus, our savior, you modeled a priesthood of service.
Make us eager to do your work—
to minister to one another's needs,
to serve the poor,
to be compassionate
where there is suffering,
and to join one another in celebration
of life with you.

Amen.

Holy Orders, like Matrimony, is a sacrament at the service of Communion. Through **Holy Orders**, men called by God are consecrated to do a particular kind of service in Christ's name—that of leading and nourishing the Body of Christ with the word of God and the grace of the sacraments. There are three degrees, or orders, of this ministry in the Catholic church:

• the episcopate, the order of bishops
• the presbyterate, the order of priests
• the diaconate, the order of deacons

Ordained ministers help the community be in touch with God and live out the mission of Jesus Christ in the world. Representing Jesus, they serve as spiritual guides to the Kingdom of God.

Before we examine the role of such spiritual guides, however, let's begin by following up on a story that is probably familiar to you, about another kingdom and the guide to that kingdom.

**After her whirlwind visit**

to Oz, Dorothy continued to live in Kansas, first on the farm owned by her aunt and uncle, and later in the town nearby. Soon Dorothy became a cherished member of the farm community. In her life as a mother, then as a grandmother, and as the town's favorite "adopted aunt," Dorothy was someone to whom people both young and old could turn when they felt down or hurt.

Invariably, Dorothy would be asked to retell the story of Oz—no matter how many times her listeners had heard it before. The children were especially enthralled by Dorothy's tales about the magical land over the rainbow—a land of witches, Munchkins, talking lions, and tin woodsmen with real hearts. They found these images startling but irresistibly alluring. Ⓐ

Dorothy captivated the adults with her special talent for painting a vivid picture of the courage of the lion, the wisdom of the scarecrow, the generosity of the tin man, and the goodness of Glinda the witch. People who heard her stories—really heard them—discovered deep truths in them and were often transformed by the rich messages they contained. In their enthusiasm the people of the community could not help but share with others the stories they had been told.

Once, a small child who had been listening to Dorothy with spellbound attention quietly whispered, "Can I go to Oz, too?" Dorothy responded with a gleam in her eye, "Why, Oz is all around you. Just look at the people you know—if you see courage, wisdom, and goodheartedness, then

## you've found Oz!"

*a spiritual guide*

Ⓐ If you could choose a spiritual guide either from history or from the world today, someone to be present and talk with you in your everyday life, whom would you choose—other than Jesus? Explain your choice of a spiritual guide in writing.

# What Does Holy Orders Celebrate?

## A Doorway to Sacred Mystery

In the above embellishment on Frank Baum's well-known tale, *The Wizard of Oz,* Dorothy in later life serves her community as a doorway into the mystery of Oz and its lessons. That image can be a metaphor for us of what ordained ministers do in the church. Ⓑ

Bishops, priests, and deacons lead people to encounter and experience the mystery of God. Like Jesus, they serve as mediators of God's love and grace, doorways into the heart of God.

To better understand the unique role of ordained ministers in the Catholic church, we'll first consider Jesus' own ministry, the ministry that every Christian is called to continue in his name.

## The Ministry of Jesus

Holy Orders celebrates the ministry of Jesus as **priest, prophet,** and **servant-leader.** These three roles of Jesus have shaped the Catholic understanding of the ministry of all God's people and of the ordained ministry in particular.

### Jesus the High Priest: Different from the Rest

The early Christian communities did not have a distinct class of priests, as Judaism did. Instead they viewed Jesus as the one and only high priest, and saw all believers as sharing in his priesthood.

The image of Jesus as the one true high priest comes from the New Testament's Letter to the Hebrews. The author of the letter wrote to Jewish Christians

*parallels*

Ⓑ Looking back at the story of Dorothy in her Kansas community, draw some parallels between her role as a "guide to Oz" and a priest's role as a "guide to God's Kingdom."

a connection to God

**C** Prophets, even the most nonviolent of them, like Mohandas K. Gandhi, Martin Luther King Jr., and Oscar Romero, usually face adversity and often die by violence. Servant-leaders, like Dorothy Day and Mother Teresa, go through life pretty much penniless. Yet none of the persons mentioned here would have chosen to live otherwise. Research the writings of one of these persons and record the reasons given for that person's living as he or she did.

🎨 *Student art:* Photo by Jessica Hodges, Shawe Memorial High School, Madison, Indiana

after the Romans' destruction of the Jerusalem Temple in the year A.D. 70. The letter compares Jesus to the Jewish high priest, the head of the priestly class. Priests offered animal sacrifices at the Temple to reconcile the Jewish people with God—to bring them back into a faithful relationship with God. However, as the author of Hebrews claims, Jesus' sacrifice of his own life on the cross *permanently* restored people's relationship with God, which had been broken by sin. Unlike the sacrifices of the Jewish priests, Jesus' sacrifice did not have to be repeated over and over. Thus the Temple, destroyed by the time Hebrews was written, was no longer needed: "We have been sanctified through the offering of the body of Jesus Christ once for all" (Hebrews 10:10).

This image of Jesus as the one true high priest offering himself in sacrifice on the cross was soon linked to Christians' celebration of the eucharistic meal. In the process a lasting connection was forged between the notion of sacrifice, the Eucharist, and leadership in the church. Celebrating the Eucharist was the central expression of faith for Christians. So presiding at eucharistic celebrations (which commemorate Jesus' life-giving sacrifice) became the central priestly function of Christian leaders, and it still is.

### Jesus as Prophet: A Living Reminder

A prophet is someone who unceasingly reminds people about God and God's ways. Jesus, and the message that he preached to the people of his native Palestine, was truly prophetic: God's word was revealed not only in Jesus' spoken words but in the flesh-and-blood reality of his life.

Ordained ministers serve as living reminders of Christ's prophetic message. When they preside at the Eucharist, preach the word of God, visit the sick, witness a couple's marriage, or lead prayer at a funeral service, they do so in Jesus' name, sharing in his prophetic ministry. **C**

### Jesus as Leader: One Who Serves

Even before the Resurrection, Jesus' disciples had a strong sense that he was the Messiah, the Anointed One sent by God to usher in God's Reign. But Jesus did not meet the expectations they had of a messiah-king, a mighty ruler. His kind of leadership confounded them.

Jesus flatly rejected the desire of many of his followers to make him a political or military ruler. He did not trick, coerce, terrorize, or manipulate people in any way to get them to follow him. Instead, he treated them with compassion and respect, forgave their sins, healed their wounds, and gave them nourishment for both body and soul. He was seldom seen with the respected, powerful, and influential people in the community. He was ridiculed and viewed with suspicion for associating with poor or ill people, women, "obvious sinners" like tax collectors, and others who lived on the margins of society. **D**

Jesus turned the disciples' expectations of him as a leader upside-down. Perhaps no incident shows this better than the story of Jesus washing the feet of the disciples at the Last Supper:

During supper Jesus . . . got up from the table, took off his outer robe, and tied a towel around himself. Then he poured water into a basin and began to wash the disciples' feet and to wipe them with the towel that was tied around him. He came to Simon Peter, who said to him, "Lord, are you going to wash my feet?" Jesus answered, "You do not know now what I am doing, but later you will understand." Peter said to him, "You will never wash my feet." Jesus answered, "Unless I wash you, you have no share with me." Simon Peter said to him, "Lord, not my feet only but also my hands and my head!" . . .

After he had washed their feet, had put on his robe, and had returned to the table, he said to them, "Do you know what I have done to you? You call me Teacher and Lord—and you are right, for that is what I am. So if I, your Lord and Teacher, have washed your feet, you also ought to wash one another's feet. For I have set you an example, that you also should do as I have done to you. Very truly, I tell you, servants are not greater than their master, nor are messengers greater than the one who sent them." (John 13:2–16)

A nineteenth-century depiction of Jesus washing Peter's feet at the Last Supper

*qualities of a leader*

D List four qualities that you think are necessary for leadership. For each one, write a sentence explaining its importance to you. Did the Apostle Peter ever fail in any of these qualities? After all, on three occasions he denied even knowing Jesus, and in some Gospel accounts he can seem unreliable and contradictory. What quality or qualities did Peter possess that so redeemed him as a leader?

answer as a priest

**E** Imagine yourself as a priest who has been asked to write a newspaper column responding to the following questions:

• What are your greatest joys as a priest?

• What are your greatest difficulties as a priest?

• If you could change anything about how people treat you as a priest, what would you change, if anything?

Write down your answers, and then ask a priest these same questions. Record his responses and compare your answers with his. Which response did you most closely agree on? Which did you differ on?

Loving service to one another, Jesus teaches his followers, is to be the hallmark of Christian life and leadership. Ordained ministers are to lead in part by the example of loving service they set. **E**

## The Church: A Priestly People

The New Testament tells us that every person who has been baptized into the Body of Christ is called to share in the ministry of Jesus as a member of a holy and royal priesthood (see 1 Peter 2:5,9). This **priesthood of all believers** (also called the common priesthood of the baptized) means that every Christian can minister in a priestly role (reconciling people with God), a prophetic role (proclaiming God's truth), and a servant-leader role.

If these ministry roles belong to the whole Christian community, why does the Catholic church have *ordained* ministers? How is the ministry of a bishop, a priest, or a deacon different from the ministry of all baptized persons?

## Ordained Ministers: Representing Christ

The ministry of the ordained, particularly of bishops and their coworkers, priests, differs from the ministry of all believers in an essential way. Holy Orders confers on men a sacred power for the service of the faithful, a power that comes to them from Christ through his church. The authority given them can be traced back to the Apostles, and in the Catholic church, bishops are considered the successors of the Apostles.

since the

By the sacrament of Holy Orders, **apostolic succession** is assured—that is, through this sacrament there is a continuous link between the authority given the Apostles by Christ and the authority of validly ordained bishops through the ages. F

Priests and bishops represent Christ and act in the name of Christ. This does not mean they are flawless or even better than everyone else; they may be as weak and sinful as the next person. But when they preside in celebrating the sacraments, we are assured that Jesus Christ himself acts through them. When they teach in union with the whole church, Christ teaches through them.

Thus the authority that Jesus handed on to his Apostles has been passed on for almost two thousand years through the consecration of bishops, who in turn consecrate priests as their coworkers and deacons to help them. The ordained ministry is essential to the church's structure and mission of carrying on the work of Christ.

### Ordination: For Men

Jesus chose men, not women, to be his Apostles, and the Apostles did the same when they chose the ones who would succeed them. For this reason Catholic teaching is that the church is bound by Jesus' choice to ordain only men and thus the ordination of women is not possible.

# The Functions of the Ordained

### Bishops

As successors of the Apostles, the world's bishops form the "college" of bishops, united with the pope as a sign of the oneness of the universal church. Bishops, who have the fullness of Holy Orders, are entrusted with these key tasks:

1. **leading worship and sacraments** (priestly function)
2. **teaching** and applying the truth of the Gospel to their own times (prophetic function)
3. **pastoral governance** (servant-leader function)

Bishops are entrusted with the oversight of dioceses, caring for the spiritual needs of the people in their diocese and fostering a unity of faith with the wider church.

### Priests

Priests are coworkers with the bishop of their diocese, so they share with him and their fellow priests the responsibility for worship, teaching, and governing. Whereas the bishop oversees a diocese, priests generally minister within a parish, a school, or another setting within a diocese.

### Deacons

Deacons are directly connected with a bishop, whom they serve by helping him and his coworkers, the priests, to carry out their tasks. They may proclaim the Gospel and preach, assist the bishop and priests at the Eucharist, preside at funerals and wakes, Baptisms and marriages, bring Communion to the sick, do works of charity and compassion, and in other ways serve.

*Student art:* Photo by Thomas Eyre, Bishop Shanahan High School, Downingtown, Pennsylvania

F Imagine that you want to pass on your most precious possession to people who will care for it after you are gone. How do you feel about entrusting it to others? Will you say anything to ensure that they will care for it well?

# Models of Ordained Ministry

Saint Jean Vianney, the patron saint of priests

A few examples from history show how ordained men have lived out Jesus' ministry as priest, prophet, and servant-leader:

**Laurence, prophetic deacon.**  Saint Laurence, a deacon, lived before Christianity was legal and therefore during a time when persecution of Christians still occurred. According to legend, the prefect (political leader) of Rome heard that the Christian church possessed great wealth. He ordered Laurence to hand over the church's riches to the emperor. Laurence agreed but told him that he would need a few days to gather them together. Laurence then set out to bring together homeless, poor, and crippled persons, persons afflicted with diseases like leprosy, and widows and orphans—all the needy of Rome who were then being supported by the church. When large groups of these people were gathered, he invited the Roman official to come and see the "wealth" of the church. For making his point so strikingly, Laurence was martyred by the angry prefect.

**Nicholas, bishop as servant-leader.**  Probably the most famous bishop in all the world is Saint Nicholas, whom North Americans know as Santa Claus. During the fourth century, Nicholas served as bishop of Myra, in what is today the country of Turkey. Although he was born to wealthy parents, Nicholas grew up an orphan. Always concerned for poor and sick persons, especially children, he gave away his possessions to those in need before being elected bishop of Myra. One story about Nicholas recounts his walking by a house and overhearing young children inside talking about their lack of food and money. Instinctively, the kind bishop took out his purse of money and threw it into the window to the surprised and delighted children. During one of the early persecutions of Christians under the Roman Empire, Bishop Nicholas was chained in prison. Today, Saint Nicholas is recognized as the patron saint of children.

**Jean Vianney, reconciling priest.** A model of a dedicated priest was Saint Jean Vianney (1786–1859). Vianney is not known for his great works; he wrote no books, lectured at no universities, and traveled to no distant lands. He is not known for great preaching. Sometimes he stumbled his way through his sermons or broke down in tears because he couldn't remember what he wanted to say. He simply served faithfully for most of his life as parish priest to the people of a little French village called Ars. At the time of Vianney's assignment to that parish, Ars was a town where no other priest wanted to go because the people there had a reputation for being crude and uncivilized.

During his service at Ars, Jean Vianney spent most of his time hearing confessions, leading many people to change their ways. People flocked to him because of his great yet humble holiness, and he inspired many townspeople and visitors from great distances to do good works. Jean Vianney stands out because he did so exceptionally well what priests do regularly—be present to a community and lead the people in prayer and in celebrating the sacraments. Jean Vianney is known today as the patron saint of priests.

Some ordained men are also members of a religious community or congregation, such as the Franciscans, the Jesuits, or the Benedictines. Often they take special vows—of poverty, chastity, and obedience—in addition to their commitment to the priesthood itself.

## Celibacy: The Gift of Self to God

Catholic priests and bishops are celibate—that is, they do not marry and they pledge not to have intimate sexual relationships. A man who is already married may be ordained a permanent deacon. But once ordained, a deacon who is single may not marry.

Why celibacy? Whether in the ordained ministry, religious life, or single life, the choice of celibacy is a way of giving oneself entirely to the service of God and God's people.

Certainly priests and bishops have close friendships and experience deep love; celibacy does not mean aloofness or lack of human connection. Yet for them, the total gift of self to another implied by marriage and sexual intimacy is reserved for God alone and for the service of God's Reign. It is a gift they give freely and joyfully to God and the church, although it entails sacrifice and is sometimes a struggle. Yet married and single people also have lives that involve hardship and suffering in their own ways. Ⓖ

*a struggle-free life?*

Ⓖ If it were possible to have a life free of sacrifice and struggle, do you think it would be worth living? Why or why not?

# the ministry of priesthood

## For Review

1. What are the three roles of Jesus' ministry that all God's people are called to share? Briefly describe how Jesus carried out one of those roles and how modern-day ordained ministers serve in that role.

2. What does the priesthood of all believers mean?

3. How does the ministry of the ordained differ from the ministry of all believers?

4. What is apostolic succession?

5. What are the three key tasks of bishops, which they share with priests?

6. Explain the meaning of celibacy as part of the life of a priest or a bishop.

# The Ritual of Holy Orders: Symbolic Actions and Words

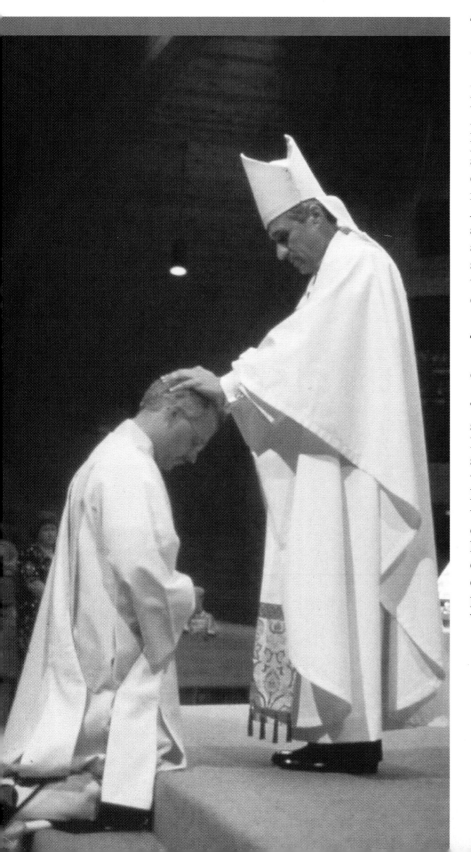

## The Whole Church Community

Just as it is with all the other sacraments, the church community as a whole is a primary symbol in Holy Orders. At one point in the ritual, those to be ordained as deacons, priests, or bishop are presented to the presiding bishop for his approval in the name of the institutional church. At the same time, the ordaining bishop asks the people in the assembly for their approval of the candidates. This emphasizes that ordained ministry flows out of the whole community's responsibility to carry on the ministry of Christ. ⊞

## The Laying On of Hands and Consecration

The laying on of hands is the other main symbolic action in the sacrament of Holy Orders. We have seen it also in the sacraments of Confirmation, Reconciliation, and Anointing of the Sick. The laying on of hands by the bishop, with the essential words of consecrating the candidate, symbolizes and brings about his empowerment by the Spirit. In the ordination of a priest, after the laying on of hands, the bishop offers the solemn prayer of consecration, including these words:

> **Almighty Father,**
> **grant to this servant of yours**
> **the dignity of the priesthood.**
> **Renew within him the Spirit of**
> **holiness.**

As a co-worker with the order of
bishops
may he be faithful to the ministry
that he receives from you, Lord God,
and be to others a model of right
conduct.

In Holy Orders, the laying on of hands also emphasizes that the power and responsibility of the office are shared:

- At the ordination of a bishop, the presiding bishop and all the other bishops present (there must be two more) lay their hands on the head of the bishop-elect.
- At the ordination of a priest, all the other priests present lay their hands on the head of the one being ordained after the bishop has laid hands on him and said the words of consecration.
- The laying on of hands at the ordination of a deacon is done only by the bishop, but the action still symbolizes the deacon's sharing in the ordained ministry of the church.
- All ordination rituals include a sign of peace among the bishops, priests, and deacons present.

Through these actions, the **collegiality** of ministry is emphasized; that is, bishops, priests, and deacons are part of an order, or college, with shared, interrelated responsibilities, and they are to collaborate with one another as brothers.

# Three Orders, Three Rituals

Each of the three orders of ordained ministers—bishop, priest, and deacon—has its own ceremony.

At their ordination, bishops receive the Book of the Gospels; their head is anointed with sacred oil; they are given a ring, which signifies marriage to the church; they receive a miter (a type of hat symbolizing authority) and a shepherd's staff, a symbol of the leadership style of Jesus, the good shepherd.

The ritual of ordination for priests includes clothing them in the official vestments of the office, anointing their hands with oil, and presenting them with a paten (plate) and a chalice holding the bread and wine, signs of their role in the Eucharist. ⊡

Deacons, like new priests, are also dressed in their vestments during their ordination ritual. They also receive the Book of the Gospels, a symbol of the ministry of preaching that is part of a deacon's official role in the church.

the newly ordained

Ⓗ How well do you think the church community of a diocese really knows the persons who have been recently ordained in the diocese? List five suggestions for how the community could get to know new priests before their ordination. Interview a recently ordained priest on what his first assignment was like. He may have some surprising (and funny) stories to tell you!

⊡ Ask a priest to recall his ordination ceremony and describe to you the words or symbolic actions that had the most meaning for him.

## rituals of ordination

**For Review**

7. In the ritual of Holy Orders, what symbolizes and brings about the candidate's empowerment by the Holy Spirit?

8. What is collegiality in the context of Holy Orders?

9. Describe two symbols used in the ordination of a bishop and two in the ordination of a priest.

All Holy Men & Women pray for us

## Holy Orders in Words and Symbols

### Ordination of a Priest

**The Litany of the Saints**

[The candidate for the priesthood prostrates himself in humility before God, as the congregation sings the litany to ask the help of all God's beloved ones for him.]

Almighty Father, grant to this servant of yours the Dignity of the Priesthood

Holy Mary, Mother of God
  pray for us
Saint Michael
  pray for us . . .
All holy men and women
  pray for us

### The Laying On of Hands
[This is done in silence first by the bishop, then by the other priests present.]

### Prayer of Consecration
Almighty Father,
grant to this servant of yours
the dignity of the priesthood.
Renew within him the Spirit of holiness.
As a co-worker with the order of bishops
may he be faithful to the ministry
that he receives from you, Lord God,
and be to others a model of right conduct.

### Receiving of Vestments
[The hymn "Veni, Creator Spiritus" ("Come, Holy Spirit,") may be sung as the new priest is being vested in stole and chasuble and the bishop is anointing his hands.]

### Anointing of Hands
The Father anointed our Lord Jesus Christ
through the power of the Holy Spirit.
May Jesus preserve you to sanctify the Christian
  people
and to offer sacrifice to God.

### Presentation of the Gifts of Bread and Wine
Accept from the holy people of God the gifts to
  be offered to him.
Know what you are doing, and imitate the mystery
  you celebrate:
model your life on the mystery of the Lord's cross.

# Holy Orders' History

## The First Century: Charisms and Shared Leadership

The Catholic church traces ordained ministry back to the Apostles, chosen by Jesus to follow him most closely and later to lead the community after he was gone. But the current structure of ordained ministry—with bishops, priests, and deacons—took time to evolve in the early church.

In the Christian communities of the first century, which sprang up throughout the Mediterranean world, many types of ministry and leadership were present. Some of these were performed by both men and women. Often, specific duties fell to those who exhibited a particular **charism** (that is, a talent or gift) for that role. Some people, for example, had a charism for taking care of widows, orphans, and others in need. Others had a charism for prophecy; still others, for leading prayer. The person at whose home the people gathered often led the community at the Eucharist. ▯

Early on, it became common to appoint or elect either a person or a group to take the leadership role both in coordinating the various service activities of local communities and in presiding at the Eucharist. Appointed or elected persons were known individually as bishops (meaning "overseers") or, if they were a group, as presbyters (literally, "elders"). Deacons ("servants") assisted the bishops in works of charity and in the celebration of the Eucharist. Thus, the three holy orders recognized by the Catholic church today had their roots in early Christian communities. Other ministries existed as well in the early church, and some of these came to be recognized as having official status.

From the beginning, leadership in the Christian churches was a shared ministry. Those who held leadership positions in one local community shared their authority with the individual leaders or group of leaders of other communities.

## The Second to the Sixth Centuries: Changes in Roles and Power

From the second century to the sixth century, church leadership roles became more specialized. Ordination rites developed for each kind of ministry. Toward the end of this period, the orders of bishops and presbyters (later called "priests") gained more prominence.

By the sixth century, the role of deacon was by and large absorbed into the functions of the presbyters. Rather than being an official order in and of itself, the diaconate was made part of the process of becoming a priest.

In this period the power and authority of priests increased. Bishops delegated more and more responsibility to priests in order to keep up with the growing number of church communities. Also, priests—along with bishops—acted as judges and counselors in the Roman government. Thus priestly ministry became more associated with worldly power and authority.

*a certain charism*

▯ Name two people you know who exhibit a particular charism or talent for helping others. Describe the special talent each person shows, and list the approach, characteristics, and actions that make her or him so effective.

# Women in Ministry in the Early Church

STS. PERPETUA and FELICITY

In Saint Paul's Letter to the Romans, we read:

> I commend to you our sister Phoebe, a deacon of the church at Cenchreae, so that you may welcome her in the Lord as is fitting for the saints, and help her in whatever she may require from you, for she has been a benefactor of many and of myself as well. (16:1–2)

Just who Phoebe was, and in what capacity she helped Paul, we do not know. But in the same letter, we find many more references to women who obviously played significant roles in the early church, among them a woman named Prisca:

> Greet Prisca and Aquila [Prisca's husband], who work with me in Christ Jesus, and who risked their necks for my life, to whom not only I give thanks, but also all the churches of the Gentiles. Greet also the church in their house. (16:3–5)

Information about the precise roles played by women in the early church is sketchy, although the New Testament does indicate that a number of women like Phoebe and Prisca were influential leaders.

The most amazing stories about early church women are the accounts of martyrs such as Perpetua, mother of a newborn, and her pregnant servant, Felicity, both of whom gave their lives rather than renounce their faith. (Listen for their names during one version of the Canon of the Mass.) Women also served in forms of ministry—such as prophecy—that were important and widespread at the time but that later did not become institutionalized as official ministries.

## The Sixth Century to the Reformation: The Class of the Clergy

From the sixth century up through the Protestant Reformation (sixteenth century), bishops and priests became more set apart from the rest of the church community. The influence of monastic life had a great deal to do with this distinction. Some early Christians felt drawn to living apart from society in caves, in the desert, or in isolated communities called monasteries. Through their solitude, they tried to experience Christ in a more intimate way, and the lifestyle fostered holiness and wisdom. Some monks were also priests, but the vast majority of priests were not monks.

The priesthood began to mirror characteristics of monastic life. That is, priests, like monks, dressed differently from other people and followed many of the spiritual practices and prayers of monasticism. Living a celibate life, considered an ideal for ordained ministers since the fourth century, became a requirement for ordination in the twelfth century, as it had been all along for monastic vocations.

By the end of the twelfth century, being a priest meant membership in a separate class known collectively as the clergy. More and more, the sacraments became the realm of the clergy, with the laity participating mostly as passive observers in public worship. This pattern changed little during the Middle Ages and persisted well into the modern era.

## Reforms with the Council of Trent

One condition that spurred the Protestant Reformation, led by the monk and priest Martin Luther, was the serious state of disarray in the clergy. Luther and other reformers protested, among other things, that many priests were not well trained and were careless in their duties; that bishops often abused their religious authority to gain political influence; and that a general condition of immorality pervaded the clergy.

Responding indirectly to these criticisms, in the mid-sixteenth century, the Catholic church's Council of Trent set out to establish a more pious and better-educated clergy than had existed during the Middle Ages. The council decreed that seminaries were to be established in each diocese, and bishops were obliged to be residents of their own dioceses. Except for the work of non-clergy religious orders, however, ministry and leadership within the church were still mainly in the hands of ordained persons until the Second Vatican Council.

the monastic influence

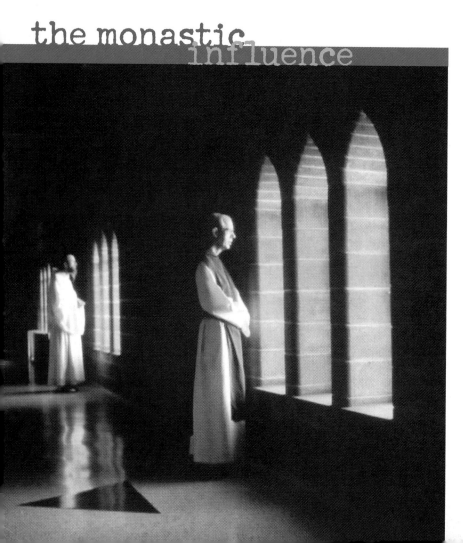

# Since Vatican Council II

### A Return to Shared Ministry

As mentioned in chapter 6, the Second Vatican Council of the 1960s sought to get back to some of the root traditions of the early church. Included in these efforts were changes in emphasis in the church's understanding of ordained ministry. Once again, service was stressed more than power and authority. Mutual decision making, among the clergy and within the community, was now called for. Additionally, the Second Vatican Council renewed the church's recognition that many facets of Christ's priesthood are the shared responsibility of ordained persons and laypeople together. Bishops, priests, and deacons were encouraged to work along with laypeople in helping to provide for the spiritual needs of the community. The role of permanent deacon, which had disappeared after the sixth century, was restored, and the permanent diaconate was opened to married men.

### Broadening the Ministries of the Church

The Second Vatican Council's call for involvement of laypeople has given rise to lay participation in various ministries previously reserved for ordained persons. Now when Catholics walk into a church, they expect to see their friends and neighbors distributing Communion, reading the Scriptures from the pulpit, and even serving as ordained deacons. Catholics who are sick or hospitalized are not surprised to find a group of laypeople visiting to pray with them or to bring them Communion. Laywomen and laymen direct retreats, teach religion, serve as spiritual directors, and hold administrative positions in Catholic schools, parishes, and dioceses.

*Student art:* Photo by Jessica Hodges, Shawe Memorial High School, Madison, Indiana

### Ordained Ministry as Essential

The emergence of new forms of lay ministry is a sign that the Holy Spirit is at work in the church, moving God's people to fuller participation in the priesthood of Jesus Christ. Many of the functions that used to be done almost entirely by priests are now being done by laypeople. But this welcome change does not obscure the distinct and essential role of ordained ministers. By the sacrament of Holy Orders, they are empowered to teach, to preside at the sacraments, and to govern in the name of Jesus Christ.

*teens in ministry*

K Find out what ministry opportunities exist for teenagers in your local church.

## Holy Orders' history

### For Review

10. To whom does the Catholic church trace its ordained ministry?

11. Describe leadership roles in the early Christian communities.

12. How did monastic life influence the development of the ordained ministry?

13. How did the Council of Trent respond indirectly to the criticisms that Luther and others had of the clergy?

14. What changes in emphasis in the ordained ministry and lay ministry came from the Second Vatican Council?

# Challenges Ahead

Participants in a Family Peace Weekend, held each summer near Toronto, Ontario, celebrate Mass with "Bishop Nick"—Nicholas De Angelis, auxiliary bishop of the Archdiocese of Toronto.

As the church continues to read and respond to the "signs of the times," encouraged in such efforts by Vatican Council II, it must continue to examine the role of ordained ministers and its understanding of Christian ministry in general. Many challenges face the church in carrying on the mission and ministry of Jesus:

- How can ordained ministers and laypeople best function together as a unified priestly people carrying on Jesus' work of service and worship? How can they support one another in their distinct but complementary priestly roles?
- How can the church turn its apparent crisis of a shortage of priests into an opportunity for positive growth and change?
- In what ways can the church better help its members recognize a possible calling to the priesthood and support them in their discernment?

Ordained ministry and lay ministry will evolve in this new century, just as the church itself will grow and develop in ways that may be beyond our imagination. That is the mystery and grace of a community that is guided by the Holy Spirit. ⌶

⌶ Project ahead in your imagination to what the church could be like in the year 2050. Describe some of the features you imagine, and how they might be both alike and different from the way the church of the present is.

# Conclusion

## the sacrament of you

**Jesus, our companion,** this course has come to an end,
but our journey with you continues.
Help us celebrate your sacramental presence.
May you continue to nourish your church
through the seven sacraments.
And may we always serve as signs of your love.
**Amen.**

In the seven sacraments, God's powerful, loving presence becomes visible and tangible in our world, and is celebrated by the rituals of the Catholic church. Ultimately, these special means of grace are meant to transform *us* into living, breathing sacraments, manifesting God's love to those around us.

Let's reflect for a moment on one woman who let God's love shine through her. Many Christians in North America and Africa who had the privilege of meeting Sr. Thea Bowman, FSPA, recall how vividly she conveyed God's grace in her life.

# visible &
# tangible

**A native of Canton, Mississippi,**

Thea (then named Bertha), while in her pre-teens, surprised her Protestant African American parents by deciding to become Catholic. A few years later, she joined a religious order, the Franciscan Sisters of Perpetual Adoration, which ran the Catholic school she attended. As a sister, Thea taught at Catholic schools and colleges in Wisconsin, Mississippi, and Louisiana. She became nationally known as a speaker and preacher on African American theology, spirituality, and arts, with a special love for leading and singing the music of her African American roots.

A reporter from the secular press, obviously moved by Sister Thea, summed up her remarkable charism in these words, written two years after Thea's death in 1990 at the age of fifty-two:

Right to the end, despite years of debilitating bone cancer, Thea was preaching, teaching and singing praises to her God.

When Thea was around, you didn't doubt there was a God. You could see him in the warm, welcoming acceptance of her eyes.

You could hear him in her clear, strong voice and in her laughter.

Even with her hair gone, bald from the chemotherapy, she was a work of art in native African dress.

God made her and it was all good.

She made people clap their hands and sing. Even TV newsman Mike Wallace and stodgy Roman Catholic bishops were helpless against the joy that radiated from Thea.

"Black is beautiful," Thea said. And it was so.

In Thea's eyes, white was beautiful, too. And red. And yellow. God doesn't make junk. We are all worthy. (Hollnagel, *La Crosse Tribune*)

Sister Thea was a sacrament of God's love for the world, and continues to keep shining God's light today through the memory others have of her. Yet Thea would want everyone to recognize that we all can be sacraments, if we are open to God's grace

# transforming us.

# You—A Sacrament

You are a sacrament. People meet God through you. You make God visible in the world. You may not be aware of when or how you reveal God, but you do. With openness to God's powerful life within you, like Sr. Thea Bowman, you can become an ever more radiant sign of God's presence. Ⓐ

This course has looked in detail at sacrament as a fundamental religious concept. It has also explored the meaning of sacrament as Christians understand it and as Catholics understand it in the seven sacraments.

Along the way you have been invited to examine your own life in light of this course. This concluding section invites you to look at five specific areas of your existence and to try to see them sacramentally. These five areas are awareness, celebration, community, service, and life.

## Sacramental Awareness

To see God we must see with the eyes of faith. Underlying all sacraments is sacramental awareness. As sacraments we view life with the loving eyes with which God sees us.

- We wonder about the mysteries of life and death.
- We listen intently to nature, silence, and other people.
- We look closely at the familiar until it appears fresh and new.
- We see God in a flower or in a friend or in a stranger—in all of creation.
- We say, "There is more to life than meets the eye."

a role model

Ⓐ Think about someone who has been a role model for you. Then briefly describe in writing a moment when you noticed that person revealing God to others.

Sr. Thea Bowman, in her native Mississippi, toward the end of her life

With sacramental awareness, we view all of God's creation as sacred.

*Student art:* Colored pencil by Natalie Bru, Saint Brendan High School, Miami, Florida

sign of faithfulness

**B** In your opinion what is the greatest indicator that a Christian community is trying to be faithful to its identity as the Body of Christ?

# Sacramental Celebration

Every sacrament is a celebration, filled with joy, peace, and love. As sacraments ourselves, we can also be a celebration.
- We celebrate God's gift of life by enjoying it to the fullest.
- We celebrate the sacredness of each moment.
- We glory in our body, mind, senses, and emotions.
- We celebrate our becoming fully human and tapping into our potential for love, goodness, truth, and beauty.
- We consider the value of things, not just their cost.
- We take time to play and pray.

# Sacramental Community

People are not Christian all by themselves. Likewise, we cannot be sacraments by ourselves. The human face of God is a family portrait—including the kind grandmother as well as the brother who always manages to say the wrong thing. Sacramental community includes rather than excludes others. Sacraments exist within a community that strives to be the Body of Christ.

- We peel away our protective armor of selfishness.
- We invite others into our circle and open the door to new friendships.
- We celebrate the Body of Christ—its past, present, and future.
- We find God in shared meals and shared lives.
- We glory in the uniqueness of each person. **B**

# Sacramental Service

Jesus was a man for others. Being a sacrament, therefore, means living a life of service. Sacramental awareness challenges us to act on behalf of those in need. Being a sacrament through service translates God's word into human body language.
- We realize that "if one suffers, all suffer."
- We ask, "What more can I do?"
- We see poor, needy, and forgotten persons and call them brothers and sisters.
- We work to move the world along toward its goal of becoming God's Kingdom.
- We treat others with respect—looking at them as loved by God.

# Sacramental Life

Life is growth and development. Each of the seven sacraments is a celebration of a passage from one kind of life to another. As sacraments, we seek the new life that comes from sharing our life with others.
- We live with a spirit of zest and adventure.
- We welcome each new day.
- We celebrate a God who is always ahead of the crowd.
- We have faith that resurrection follows every cross.
- We say yes to life.

# Celebrating God's Presence

Fishes, asking what water was, went to a wise fish.

He told them that it was all around them, yet they still thought that they were thirsty. (An anonymous Sufi saying)

Then Jacob woke from his sleep and said, "Surely the Lord is in this place—and I did not know it!" (Genesis 28:16)

The Christian church is like a wise fish. It began with a group of people so convinced and so excited by Jesus' message that at every opportunity they celebrated the continuing, living presence of God in their life: The Lord is here! They celebrated meals, new members, individuals' talents, healings, weddings, and commit-

ments. The Catholic church today continues to celebrate all these occasions. [C]

When you hear the word *sacrament*, remember that it refers to those ways that God reaches out to us in friendship. When we see God in our life and respond through prayer, celebration, sharing, and service, we become living sacraments. When we celebrate the seven sacraments of Baptism, Confirmation, the Eucharist, Reconciliation, Anointing of the Sick, Matrimony, and Holy Orders, we are joining with the church past and present in making Christ alive and visible in the world. And by being a sacramental presence ourselves, we help make those around us more aware of God's love.

your perceptions

[C] Have you participated in any of the church's seven sacraments while taking this course? If so, how did the material you learned in this course affect the way you perceived or experienced those sacraments?

living sacraments

*Italic* numbers are references to photos.

Reconciliation ritual: confession process of, 213; and confidentiality, 230; in the early church, 227; for excommunicated persons, 228–229; less celebration of, 230; minister of, 221; nonsacramental form of, 226; origins of private, 229–230; parish rooms for, 222; penance of, 216; preparation for, 214, 215, 223; three forms of, 221–223; words spoken at, 224

Red Sea crossing, 137

Reign of God, 86–87, 269–270

Resurrection, 79, 80, 197–198, 246, 261

reverence (gift of the Holy Spirit), 163

right judgment (gift of the Holy Spirit), 162

rings: blessing and exchange of, 273, 274

Rite of Christian Initiation of Adults (RCIA), 161; four stages of, 151–152

rituals: characteristics of, 41–46; Christian mingled with pagan, 101; community setting of, 46–47; of early Christians, 100–101, 137, 145–147, 171, 198–199, 227–229, 253–254, 278; play's connection to, 39–40; practical actions versus, 38; prayer as, 56–58; prehistoric roots of, 48–49; recognized as sacraments, 50–51, 101, 108; routines versus, 38–39; symbolic meaning of, 37–38, 41; as worship, 48–49, 110

Roman Empire, 102–104

Romans, Letter to the, 297

Rome, 103, 104

routines, 38–39

**S**

sacramental awareness: how to experience, 11, 305; listening skills for, 17–18; through prayer, 58–59, 63; reasons for lack of, 10; responding skills for, 18; symbolic thinking as, 33

sacramental moments, 19–20

sacramentals, 112, 113

sacrament(s): Augustine's view of, 103–104; Christian life as, 305–306, 307; the church as, 84, 86, 88; daily life experience of, 19–20; God's presence through, 14, 73, 307; Jesus Christ as, 76, 78–80, 90–91; our body as, 70; at the service of Communion, 258, 284; two approaches to, 14, 73. *See also* seven sacraments

sacraments of initiation: the church's role in, 152–153; for early Christians, 145–147; infant's experience of, 149; life experiences reflecting, 124–128, 156–157; names of, 124; order of conferring, 172; in RCIA, 151–152; as separate sacraments, 147–148, 171. *See also* Baptism; Confirmation; Eucharist

*sacramentum* (Latin term), 101, 108

sacred, the: awareness of, 11, 17–18; defined, 10; oil's connection to, 139; prayer's experience of, 58–59, 63; reasons for dullness to, 10

sacrifice: ancient rituals of, 48–49; and the Eucharist, 180, 286

Saint-Exupéry, Antoine de, *The Little Prince*, 42

Saint Maurice Cathedral (Angers, France), *199*

salvation: through Baptism, 124, 129–130, 135; for non-Christians, 135

Samuel, 14

Santa Maria Maggiore, basilica of (Rome), *102*

Scholasticism, 114

scriptural meditation, 65–66

seal (permanent character), 134, 156; sacraments with, 103

seal of confession, 230

second Baptism, 228–229

Second Vatican Council. *See* Vatican Council II

seder, Passover, 178, 179, 197

servant-leader: Jesus as, 286–288; pastoral governance function of, 289

service: Jesus' example of, 286–288; sacramental life of, 306; sacraments of, 258, 284; suffering linked to, 244–245; Vatican Council II on, 299

seven sacraments: correct form for, 108–109; Council of Trent on, 112, 114–115; in Dark Ages, 104–105; definition of, 92; as divinely efficacious, 91; human disposition to, 91–92, 110; and Jesus' seven actions, 90; and life's crossings, 120–121; magical view of, 109–110; as means of grace, 108, 114; official designation of, 50–51, 108; with permanent seal, 103, 134, 156; ritual expression of, 37–38; as symbols, 33; twofold function of, 90; Vatican Council II on, 117–118. *See also* sacrament(s); sacraments of initiation

sexual intercourse, 262; and celibacy, 291; and fidelity, 265; as love ritual, 271–272

The quotation on page 87 is from *The Eucharist and Human Liberation,* by Tissa Balasuriya (Maryknoll, NY: Orbis Books, 1979), page 26. Copyright © 1977 by the Centre for Society and Religion, Colombo, Sri Lanka.

The quotation from the *Dogmatic Constitution on the Church* on page 88 is from *The Documents of Vatican II,* edited by Walter M. Abbott (New York: America Press, 1966), number 1. Copyright © 1966 by America Press.

The story on page 89 is based on *New Eyes for Reading,* edited by John S. Pobee and Barbel Von Wartenberg-Potter (Bloomington: Meyer-Stone, 1987), pages 35–36. Copyright © 1987 by Meyer-Stone.

The quotation on page 92 and the quotation from the *Dogmatic Constitution on the Church* on page 176 are from the *Catechism of the Catholic Church,* by the Libreria Editrice Vaticana, translated by the United States Catholic Conference (USCC) (Washington, DC: USCC, 1994), numbers 1131 and 11. English translation copyright © 1994 by the USCC-Libreria Editrice Vaticana.

The rites excerpts on pages 140–141, 168–169, 194–195, 224, 226, 249, 250–251, 274–275, 292, and 294–295 are from the English translation of the *Rite of Baptism for Children* © 1969, International Committee on English in the Liturgy (ICEL); the English translation of *Rite of Christian Initiation of Adults,* copyright © 1985, ICEL; the English translation of *Rite of Confirmation,* second edition, copyright © 1975, ICEL; the English translation of *The Roman Missal,* copyright © 1973, ICEL; the English translation of *Rite of Penance,* copyright © 1974, ICEL; the English translation of *Pastoral Care of the Sick,* copyright © 1982, ICEL; the English translation of the *Rite of Marriage,* copyright © 1969, ICEL; and the English translation of *Ordination of Deacons,*

*Priests, and Bishops,* copyright © 1975, ICEL. All rights reserved. Used by permission.

The quotation on page 150 is from "World Youth Day '97: Pilgrimage to Paris," by Jerry Daoust, *St. Anthony Messenger Press* (December 1997). Copyright © 1997 by Jerry Daoust. Used by permission of the author.

The story on pages 176–177 is from "Send Me," by Joseph J. Juknialis, *Modern Liturgy* 5, no. 4:26–27. Copyright © 1978 by Resource Publications.

The story of the Corn Mother on page 177 is from "Native Americans and the Land: 'The End of Living, and the Beginning of Survival,'" by George E. Tinker, *Word and World* (6 June 1986): 143. Copyright © 1986 by Luther-Northwestern Theological Seminaries.

The story on page 181 is an old Hasidic tale retold by Martin Buber and cited by Rabbi Laurence Kushner in *Context,* (15 December 1991).

The quotation on page 188 is from "Why Is the World Hungry?" by Wendy Bauers Northup, *Youth Update* YU 0688 (June 1988). Reprinted by permission of St. Anthony Messenger Press, 1615 Republic Street, Cincinnati, Ohio 45210; phone 800-488-0488.

The quotation on page 219 is from "Bless Me, Father, I'm Not Sure I Want to Be Here!" by Kathleen M. Paiva, *Youth Update* (October 1982).

The quotation on page 240 is from *Doors to the Sacred,* by Joseph Martos (Tarrytown, NY: Triumph Books, 1991), page 339. Copyright © 1981, 1982, 1991 by Joseph Martos.

The story on pages 242–243 is by Laura Collins of Merion Mercy Academy, Merion Station, Pennsylvania.

The story on pages 258–259 is adapted from "The Gift of the Magi," by O. Henry [William Sydney Porter], in *The Complete Works of O. Henry* (Garden City, NY: Doubleday & Company, 1953), pages 7–11. Copyright © 1953 by Doubleday & Company.

The quotation on pages 261–262 is from *Building Christian Families,* by Mitch and Kathy Finley (Allen, TX: Thomas More Press, 1984, 1996), pages 65–67. Copyright © 1984, 1996 by Mitch and Kathy Finley. Used by permission of the authors.

The quotation on page 267 is from *The Velveteen Rabbit,* by Margery Williams (New York: Avon Books, 1975), pages 16–17.

The quotation on page 304 is from "New Book Recounts Life of Cherished Nun," by Gayda Hollnagel, *La Crosse Tribune* (1 February 1992), as quoted in *Sister Thea Bowman, Shooting Star: Selected Writings and Speeches,* edited by Celestine Cepress, FSPA (Winona, MN: Saint Mary's Press, 1993), page 11. Used by permission.

**Photo and Art Credits**

We appreciate the hundreds of students from Catholic high schools around the United States who submitted their artworks and photography for possible use in this text. Unfortunately we could not use all the submitted works. The following students' works appear on the pages indicated:

Jacinto Astiazarán: page 211
Lauren Aumiller: page 19
Michelle Barrack: page 43
Virginia Bernard: page 27
Rebecca Bignell: page 21
Erin Bode: page 201
Patrick Brinkman: page 12
Cara A. Brown: pages 37, 40
Natalie Bru: page 306
Erin Burke: page 17

Matt Carroll: pages 52–53
Francesca Caruso: page 81
Jason W. Chan: pages 61, 255
Christine Della Cioppa: page 186
Samantha Conte: page 136
Sarah Cooper: page 146
Leah Deeg: page 39
Tracy deEscobar: page 263
Nina Eaglin: page 164
Thomas Eyre: pages 105, 185, 266, 289
Margaret Ferguson: pages 71, 239
Amy Foote: page 133
Virginia Foy: pages 9, 79
Jacqueline Gordon: page 268
Meg Greene: page 149
Colleen Hagan: pages 16, 58
Kim Hall: cover photo of shamrocks and pages 232–233
Greta Hauge: page 144, 280–281
Lisa Hensley: page 26
Jessica Hodges: pages 286, 299
Suzanne Marie Hogan: pages 120–121
Andrea Jablonski: page 134
Cailin Joyce: page 238
Jennifer Khouri: page 91
Andrea Kohler: page 64
Maria E. S. Lopez: page 276
Sara M. Luczak: page 162
Clare Major: cover photo of hikers and pages 20, 62, 173
Ryan Martinez: page 25
Lisa Mayor: page 246
Claire McClain: page 50
Marissa Mountcastle: page 88
Vanessa Navarro: page 57
Kristin Nienkirchen: page 187
Philip Noche: page 125
Katie O'Brien: page 153
Maureen O'Mara: page 70
Caroline Read: page 11
Laura Reestman: page 221
Megan Rulli: pages 29, 160, 210, 245
Jesse Schmidbauer: page 80
Elise Schweitzer: pages 30, 48
Swen Swenson-Graham: cover photo of water droplets and page 68
Laurel Tomasello: page 129

Lindsay Van Cleave: cover photo of shells and page 65

Lucia Wharton: page 157

Amy Wibowo: page 260

The photo accompanying the story by Laura Collins on page 242 has an unknown source; image courtesy of Laura Collins.

Barbara Allaire: page 231

James L. Amos, CORBIS: page 207 (middle)

CORBIS: pages 3, (lower right), 73, 89, 95 (top right), 117, 155, 259, 261, 267, 282 (bottom left), 285, 288, 302–303

Mary Farrell: page 229

Lowell Georgia, CORBIS: page 114

Erol Gurian, CORBIS: page 59

Pam Hasegawa, Impact Visuals: page 279

Copyright © 1991 by Marion C. Honors, CSJ: page 214

Crispin Hughes, Impact Visuals: page 119

George Hunter, Tony Stone Images: page 46

Tony Hutchings, Tony Stone Images: page 130 (top left)

Index Stock Imagery: pages 94–95, 123 (top right), 127, 174–175, 302 (middle)

SAM KITTNER/NGS Image Collection: pages 122–123

Claudia Kunin, Tony Stone Images: page 256

Arnold C. Lehrer, International Stock: page 188

Copyright Robert Lentz, 1996. Image courtesy of Natural Bridges, P.O. Box 91204, Albuquerque, NM 87199, 800-699-4482: page 297

© M. Long, Index Stock Imagery: pages 154–155

Marquette University Archives: page 72

Cindy McIntyre/Weststock: page 35

Museo del Prado, Madrid/SuperStock: page 98

Mark Newman, International Stock: page 159

Photodisc: front cover (top right and bottom left) and pages 2-3, 6 (bottom left and top right), 7 (top), 12 (top left), 18, 22 (top), 22–23 (bottom), 23 (top), 31, 34 (top and bottom), 41, 42, 45, 54 (top), 54–55, 74 (bottom left), 74–75, 75 (middle right), 77, 122 (bottom left), 126, 161, 191, 228, 235 (top right), 256 (bottom left), 264, 265

Gene Plaisted, The Crosiers: pages 93, 107, 227, 253, 290, 292

© 1999 Gerard Pottebaum/Treehaus Communications, Inc. All rights reserved: page 305

Patrick Ramsey, International Stock: page 197

Russell, Index Stock Imagery: page 49

Santa Maria Maggiore, Rome/Canali Photobank Milan/SuperStock: page 102

Santa Maria Novella, Florence/SuperStock: page 109

© Servizio Fotografico de L'Osservatore Romano, 00120 Citta' del Vaticano, Tel. 0669.884.797, Fax 0669.884.998, e-mail: photo@ossrom.va: page 150

James L. Shaffer: pages 85, 86, 101, 196, 198, 223, 273, 282–283, 298

Skjold Photographs: front cover (top left) and pages 182, 184, 215, 216, 217, 220

Sean Sprague, Impact Visuals: page 189

Paul A. Souders, CORBIS: page 116

SuperStock: back cover (lower middle) cover wrap, front cover (top left) and pages 1, 1 (center), 54 (bottom), 67, 84, 97, 106, 111, 130 (top right), 131, 155 (bottom left), 158, 167, 174, 177, 179, 199, 206–207, 209, 218, 234, 234–235, 240, 247, 257, 307

Tate Gallery, London/ET Archive, London/SuperStock: page 287

All rights reserved Vie de Jésus MAFA, 24 rue du Maréchal Jaffre, F-78000 VERSAILLES: pages 83, 248

W. P. Wittman Limited: pages 87, 94 (bottom left), 100, 104, 112, 113, 138, 139, 142, 147, 148, 151, 163, 170, 178, 180, 183, 192, 193, 202, 204–205, 212, 219, 237, 269, 271, 283, 300–301

Matt PATTOLI